Hornbook Series
Nutshell Series

and

Black Letter Series

of

WEST PUBLISHING COMPANY
P.O. Box 64526
St. Paul, Minnesota 55164–0526

Accounting

FARIS' ACCOUNTING AND LAW IN A NUTSHELL, 377 pages, 1984. Softcover. (Text)

Administrative Law

GELLHORN AND BOYER'S ADMINISTRATIVE LAW AND PROCESS IN A NUTSHELL, Second Edition, 445 pages, 1981. Softcover. (Text)

Admiralty

MARAIST'S ADMIRALTY IN A NUTSHELL, Second Edition, 379 pages, 1988. Softcover. (Text)

SCHOENBAUM'S HORNBOOK ON ADMIRALTY AND MARITIME LAW, Student Edition, 692 pages, 1987. (Text)

Agency—Partnership

REUSCHLEIN AND GREGORY'S HORNBOOK ON THE LAW OF AGENCY, PARTNERSHIP AND OTHER UNINCORPORATED BUSINESS ORGANIZATIONS, 625 pages, 1979, with 1981 pocket part. (Text)

STEFFEN'S AGENCY-PARTNERSHIP IN A NUTSHELL, 364 pages, 1977. Softcover. (Text)

American Indian Law

CANBY'S AMERICAN INDIAN LAW IN A NUTSHELL, Second Edition, 336 pages, 1988. Softcover. (Text)

Antitrust—see also Regulated Industries, Trade Regulation

GELLHORN'S ANTITRUST LAW AND ECONOMICS IN A NUTSHELL, Third Edition, 472 pages, 1986. Softcover. (Text)

HOVENKAMP'S BLACK LETTER ON ANTITRUST, 323 pages, 1986. Softcover. (Review)

HOVENKAMP'S HORNBOOK ON ECONOMICS AND FEDERAL ANTITRUST LAW, Student Edition, 414 pages, 1985. (Text)

SULLIVAN'S HORNBOOK OF THE LAW OF ANTITRUST, 886 pages, 1977. (Text)

Appellate Advocacy—see Trial and Appellate Advocacy

Art Law

DUBOFF'S ART LAW IN A NUTSHELL, 335 pages, 1984. Softcover. (Text)

Banking Law

LOVETT'S BANKING AND FINANCIAL INSTITUTIONS LAW IN A NUTSHELL, Second Edition, 464 pages, 1988. Softcover. (Text)

Civil Procedure—see also Federal Jurisdiction and Procedure

CASAD'S RES JUDICATA IN A NUTSHELL, 310 pages, 1976. Softcover. (Text)

CLERMONT'S BLACK LETTER ON CIVIL PROCEDURE, Second Edition, 332 pages, 1988. Softcover. (Review)

EHRENZWEIG, LOUISELL AND HAZARD'S JURISDICTION IN A NUTSHELL, Fourth Edition, 232 pages, 1980. Softcover. (Text)

FRIEDENTHAL, KANE AND MILLER'S HORNBOOK ON CIVIL PROCEDURE, 876 pages, 1985. (Text)

KANE'S CIVIL PROCEDURE IN A NUTSHELL, Second Edition, 306 pages, 1986. Softcover. (Text)

KOFFLER AND REPPY'S HORNBOOK ON COMMON LAW PLEADING, 663 pages, 1969. (Text)

SIEGEL'S HORNBOOK ON NEW YORK PRACTICE, 1011 pages, 1978, with 1987 pocket part. (Text)

Commercial Law

BAILEY AND HAGEDORN'S SECURED TRANSACTIONS IN A NUTSHELL, Third Edition, 390

Commercial Law—Continued pages, 1988. Softcover. (Text)

HENSON'S HORNBOOK ON SECURED TRANSACTIONS UNDER THE U.C.C., Second Edition, 504 pages, 1979, with 1979 pocket part. (Text)

NICKLES' BLACK LETTER ON COMMERCIAL PAPER, 450 pages, 1988. Softcover. (Review)

SPEIDEL'S BLACK LETTER ON SALES AND SALES FINANCING, 363 pages, 1984. Softcover. (Review)

STOCKTON'S SALES IN A NUTSHELL, Second Edition, 370 pages, 1981. Softcover. (Text)

STONE'S UNIFORM COMMERCIAL CODE IN A NUTSHELL, Second Edition, 516 pages, 1984. Softcover. (Text)

WEBER AND SPEIDEL'S COMMERCIAL PAPER IN A NUTSHELL, Third Edition, 404 pages, 1982. Softcover. (Text)

WHITE AND SUMMERS' HORNBOOK ON THE UNIFORM COMMERCIAL CODE, Third Edition, Student Edition, 1386 pages, 1988. (Text)

Community Property

MENNELL AND BOYKOFF'S COM-MUNITY PROPERTY IN A NUTSHELL, Second Edition, 432 pages, 1988. Softcover. (Text)

Comparative Law

GLENDON, GORDON AND OSAKWE'S COMPARATIVE LEGAL TRADITIONS IN A NUTSHELL. 402 pages, 1982. Softcover. (Text)

Conflict of Laws

SCOLES AND HAY'S HORNBOOK ON CONFLICT OF LAWS, Student Edition, 1085 pages, 1982, with 1989 pocket part. (Text)

SEIGEL'S CONFLICTS IN A NUTSHELL, 470 pages, 1982. Softcover. (Text)

Constitutional Law—Civil Rights

BARRON AND DIENES' BLACK LETTER ON CONSTITUTIONAL LAW, Second Edition, 310 pages, 1987. Softcover. (Review)

BARRON AND DIENES' CONSTITUTIONAL LAW IN A NUTSHELL, 389 pages, 1986. Soft cover. (Text)

ENGDAHL'S CONSTITUTIONAL FEDERALISM IN A NUTSHELL, Second Edition, 411 pages, 1987. Softcover. (Text)

MANNING'S THE LAW OF

Constitutional Law—Civil Rights—Continued

CHURCH-STATE RELATIONS IN A NUTSHELL, 305 pages, 1981. Softcover. (Text)

MARKS AND COOPER'S STATE CONSTITUTIONAL LAW IN A NUTSHELL, 329 pages, 1988. Softcover. (Text)

MILLER'S PRESIDENTIAL POWER IN A NUTSHELL, 328 pages, 1977. Softcover. (Text)

NOWAK, ROTUNDA AND YOUNG'S HORNBOOK ON CONSTITUTIONAL LAW, Third Edition, 1191 pages, 1986 with 1988 pocket part. (Text)

VIEIRA'S CIVIL RIGHTS IN A NUTSHELL, 279 pages, 1978. Softcover. (Text)

WILLIAMS' CONSTITUTIONAL ANALYSIS IN A NUTSHELL, 388 pages, 1979. Softcover. (Text)

Consumer Law—see also Commercial Law

EPSTEIN AND NICKLES' CONSUMER LAW IN A NUTSHELL, Second Edition, 418 pages, 1981. Softcover. (Text)

Contracts

CALAMARI, AND PERILLO'S BLACK LETTER ON CONTRACTS, 397 pages, 1983. Softcover. (Review)

CALAMARI AND PERILLO'S HORNBOOK ON CONTRACTS, Third Edition, 1049 pages, 1987. (Text)

CORBIN'S TEXT ON CONTRACTS, One Volume Student Edition, 1224 pages, 1952. (Text)

FRIEDMAN'S CONTRACT REMEDIES IN A NUTSHELL, 323 pages, 1981. Softcover. (Text)

KEYES' GOVERNMENT CONTRACTS IN A NUTSHELL, 423 pages, 1979. Softcover. (Text)

SCHABER AND ROHWER'S CONTRACTS IN A NUTSHELL, Second Edition, 425 pages, 1984. Softcover. (Text)

Copyright—see Patent and Copyright Law

Corporations

HAMILTON'S BLACK LETTER ON CORPORATIONS, Second Edition, 513 pages, 1986. Softcover. (Review)

HAMILTON'S THE LAW OF CORPORATIONS IN A NUTSHELL, Second Edition, 515 pages, 1987. Softcover. (Text)

HENN AND ALEXANDER'S HORNBOOK ON LAWS OF CORPORATIONS, Third Edition, Student Edition, 1371 pages, 1983,

Corporations—Continued with 1986 pocket part. (Text)

Corrections

KRANTZ' THE LAW OF CORRECTIONS AND PRISONERS' RIGHTS IN A NUTSHELL, Third Edition, 407 pages, 1988. Softcover. (Text)

POPPER'S POST-CONVICTION REMEDIES IN A NUTSHELL, 360 pages, 1978. Softcover. (Text)

Creditor's Rights

EPSTEIN'S DEBTOR-CREDITOR RELATIONS IN A NUTSHELL, Third Edition, 383 pages, 1986. Softcover. (Text)

NICKLES AND EPSTEIN'S BLACK LETTER ON CREDITOR'S RIGHTS AND BANKRUPTCY, Approximately 500 pages, 1989. (Review)

Criminal Law and Criminal Procedure—see also Corrections, Juvenile Justice

LAFAVE AND ISRAEL'S HORNBOOK ON CRIMINAL PROCEDURE, Student Edition, 1142 pages, 1985, with 1988 pocket part. (Text)

LAFAVE AND SCOTT'S HORNBOOK ON CRIMINAL LAW, Second Edition, 918 pages, 1986. (Text)

LOEWY'S CRIMINAL LAW IN A NUTSHELL, Second Edition, 321 pages, 1987. Softcover. (Text)

LOW'S BLACK LETTER ON CRIMINAL LAW, 433 pages, 1984. Softcover. (Review)

Decedents' Estates—see Trusts and Estates

Domestic Relations

CLARK'S HORNBOOK ON DOMESTIC RELATIONS, Second Edition, Student Edition, 1050 pages, 1988. (Text)

KRAUSE'S BLACK LETTER ON FAMILY LAW, 314 pages, 1988. Softcover. (Review)

KRAUSE'S FAMILY LAW IN A NUTSHELL, Second Edition, 444 pages, 1986. Softcover. (Text)

Education Law

ALEXANDER AND ALEXANDER'S THE LAW OF SCHOOLS, STUDENTS AND TEACHERS IN A NUTSHELL, 409 pages, 1984. Softcover. (Text)

Employment Discrimination—see also Women and the Law

PLAYER'S FEDERAL LAW OF EMPLOYMENT DISCRIMINATION IN A NUTSHELL, Second Edition, 402 pages, 1981. Softcover.

Employment Discrimination—
Continued

(Text)

PLAYER'S HORNBOOK ON EM-
PLOYMENT DISCRIMINATION
LAW, Student Edition, 708
pages, 1988. (Text)

**Energy and Natural Resources
Law**—see also Oil and Gas

Environmental Law—see also
Energy and Natural Re-
sources Law; Sea, Law of

FINDLEY AND FARBER'S ENVI-
RONMENTAL LAW IN A NUT-
SHELL, Second Edition, 367
pages, 1988. Softcover.
(Text)

RODGERS' HORNBOOK ON ENVI-
RONMENTAL LAW, 956 pages,
1977, with 1984 pocket part.
(Text)

Equity—see Remedies

Estate Planning—see also
Trusts and Estates; Taxa-
tion—Estate and Gift

LYNN'S AN INTRODUCTION TO
ESTATE PLANNING IN A NUT-
SHELL, Third Edition, 370
pages, 1983. Softcover.
(Text)

Evidence

BROUN AND BLAKEY'S BLACK
LETTER ON EVIDENCE, 269
pages, 1984. Softcover. (Review)

GRAHAM'S FEDERAL RULES OF
EVIDENCE IN A NUTSHELL, Sec-
ond Edition, 473 pages, 1987.
Softcover. (Text)

LILLY'S AN INTRODUCTION TO
THE LAW OF EVIDENCE, Second
Edition, 585 pages, 1987.
(Text)

MCCORMICK'S HORNBOOK ON
EVIDENCE, Third Edition, Student Edition, 1156 pages,
1984, with 1987 pocket part.
(Text)

ROTHSTEIN'S EVIDENCE IN A
NUTSHELL: STATE AND FEDER-
AL RULES, Second Edition, 514
pages, 1981. Softcover.
(Text)

**Federal Jurisdiction and Pro-
cedure**

CURRIE'S FEDERAL JURISDIC-
TION IN A NUTSHELL, Second
Edition, 258 pages, 1981.
Softcover. (Text)

REDISH'S BLACK LETTER ON
FEDERAL JURISDICTION, 219
pages, 1985. Softcover. (Review)

WRIGHT'S HORNBOOK ON FED-
ERAL COURTS, Fourth Edition,
Student Edition, 870 pages,
1983. (Text)

Future Interests—see Trusts and Estates

Health Law—see Medicine, Law and

Human Rights—see International Law

Immigration Law

WEISSBRODT'S IMMIGRATION LAW AND PROCEDURE IN A NUTSHELL, 345 pages, 1984, Softcover. (Text)

Indian Law—see American Indian Law

Insurance Law

DOBBYN'S INSURANCE LAW IN A NUTSHELL, 281 pages, 1981. Softcover. (Text)

KEETON AND WIDISS' INSURANCE LAW, Student Edition, 1359 pages, 1988. (Text)

International Law—see also Sea, Law of

BUERGENTHAL'S INTERNATIONAL HUMAN RIGHTS IN A NUTSHELL, 283 pages, 1988. Softcover. (Text)

BUERGENTHAL AND MAIER'S PUBLIC INTERNATIONAL LAW IN A NUTSHELL, 262 pages, 1985. Softcover. (Text)

FOLSOM, GORDON AND SPANOGLE'S INTERNATIONAL BUSINESS TRANSACTIONS IN A NUTSHELL, Third Edition, 509 pages, 1988. Softcover. (Text)

Interviewing and Counseling

SHAFFER AND ELKINS' LEGAL INTERVIEWING AND COUNSELING IN A NUTSHELL, Second Edition, 487 pages, 1987. Softcover. (Text)

Introduction to Law—see Legal Method and Legal System

Introduction to Law Study

DOBBYN'S SO YOU WANT TO GO TO LAW SCHOOL, Revised First Edition, 206 pages, 1976. Softcover. (Text)

HEGLAND'S INTRODUCTION TO THE STUDY AND PRACTICE OF LAW IN A NUTSHELL, 418 pages, 1983. Softcover (Text)

KINYON'S INTRODUCTION TO LAW STUDY AND LAW EXAMINATIONS IN A NUTSHELL, 389 pages, 1971. Softcover. (Text)

Juvenile Justice

FOX'S JUVENILE COURTS IN A NUTSHELL, Third Edition, 291 pages, 1984. Softcover. (Text)

Labor Law—see also Employment Discrimination, Social Legislation

GORMAN'S BASIC TEXT ON LABOR LAW—UNIONIZATION AND COLLECTIVE BARGAINING, 914 pages, 1976. (Text)

LESLIE'S LABOR LAW IN A NUTSHELL, Second Edition, 397 pages, 1986. Softcover. (Text)

NOLAN'S LABOR ARBITRATION LAW AND PRACTICE IN A NUTSHELL, 358 pages, 1979. Softcover. (Text)

Land Finance—Property Security—see Real Estate Transactions

Land Use

HAGMAN AND JUERGENSMEYER'S HORNBOOK ON URBAN PLANNING AND LAND DEVELOPMENT CONTROL LAW, Second Edition, Student Edition, 680 pages, 1986. (Text)

WRIGHT AND WRIGHT'S LAND USE IN A NUTSHELL, Second Edition, 356 pages, 1985. Softcover. (Text)

Legal Method and Legal System—see also Legal Research, Legal Writing

KEMPIN'S HISTORICAL INTRODUCTION TO ANGLO-AMERICAN LAW IN A NUTSHELL, Second Edition, 280 pages, 1973. Softcover. (Text)

REYNOLDS' JUDICIAL PROCESS IN A NUTSHELL, 292 pages, 1980. Softcover. (Text)

Legal Profession

ARONSON AND WECKSTEIN'S PROFESSIONAL RESPONSIBILITY IN A NUTSHELL, 399 pages, 1980. Softcover. (Text)

ROTUNDA'S BLACK LETTER ON PROFESSIONAL RESPONSIBILITY, Second Edition, 414 pages, 1988. Softcover. (Review)

RYAN'S STATING YOUR CASE: HOW TO INTERVIEW FOR A JOB AS A LAWYER, 190 pages, 1982. Softcover. (Text)

WOLFRAM'S HORNBOOK ON MODERN LEGAL ETHICS, Student Edition, 1120 pages, 1986. (Text)

Legal Research

COHEN'S LEGAL RESEARCH IN A NUTSHELL, Fourth Edition, 452 pages, 1985. Softcover. (Text)

Legal Writing

SQUIRES AND ROMBAUER'S LEGAL WRITING IN A NUTSHELL, 294 pages, 1982. Softcover. (Text)

Legislation

DAVIES' LEGISLATIVE LAW AND PROCESS IN A NUTSHELL, Second Edition, 346 pages, 1986. Softcover. (Text)

Local Government

MCCARTHY'S LOCAL GOVERNMENT LAW IN A NUTSHELL, Second Edition, 404 pages, 1983. Softcover. (Text)

REYNOLDS' HORNBOOK ON LOCAL GOVERNMENT LAW, 860 pages, 1982, with 1987 pocket part. (Text)

Malpractice—see Medicine, Law and; Legal Profession

Mass Communication Law

ZUCKMAN, GAYNES, CARTER AND DEE'S MASS COMMUNICATIONS LAW IN A NUTSHELL, Third Edition, 538 pages, 1988. Softcover. (Text)

Medicine, Law and

KING'S THE LAW OF MEDICAL MALPRACTICE IN A NUTSHELL, Second Edition, 342 pages, 1986. Softcover. (Text)

Military Law

SHANOR AND TERRELL'S MILITARY LAW IN A NUTSHELL, 378 pages, 1980. Softcover. (Text)

Mortgages—see Real Estate Transactions

Natural Resources Law—see Energy and Natural Resources Law, Environmental Law

Office Practice—see also Interviewing and Counseling

HEGLAND'S TRIAL AND PRACTICE SKILLS IN A NUTSHELL, 346 pages, 1978. Softcover (Text)

Oil and Gas

HEMINGWAY'S HORNBOOK ON OIL AND GAS, Second Edition, Student Edition, 543 pages, 1983, with 1986 pocket part. (Text)

LOWE'S OIL AND GAS LAW IN A NUTSHELL, Second Edition, 465 pages, 1988. Softcover. (Text)

Partnership—see Agency—Partnership

Patent and Copyright Law

MILLER AND DAVIS' INTELLECTUAL PROPERTY—PATENTS, TRADEMARKS AND COPYRIGHT IN A NUTSHELL, 428 pages, 1983. Softcover. (Text)

Products Liability

PHILLIPS' PRODUCTS LIABILITY IN A NUTSHELL, Third Edition,

Remedies—Continued
320 pages, 1985. Softcover. (Text)

Sea, Law of
SOHN AND GUSTAFSON'S THE LAW OF THE SEA IN A NUTSHELL, 264 pages, 1984. Softcover. (Text)

Securities Regulation
HAZEN'S HORNBOOK ON THE LAW OF SECURITIES REGULATION, Student Edition, 739 pages, 1985, with 1988 pocket part. (Text)

RATNER'S SECURITIES REGULATION IN A NUTSHELL, Third Edition, 316 pages, 1988. Softcover. (Text)

Social Legislation
HOOD AND HARDY'S WORKERS' COMPENSATION AND EMPLOYEE PROTECTION IN A NUTSHELL, 274 pages, 1984. Softcover. (Text)

LAFRANCE'S WELFARE LAW: STRUCTURE AND ENTITLEMENT IN A NUTSHELL, 455 pages, 1979. Softcover. (Text)

Sports Law
SCHUBERT, SMITH AND TRENTADUE'S SPORTS LAW, 395 pages, 1986. (Text)

Taxation—Corporate
WEIDENBRUCH AND BURKE'S FEDERAL INCOME TAXATION OF CORPORATIONS AND STOCKHOLDERS IN A NUTSHELL, Third Edition, approximately 325 pages, 1989. Softcover. (Text)

Taxation—Estate & Gift—see also Estate Planning, Trusts and Estates
MCNULTY'S FEDERAL ESTATE AND GIFT TAXATION IN A NUTSHELL, Fourth Edition, approximately 479 pages, 1989. Softcover. (Text)

Taxation—Individual
HUDSON AND LIND'S BLACK LETTER ON FEDERAL INCOME TAXATION, Second Edition, 396 pages, 1987. Softcover. (Review)

MCNULTY'S FEDERAL INCOME TAXATION OF INDIVIDUALS IN A NUTSHELL, Fourth Edition, 503 pages, 1988. Softcover. (Text)

POSIN'S HORNBOOK ON FEDERAL INCOME TAXATION, Student Edition, 491 pages, 1983, with 1987 pocket part. (Text)

ROSE AND CHOMMIE'S HORNBOOK ON FEDERAL INCOME TAXATION, Third Edition, 923 pages, 1988. (Text)

Taxation—State & Local

GELFAND AND SALSICH'S STATE AND LOCAL TAXATION AND FINANCE IN A NUTSHELL, 309 pages, 1986. Softcover. (Text)

Torts—see also Products Liability

KIONKA'S BLACK LETTER ON TORTS, 339 pages, 1988. Softcover. (Review)

KIONKA'S TORTS IN A NUTSHELL: INJURIES TO PERSONS AND PROPERTY, 434 pages, 1977. Softcover. (Text)

MALONE'S TORTS IN A NUTSHELL: INJURIES TO FAMILY, SOCIAL AND TRADE RELATIONS, 358 pages, 1979. Softcover. (Text)

PROSSER AND KEETON'S HORNBOOK ON TORTS, Fifth Edition, Student Edition, 1286 pages, 1984 with 1988 pocket part. (Text)

Trade Regulation—see also Antitrust, Regulated Industries

MCMANIS' UNFAIR TRADE PRACTICES IN A NUTSHELL, Second Edition, 464 pages, 1988. Softcover. (Text)

SCHECHTER'S BLACK LETTER ON UNFAIR TRADE PRACTICES, 272 pages, 1986. Softcover. (Review)

Trial and Appellate Advocacy—see also Civil Procedure

BERGMAN'S TRIAL ADVOCACY IN A NUTSHELL, 402 pages, 1979. Softcover. (Text)

GOLDBERG'S THE FIRST TRIAL (WHERE DO I SIT? WHAT DO I SAY?) IN A NUTSHELL, 396 pages, 1982. Softcover. (Text)

HEGLAND'S TRIAL AND PRACTICE SKILLS IN A NUTSHELL, 346 pages, 1978. Softcover. (Text)

HORNSTEIN'S APPELLATE ADVOCACY IN A NUTSHELL, 325 pages, 1984. Softcover. (Text)

JEANS' HANDBOOK ON TRIAL ADVOCACY, Student Edition, 473 pages, 1975. Softcover. (Text)

Trusts and Estates

ATKINSON'S HORNBOOK ON WILLS, Second Edition, 975 pages, 1953. (Text)

AVERILL'S UNIFORM PROBATE CODE IN A NUTSHELL, Second Edition, 454 pages, 1987. Softcover. (Text)

BOGERT'S HORNBOOK ON

Advisory Board

THE LAW OF SCHOOLS, STUDENTS, AND TEACHERS IN A NUTSHELL

By

KERN ALEXANDER
University of Florida

and

M. DAVID ALEXANDER
Virginia Tech University

ST. PAUL, MINN.
WEST PUBLISHING CO.
1984

Library of Congress Cataloging in Publication Data

Alexander, Kern.
    The law of schools, students, and teachers in a nutshell.

    (Nutshell series)
    Includes index.
    1. Educational law and legislation—United States.
I. Alexander, M. David. II. Title. III. Series.
KF4119.3.A43   1984   344.73'07   84–2409
                            347.3047
ISBN 0–314–80555–9

        Alexander & Alexander Schs., Studs., Tchs. ns
        3rd Reprint—1989

PREFACE

To capture the essence of education law and place it neatly in a nutshell is no mean undertaking. The expanding boundaries of this field of law are evolving at such a rapid pace that it is virtually impossible to sift through all the precedents much less reduce them to a cogent package of pertinence which will make sense to students, teachers, and others.

Now that the job of synthesizing all the cases is completed, we already see that the dynamic flow of the law will greatly expand and embellish many of these precedents. We feel, however, that the restatement of the law as we have given it will continue to provide a firm foundation on which readers of the book can continue to rely. In any event, the preparation of a book on law requires that the authors exercise a considerable amount of discretion in the identification and interpretation of precedents, and most persons who have written books on the law will freely admit to their vulnerability in attempting to glean from judicial expositions actual and appropriate meanings.

With this awareness, and fully convinced that four heads are much better than two, the authors often called on Samuel Alexander, who happens also to be our father and a school law specialist in his own right, and on Dr. Mary Jane Connelly, professor of educational administration at Glassboro State College, New Jersey, to assist in the analysis of the law and editing of the manuscript.

PREFACE

Without their assistance the task would probably never have been completed. We also want to acknowledge the support of our mother, Emma McCune Alexander, also an educator, who beyond her essential role of bringing us into this world and rearing us with love and understanding, also provided us with valuable educational insights. We also acknowledge the prompt and efficient assistance we received from Nancy McDavid of Brooker, Florida, and Paulette Gardner of Blacksburg, Virginia, in typing and further editing of the manuscript.

K. ALEXANDER
M. D. ALEXANDER

Gainesville, Florida
January 11, 1984

OUTLINE

CHAPTER 2. THE INSTRUCTIONAL PROGRAM—Continued

CHAPTER 3. RIGHT TO AN EDUCATION AND PROCEDURAL DUE PROCESS

CHAPTER 12. CIVIL LIABIITY

CHAPTER 13. STUDENT RECORDS, DEFA-MATION, AND PRIVACY

CHAPTER 15. TERMS AND CONDITIONS OF TEACHER EMPLOYMENT

CHAPTER 16. CONSTITUTIONAL RIGHTS OF TEACHERS

CHAPTER 17.   TEACHER DISMISSAL—Continued

TABLE OF CASES

References are to Pages

TABLE OF CASES

TABLE OF CASES

TABLE OF CASES

TABLE OF CASES

TABLE OF CASES

THE LAW OF SCHOOLS, STUDENTS, AND TEACHERS IN A NUTSHELL

*

INTRODUCTION

During the last generation Americans have witnessed an explosion of litigation affecting education. Courts have become much more actively involved in aspects of education which were heretofore left entirely to the discretion of school administrators and school boards. Teachers', students' and parents' rights have been asserted in legal actions against school authority producing a vastly expanded field of judicial precedents which have tended to reshape American education.

These precedents have materially affected the way Americans view their public schools. Gallup polls taken annually over the last decade for the Phi Delta Kappa, a professional education fraternity, have indicated that the average American citizen believes that the number one problem in public schools is pupil control and discipline. Teachers attribute the problems of discipline to the pervasive expansion of student rights and the corresponding limits on school authority to control student behavior.

School authorities, further, maintain that the complexity of legal precedents governing school and student relations creates such a degree of uncertainty in control of students, that many teachers and school administrators are hesitant to control student behavior for fear of potential litigation. Such uncertainty generally results in an extraordinary expenditure of teacher or administrator time in providing students with extensive legal process or has, at times, resulted in

[1]

ignoring student infractions of rules resulting many times in school disruption.

Such problems have precipitated a national debate over the conduct of the public schools. Widely circulated research reports have maintained that private schools are academically superior to public schools because the private schools are not fettered with student constitutional safeguards and private school teachers and administrators can act quietly and decisively in ridding their schools of disruptive students through banishment. Because of individual constitutional safeguards, public schools have no such peremptory options. Thus, the great constitutional principles of the Bill of Rights so revered and honored by Americans since 1791 have frequently been cited as the reason for the lack of quality education in America's public schools.

Yet, judicial precedents extending students' rights have, in most cases, been rational and logical applications of guaranteed constitutional rights and interests to which all persons are entitled, including students, against unwarranted governmental intrusion.

No one can reasonably argue that an arbitrary action by a teacher or administrator denying a public education to a child should go unredressed by the courts. Or that denial of an education to a child merely because he or she is handicapped and his or her education would be more expensive than a regular child's is not an affront to the individual's constitutional interests. To argue that children do not have a right to be free from state-sanctioned religious indoctrination is likewise an offense against any rational consideration of individual liberty. Too, to assert that it does not offend a child's right of privacy to strip them of their clothes and search them is an effrontery to commonly accepted principles of decency and moral behavior. Certainly, no one will deny that denial of equal education on the basis of race or sex should be condoned in this or any other society. Yet, all of these encroachments on the student's rights have been, at times, practiced in America's educational system.

Operating within their constitutional mandate to protect individual rights, the courts have stemmed such practices in the public schools. In so doing they have cast aside the older legal concept that education was a privilege, bestowed by the state on students, which could be withdrawn at any time. Today, the courts view each student as having a constitutional interest in education which cannot be denied except where the state's interest is preeminent. Interests, between the student and the school are thus balanced and weighed as to the benefits gained and the detriments suffered by both parties. From this "balancing of interests" a new student and school constitutional relationship is fashioned.

The expansion of individual interests in constitutional law has not only affected the student, but has significantly reshaped the teacher and school relationship as well. Application of constitutional principles of freedom of speech and expression are at least as essential to teaching as they are to learning. The preservation of "academic freedom" to expand the horizons of knowledge is the essence of education. Neither school boards nor parents will be allowed by

[*3*]

the courts to "cast a pall of orthodoxy" over the classroom. Teachers by pursuit of their profession are, also, vested with substantive due process interests which cannot be arbitrarily denied by school board action no matter how great the community or political pressure. Court decisions have thus been instrumental in expansion and preservation of teacher interests and rights in the furtherance of education.

This book is about these issues: the judicial balancing of the interests between the public school, as a state agency, and the students and teachers as individuals. It is also about student and teacher relationships in the common law context of the teacher standing *in loco parentis*, to control, nurse, and teach the child through the twelve critical years of elementary and secondary education. The respective relationships are delineated according to judicial precedents. By reading and understanding this book, students, teachers, school officials, and parents will better understand and appreciate their legal responsibilities in the American educational process.

CHAPTER 1

ATTENDANCE IN PUBLIC SCHOOLS

§ 1.1 INTRODUCTION

Provision for attendance in free public schools is provided for in state constitutions. Within the scope of constitutional provisions legislatures enact laws which prescribe the admission requirements. Some constitutional provisions designate an age span, such as between six and twenty years of age, for which the state shall provide an education. These constitutional provisions are viewed by the courts as requiring state legislatures to provide for public education covering at least this age group, but does not prohibit the legislature from expanding educational opportunity beyond the specified ages. For example, courts have held that a legislature has the implied authority to create kindergarten programs for children below the age of six years. In re Kindergarten Schools, 32 P. 422 (Colo. 1893). Similarly, expansion of vocational education programs for adults has been held to be within legislative prerogative, even though the state constitution defined public education as covering only ages four through twenty years. In this case, the Supreme Court of Wisconsin said that: "The constitutional provision [that] the Legislature shall provide for establishment of district schools and that such schools shall be free to all children between the ages of four and twenty years does not impliedly prohibit free education for persons beyond the age of twenty and under

[5]

the age of four." Manitowoc v. Manitowoc Rapids, 231 Wis. 94, 285 N.W. 403 (1939).

Courts have, generally, acceded to expansion of educational opportunity through reliance on broad implication of either the state constitution or statute. In the famous *Kalamazoo* case, the precedent which helped form public secondary schools in America, the court relied on broad implication of state policy, not explicit statute, to support its conclusion that a local school district could, with consent of the voters, expand its educational program to include high school. Stuart v. School District No. 1 of the Village of Kalamazoo, 30 Mich. 69 (1874).

§ 1.2 ADMISSION

As the educational program is expanded, all persons in the particular age group are entitled to attend the public school. A state cannot set up unreasonable attendance classifications of persons within the age groups. For example, the public schools in one sector of the state cannot be closed down and vouchers from public funds given to students to attend private schools, with the result that schools are racially segregated. Griffin v. County School Board of Prince Edward County, 377 U.S. 218, 84 S.Ct. 1226 (1964). When the state makes the decision to provide an educational program, it must do so uniformly and denial of attendance cannot be for a discriminatory purpose.

§ 1.21 Restrictions

States can impose restrictions on admission to public schools which are reasonably related to the state's purpose of providing a free public education. Such restrictions have been upheld when related to the maintenance of the health and protection of the public welfare. Also, residence requirements for reasonable classifications of children have been upheld. Residence statutes which require children to attend school in one school district rather than in another have been dealt with liberally by the courts. A school district has a right to question the *bona fides* of the residency of its students. Where a student changes guardianship solely to attend school in another school district, the validity of the change in residence may be rejected by the receiving school board. In the Matter of Proios, 111 Misc.2d 252, 443 N.Y.S.2d 828 (1981).

§ 1.22 Residence

Most state laws require children to attend school in the district in which the student resides with his parents or guardian or person having lawful control of him. If a child lives with a custodian, but his parents are in residence in another school district, he must attend school in the district where his parents reside. The United States Supreme Court has held that a *bona fide* residence requirement which is appropriately defined and uniformly applied furthers the state interest in assuring that educational services of the state are enjoyed only by the state's residents. Morales v. Bynum, ___ U.S. ___, 103 S.Ct. 1838 (1983).

"Residence" generally requires both physical presence and an intention to remain. The Supreme Court of Maine provided the best definition over a century ago, "When . . . a person voluntarily takes up his abode in a given place, with intention to remain permanently, or for an indefinite period of time; or, to speak more accurately, when a person takes up his abode in a given place, without any present intention to remove therefrom, such place of abode becomes his residence." Inhabitants of Warren v. Inhabitants of Thomaston, 43 Me. 406 (1857).

§ 1.23 Domicile

The word "domicile" is derived from the Latin "domus" meaning home or dwelling house. The word may be defined by law as the true place of habitation, for example, a Washington statute which was upheld as constitutional by the United States Supreme Court defined "domicile" as "a person's true, fixed and permanent home and place of habitation. It is the place where he intends to remain, and to which he expects to return when he leaves without intending to establish a new domicile elsewhere." Sturgis v. Washington, 414 U.S. 1057, 94 S.Ct. 563 (1973). A *bona fide* residence requirement may have the same legal connotation as domicile. Domicile and residence are usually in the same place, but the terms are not identical. A person may have two residences, but can have only one domicile. Whether the term "residence" or "domicile" is used, the key is the "intention to remain."

§ 1.24 Constitutional Classification

Classification of persons by geographical boundaries does not constitute a "suspect" classification requiring strict scrutiny to show a compelling reason to so classify. Domicile requirements are not unconstitutional if the classification is rationally related to a legitimate state purpose. The Supreme Court affirmed a lower federal court decision which held valid a state university regulation which declared that no student could be eligible for resident classification " . . . unless he had been a bona fide domiciliary of the state for at least a year immediately prior thereto . . . " The rule required that the student show permanent residence and that his presence in the state was not solely for the purpose of attending the state university. Starns v. Malkerson, 401 U.S. 985, 91 S.Ct. 1231 (1970).

§ 1.25 Irrebuttable Presumption

A Connecticut residence requirement for university students was held to be unconstitutional as violating due process because it created an "irrebuttable presumption" of nonresidency for all students whose legal addresses were outside the state before they applied for admission. This meant that nonresident students could not gain resident status so long as they were students because the law created a presumption of nonresidence for all those who attended the state university. The nonresident students could not rebut this presumption even though they intended to continue to live in the state after graduation. Vlandis v. Kline, 412 U.S. 441, 93 S.Ct. 2230 (1973).

§ 1.26 Validity of Residence

In Morales v. Bynum, supra, the United States Supreme Court upheld a Texas statute which denied tuition-free admission to minors who live apart from their parent or guardian for the "primary purpose of attending public free schools." In this case, Roberto Morales, who was born in McAllen, Texas in 1969, a citizen of the United States by birth, was denied tuition-free admission in the McAllen Independent School District because his parents no longer lived in Texas and now resided in Mexico. He moved to McAllen where he lived with his sister who was his custodian but not his legal guardian. The Court held that denial of admission was not violative of equal protection because the State of Texas had a substantial interest in maintaining school quality by imposing *bona fide* residence requirements. The Court said that: "Absent residence requirements, there can be little doubt that the proper planning and operation of the schools would suffer significantly."

§ 1.27 Illegal Aliens

If, however, state law regarding residency works to completely deny school attendance in all districts of a state, the constitution may be violated. Children of illegal aliens have been held to have a right to attend the public schools of Texas when the alternative was that they would receive no public education at all. Plyler v. Doe, 457 U.S. 202, 102 S.Ct. 2382 (1982). In this case plaintiffs, illegal aliens, challenged a state statute in Texas which withheld state school funds for the education of children who were not legally admitted into the United States and which authorized local school districts to deny their enrollment. The plaintiffs claimed that the statute violated the Equal Protection Clause of the Fourteenth Amendment which states that no state shall "deny to any person within its jurisdiction the equal protection of the laws." The state of Texas in defense maintained that the provision in the Clause "within its jurisdiction" excluded consideration of aliens and, further, contended that such a classification was rational because it was in the state's interest to preserve its limited resources for education for those children who were legal residents of the state. In ruling on the first issue, the Court said that the phrase "within its jurisdiction" was meant to confirm the understanding that the protection of the Fourteenth Amendment extended to anyone, citizen or stranger, who is subject to the laws of the state. Since illegal aliens were within the state's boundaries, they were subject to its laws. The Supreme Court pointed out that even though undocumented aliens are not a "suspect class" under the Constitution and that education is not a fundamental right, such a statute would result in a lifetime of hardship for those affected. The Court noted that the children could not be denied services because their parents were illegal aliens and to subject them to such deprivation could not be justified on rational grounds. In arriving at this conclusion, the Court went to great lengths to expound the importance and virtues of public education and, while not declaring it fundamental, apparently elevated it to a level of importance substantially greater than other governmental functions. The Court said that the deprivation of education was not the same as denial of other social benefits of government. Public education plays a pivotal role "in maintaining the fabric of our society and in sustaining our political and cultural heritage"; the denial of education takes an "inestimable toll on the social, economic, intellectual, and psychological well-being of the individual." For the state to impose such an obstacle on a child is to impose a lifetime handicap. In balancing the educational interest of the alien child against the interest of the state, the Court found little contest.

§ 1.3 COMPULSORY ATTENDANCE

An educated citizenry is of paramount importance to perpetuate a democratic society. Experience throughout history has shown that those societies with high levels of illiteracy and ignorance among their people are most susceptible to domination and tyranny. James Madison observed that no nation can expect to have a popular government without popular information and Jefferson in his *Preamble to a Bill for the More General Diffusion of Knowledge* (1779) admonished that the most effectual means of preventing tyranny is "to illuminate, as far as practicable, the minds of the people."

Mass education is not only the best and surest means of preservation of liberty, but it is also essential to the economic and social welfare of the people. Horace Mann probably expressed it best in 1848 when he said that: "For the creation of wealth, then—for the existence of a wealthy people and a wealthy nation—intelligence is the grand condition. . . . The greatest of all arts of political economy is to change a consumer into a producer; and the next greatest is to increase the producing power—an end to be directly attained, by increasing his intelligence."

On these grounds the legislatures and the courts of the nation have justified mass general education of all the people. To accomplish this compulsory school attendance laws have been enacted throughout the nation. Those who have advanced ideas which would result in deschooling society have been given little serious consideration by thoughtful and forward-looking leaders of society.

§ 1.31 Parens Patriae

Legal rationale for compulsory education is found in the common law doctrine of *parens patriae,* which means that the state is the father or guardian for minors or others—"to the end that the health, patriotism, morality, efficiency, industry, and integrity of its citizenship may be preserved and protected." Strangway v. Allen, 194 Ky. 681, 240 S.W. 384 (1922). An Illinois court has explained *parens patriae* in this manner. "It is the unquestioned right and imperative duty of every enlightened government, in its character of *parens patriae,* to protect and provide for the comfort and well-being of such of its citizens . . . The performance of these duties is justly regarded as one of the most important of governmental functions, and all constitutional limitations must be so understood as not to interfere with its proper and legitimate exercise." County of McLean v. Humphrey, 104 Ill. 378 (1882).

This power of the state to protect and educate the populace, generally, supersedes the custodial authority of the parent over the child. Parents have undoubted inherent rights to rear and control their own children, but these rights may be legitimately restricted by the

[*13*]

state when parental prerogatives are exercised to the detriment of the child. The courts have long recognized that parents may not always act in the best interest of their children. The United States Supreme Court pointed out in 1962 that ". . . experience has shown that the question of custody, so vital to a child's happiness and well-being, frequently cannot be left to the discretion of the parents." Ford v. Ford, 371 U.S. 187, 83 S.Ct. 273 (1962).

The United States Supreme Court most clearly enunciated this power of the state by upholding a Massachusetts child labor law in 1943 under which a parent was convicted of contributing to the delinquency of a minor. The parent had continued to force the child to work and would not permit the child to attend school, in spite of the law. In this case, Prince v. Massachusetts, 321 U.S. 158, 64 S.Ct. 438 (1943), the Court said: "[T]he family itself is not beyond regulation in the public interest . . . acting to guard the general interest in a youth's well-being, the state as *parens patriae* may restrict the parents' control by requiring school attendance, regulating or prohibiting the child's labor and in many other ways."

§ 1.4 LIMITATIONS ON STATE POWER

The legal competence of the state to compel children to attend school is well established, but the power of the state is not unlimited. The state, for example, cannot require attendance solely in public schools. In Pierce v. Society of Sisters, 268 U.S. 510, 45 S.Ct. 571 (1925), the United States Supreme Court held an Oregon statute unconstitutional because it sought to compel all children between the ages of eight and sixteen years to attend public schools. Two private schools sued claiming that the law denied them their property without due process of law. The institutions claimed that they owned valuable buildings which were constructed for school purposes and that they acquired income from education programs, the success of which was dependent on long-term contracts with teachers and parents. The Supreme Court held that the law did, in fact, deprive the schools of property without due process. The Court agreed that "the right to conduct schools was property and that parents and guardians, as a part of their liberty, might direct the education of children by selecting reputable teachers and places." The Court further said that it was clear that the statute interfered with the liberty of parents to control their children. The "fundamental theory of liberty" the Court said "excludes any general power of the state to standardize its children by forcing them to accept instruction from public teachers only." *Pierce*, therefore, recognizes and guarantees the private school's property interest and acknowledges a parental liberty interest in education of the child in other than public schools.

§ 1.41 Truancy

Compulsory attendance laws provide for enforcement by penalizing parents for their children's absences. When a child is declared a truant or a chronic or habitual truant, the school board may institute legal proceedings which may include criminal penalty of the parent. A typical definition of truant is found in an

Illinois law which reads as follows: "A 'truant' is defined as a child subject to compulsory school attendance and who is absent without valid excuse from such attendance for a school day or portion thereof." Ill.Rev.Stat.1979, Ch. 122, ¶ 27–2a.

Valid cause for absences may be variously defined by statute as illness, death in the family, family emergency or situations beyond the control of the student.

A chronic or habitual truant is usually defined as a student who has several unexcused absences during a specified period of time. In Illinois, for example, a chronic or habitual truant is a student who is absent without valid cause for fifteen of ninety consecutive days. Statute may require that absences for illness be certified by a physician. Such requirement of doctor's verification of the child's medical condition has been upheld as a valid exercise of state discretion. People ex rel. Latimer v. Board of Education, 394 Ill. 228, 68 N.E.2d 305 (1946).

Where parents took their daughter to several doctors occasionally over a two-year period, but there was no evidence that any single doctor thought she was unable to attend school and no medical excuse was ever received by the school, the court upheld conviction and fining of parents for permitting chronic truancy of their child. People v. Berger, 109 Ill.App.3d 1054, 65 Ill.Dec. 600, 441 N.E.2d 915 (1982).

§ 1.42   Home Instruction

Home instruction is not, generally, considered to fulfill the requirements of compulsory school attendance.

Statutes which provide for private school instruction as fulfillment of compulsory attendance requirements, as they must under Pierce v. Society of Sisters, supra, are not to be construed as permitting home instruction. Authority to exempt home instruction from compulsory attendance laws must be permitted by express statutory provision. A statute in California which provided for exemption for those "being instructed in a private full-time day school by persons capable of teaching" was held not to implicitly permit home instruction. People v. Turner, 121 Cal.App.2d Supp. 861, 263 P.2d 685 (1953), appeal dismissed 347 U.S. 972, 74 S.Ct. 785 (1954). The fact that there is no statutory regulation of private schools does not mean that parents can proclaim that their homes are schools in an effort to avoid enrolling their children in public schools. State v. M.M., 407 So.2d 987 (1981).

A compulsory attendance statute which required that parents send their children to a "public school," or a "private denominational or parochial school or have such . . . children taught [in a home] by a tutor or teachers of qualifications prescribed by the State Board of Education" was held to be violated by unqualified parents who attempted to have home instruction for their child. One of the parents was a high school graduate and held an Associate's degree in Industrial Technology and the other held a high school diploma from a correspondence school. The parents used teaching materials purchased from a company which marketed home study courses. The court observed that the burden of proof was on the state to show that the home instruction was not equivalent of private schools and the state in this case had success-fully carried that burden. Grigg v. Commonwealth of Virginia, 224 Va. 356, 297 S.E.2d 799 (1982). Correspondence courses for students in lieu of school attendance will not suffice to fulfill statutory requirements of continuous school attendance. State v. Garber, 197 Kan. 567, 419 P.2d 896 (1966).

Some courts have observed that the attributes of school attendance go beyond merely the instruction of children and include social interaction with other students, appropriate facilities such as libraries, laboratories and other features generally found in formal school settings but absent in homes. Student interaction is an essential ingredient of school, thus, home instruction involving only one's own children cannot constitute the equivalent of a regular school program. Stephens v. Bongart, 15 N.J.Misc. 80, 189 A. 131 (1937).

While a compulsory attendance law must allow for private school attendance, it does not necessarily need to have a similar provision for home instruction. Pierce v. Society of Sisters, supra, protected the property interest of the private school, but did not extend similar constitutional protection to home instruction. Several states' statutes do not provide for home instruction because it is believed that the sequestration of children in the home sealed off from other children and modern society will inhibit their living normal, happy, and productive lives. State v. Riddle, ___ W.Va. ___, 285 S.E.2d 359 (1981). "Cloister and shelter have its place, but not in the everyday give and take of life." Knox v. O'Brien, 7 N.J.Super. 608, 72 A.2d 389 (1950).

Denial of home instruction as a valid exemption from compulsory attendance does not violate the Equal Protection Clause of the Fourteenth Amendment. A New Mexico court held that statutory exclusion of home instruction was subject to the rational relationship test of constitutionality. State v. Edgington, 99 N.M. 715, 663 P.2d 374 (App.1983). This test requires that the state merely show that the purpose for the law is rational. Plaintiffs had argued that the more rigorous test of strict scrutiny must be applied which would require that the state bear the burden of showing a compelling interest to justify its action. This latter test is very difficult to sustain. In considering the two tests, the court concluded that because the United States Supreme Court had held that education was not a fundamental interest, San Antonio School District v. Rodriguez, 411 U.S. 1, 93 S.Ct. 1278 (1973), the lesser test was appropriate. Using this test the court reasoned that requiring children to go to school with other children was a legitimate state interest. The New Mexico court said: "By bringing children into contact with some person, other than those in the excluded group, those children are exposed to at least one other set of attitudes, values, morals, lifestyles and intellectual abilities. Therefore, we hold that the statutory classifications presented in the attendance law rationally relates to a legitimate state interest." State v. Edgington, supra.

§ 1.43   Private Schools

Exemption from compulsory attendance to attend private schools is a right of all parents as protected by due process as enunciated in Pierce v. Society of Sisters, supra. Litigation, though, frequently arises as to whether a school has the attributes which are required to qualify as a "private school" as contemplated by law. A Washington court in 1912 held that the words "to attend a private school" meant more than home instruction; it means, to be approved for exemption, the school must be "the same character of school as the public school, a regular organized and existing institution making a business of instructing children of school age in required studies and for the full time required by the laws . . . " State v. Counort, 69 Wash. 361, 124 P. 910 (1912).

According to a New Jersey court, whether an instructional program constitutes a "private school" within the meaning of statute is dependent on three tests: first, the qualifications of the parent or instructor; second, the teaching material being used; and third, whether the educational program was commensurate with that provided in public schools. Knox v. O'Brien, supra.

Home instruction conducted by a parent trained in education, where appropriate instructional materials were used for class during a regularly scheduled school day, was held to be a valid "private school" program in Illinois. People v. Levisen, 404 Ill. 574, 90 N.E.2d 213 (1950). In the absence of a home instruction statute, the burden of proof is on the parent to show that the instructional program is a "private school" and to be so adjudged it must be commensurate with that of a regular public school program.

§ 1.44   Religious Exemption

The general rule of law is that religious objection to education is not a valid reason for keeping a child away from school. The great jurist Blackstone noted that common law recognized that the most important duty of parents is to give their children "an education suitable to their station in life" and Blackstone further acknowledged the power of the state to take children from the parents to assure that the children's abilities could be developed to "the greatest advantage of the commonwealth." 1 Commentaries 451.

In 1839 the United States Supreme Court held that the right to control their own children is a parent's natural, but not an "unalienable right." Ex parte Crouse, 4 Whart. 9 (1839). In justification of compulsory attendance, as a limitation on parental control, a Pennsylvania court has said that "it must be conceded by all right thinking persons, that enforcement of the compulsory school code is a matter of paramount importance, to which the views of the individual view must yield . . ." Commonwealth v. Gillen, 65 Pa.Super. 31 (1916).

Objection to compulsory attendance cannot be simply justified by parent's claims that they have an inherent right to control their child's religious upbringing. Prince v. Massachusetts, supra. In Commonwealth v. Bey, 166 Pa.Super. 136, 70 A.2d 693 (1950), Mohammedan parents persistently refused to send their children to school on Fridays, the sacred day of that religion. The court found the parents in violation of the compulsory attendance law and said: "It [the law] permits attendance at private and parochial schools. All that it requires is continuous attendance at a day-school of the kind and character mentioned in the statute, or daily instruction by a private tutor. Since the parent may avail himself of other schools, including parochial or denominational schools, the statute does not interfere with or impinge upon the religious freedom of parents . . ."

§ 1.45   Wisconsin v. Yoder

The most important exception to the general rule, that religious belief does not exempt one from compulsory attendance laws, is found in the United States Supreme Court's decision in State of Wisconsin v. Yoder, 406 U.S. 205, 92 S.Ct. 1526 (1972). In this case the Court held that Amish children could not be compelled to attend high school even though they were within the age range of Wisconsin's compulsory attendance statute. The Amish maintained that higher learning beyond that which could be acquired in neighborhood elementary schools tended to develop values which alienated their children from God. The Amish sect believes that its members should reject the competitive spirit, deemphasize material success and insulate its youth from the modern world.

The Supreme Court, in interpreting the sweep of the First Amendment's Free Exercise Clause, observed that protection of religious beliefs is a basic freedom of such magnitude that the state's interest must be of the "highest order" if it is to overbalance the individual's religious interest. The Court placed the burden of proof on the state to show that universal compulsory education was not merely rational public policy, but, indeed, a compelling state interest.

In attempting to show a compelling interest, Wisconsin maintained that education is necessary to prepare citizens to participate effectively in our democratic system of government. In response the Court observed that the Amish community is a unique and special case which has been "highly successful as a social unit within our society" and that its members had an exemplary record as productive and law-abiding citizens. With regard to participation in the democratic process, the Court held that the brief period of education from ages fourteen to sixteen, the period in question when the Amish children would be compelled to attend high school, was not a period of time significant enough to justify "severe interference with religious freedom." According to the Court, the Amish alternative to formal secondary education had enabled the Amish to function effectively in day-to-day life of contemporary society as a "separate and sharply identifiable and highly self-sufficient community for more than 200 years in this country." Further, the Court noted that when Thomas Jefferson emphasized the need for an educated citizenry as a bulwark against tyranny, he did not necessarily have in mind education beyond a basic eighth-grade education.

In ruling for the Amish parents, however, the Court so narrowly defined the attributes of the Amish religion in exempting it from compulsory attendance that the use of *Yoder* as precedent by parents of other religions to gain similar exemptions has been generally unsuccessful. The Court set out three criteria for balancing the individual's religious interests against the public interests of the state. The court must determine (1) whether the individual's beliefs are legitimately religious and if they are sincerely held; (2) whether the state regulation unduly restricts the religious practices; (3) whether the state has a compelling interest justifying the regulation and whether the compelling interest is of such importance as to overcome the right to free exercise of religion.

The primary importance of *Yoder* is that it elevates religion to a special constitutional status as a First Amendment right which must be given particular consideration by the courts when parents and students contest state action. Importantly, it requires that the state bear the burden of showing that it has a compelling reason to justify its denial of a religious belief. In the unique case of *Yoder* and the Amish religion, the state was unable to bear this burden.

§ 1.46   Regulation of Religious Schools

The state has a legitimate interest in the quality of the educational program performed in private schools, but as indicated in *Yoder* where freedom of religion is in question the courts will apply strict judicial scrutiny. The extent of the state regulation to be permitted by the courts will depend on the state's constitution and statutes and how they are applied to the private school.

In a 1979 case, the Kentucky Supreme Court held that the state could not prosecute parents for violation of the compulsory attendance law who enrolled their children in private schools which did not employ certified teachers nor use state approved textbooks. Kentucky State Board v. Rudasill, 589 S.W.2d 877 (Ky.1979). The court decided the case purely on a state constitutional provision which stated in part: "nor shall any man be compelled to send his child to any schools to which he is conscientiously opposed . . . ." This provision, the court observed, was more restrictive on the state than the Free Exercise Clause of the First Amendment of the United States Constitution. In examining the debate at the constitutional convention at which the provision was adopted, the court found the intent of this provision was to allow parents to choose any school for their children, as a matter of conscience. The court found nothing wrong with the state mandating that private schools have instruction in several branches of study as was required of public schools, but the court would not allow the state to require the same instruments of education, certified teachers, and state-approved textbooks, to be used by private schools.

Parents again prevailed in an Ohio case in which parents were convicted of violating compulsory attendance laws because they enrolled their children in a Bible-oriented Christian school which failed to "conform to the minimum standards prescribed by the state . . . ." State v. Whisner, 47 Ohio St.2d 181, 351 N.E.2d 750 (1976). The private school had only twenty-three children who were taught by a certified teach-

[25]

er in one room. The state minimum standards in Ohio were highly restrictive regulating virtually to the minute what should be taught in private schools. These standards regulated "[t]he content of the curriculum that [was] taught, the manner in which it [was] taught, the person or persons who [taught] it, the physical layout of the building in which the students [were] taught, the hours of instruction, and the educational policies intended to be achieved through the instruction offered."

The court found these rules to be so excessive as to deny the parents their freedom of religion and the right to direct the education of their children as they saw fit. In following *Yoder* the court required that the state show a compelling reason to justify the encroachment on individual religious freedom. This burden the state was unable to sustain.

Conviction of parents for violating compulsory attendance laws has, however, been upheld in Nebraska and North Dakota. In Meyerkorth v. State, the Supreme Court of Nebraska held that statutes requiring that private school instruction be "substantially the same" as that of public schools did not violate the religious freedom of private school parents or the students. 173 Neb. 889, 115 N.W.2d 585 (1962).

The North Dakota case set a precedent almost precisely opposite that of *Whisner*. State v. Shaver, 294 N.W.2d 883 (N.D.1980). Here defendant parents were convicted of violating compulsory attendance laws for sending their children to a church-affiliated private school which was not approved by the state. The school had no certified teachers and employed a widely used self-study curriculum made up of a series of Bible-oriented learning packets. The school showed, as was the case in *Rudasill*, that the students of the private school scored higher on achievement tests than did their counterparts in public schools.

The court in applying the three-part test of *Yoder*, balancing the parents' interests against the state's, ruled against the parents. As to the tests: first, the court acknowledged that the defendants had a sincere religious belief; second, the court did not agree that the state rules placed an undue burden on the defendants' religious beliefs, but assumed arguendo that such a burden did exist in order to apply the third test, holding that the state had a "legitimate and compelling interest . . . in educating its people" and the regulation of private schools was within state prerogative.

Therefore, a state may regulate private religious schools so long as the regulations are reasonable and are not so excessive or restrictive as to constitute unwarranted interference with the individual's religious freedom. Where parents, though, are able to show that the state's requirements are too specific, then private school parents may succeed in averting conviction for violation of compulsory attendance laws.

§ 1.47 Marriage

Compulsory attendance laws do not generally apply to married persons. Courts have agreed that the nature and responsibilities of marriage are such that married persons of compulsory attendance age should be exempted. The view of the courts is best expressed in State v. Priest, which said that: "The marriage relationship, regardless of the age of the persons involved, creates conditions and imposes obligations upon the parties that are obviously inconsistent with compulsory school attendance or with either the husband or wife remaining under the legal control of parents or other persons." 210 La. 389, 27 So.2d 173 (1946).

In the eyes of the law, then, marriage emancipates the minor from control by either the parent or the state, for purposes of compulsory education.

§ 1.48 Vaccination

States have the inherent police power to enact laws to promote the health and welfare of its citizenry. State statutes, or school board rules made pursuant to statute, requiring vaccination of children against smallpox before they can enter school are a valid exercise of *parens patriae* authority. The United States Supreme Court held in 1905 that the board of health of Cambridge, Massachusetts, could require all persons to be vaccinated without offending personal liberties as guaranteed by the Fourteenth Amendment. The Court noted that individuals do not have unlimited liberty from government control, particularly where the exercise of one's freedom may result in harm to another person in the community.

CHAPTER 2

THE INSTRUCTIONAL PROGRAM

§ 2.1 INTRODUCTION

As a general rule school officials have the authority to prescribe the method of teaching, decide on what curriculum shall be offered, and what books shall be used in the school. Such authority is vested in public schools either expressly or implicitly by state law. However, this authority is not absolute and may be curtailed or modified by the courts if school officials proceed beyond the bounds of their power or act arbitrarily in violation of the constitutional rights of students or teachers. The courts, however, will not intervene in resolution of conflicts which arise from the daily operation of the schools and which do not directly involve basic constitutional values. Pratt v. Independent School District No. 831, Forest Lake, Minnesota, 670 F.2d 771 (8th Cir. 1982).

§ 2.2 CURRICULUM

Power given to school authorities by state legislatures implies discretion to prescribe course content. This power may emanate from rules of general authority which allow the local school authorities to establish the curriculum as well as requirements for promotion and graduation. Such power, of course, may be retained by the legislature, and rather than delegating to local school boards, statute may specifically

[*29*]

mandate a prescribed curriculum or graduation requirements.

§ 2.21   Reasonable Rules

The right of every student to attend school is subject to reasonable regulation. Rules have often been invalidated by the courts because they are arbitrary or capricious. By definition a reasonable rule is neither arbitrary nor capricious. So long, though, as the legal authority is appropriately delegated to local school boards, and the boards act in good faith in formulating and applying reasonable standards, boards' actions will not be overturned.

§ 2.22   Constitutionality

In deciding on the constitutionality of a statute or a rule, the courts will balance the interests of the parties involved. With regard to the school curriculum, students, parents, teachers, and the state all have interests which must be taken into consideration.

The student's interest is an obvious one of self-interest which must be accommodated if the educational process is served. As the guardian of the child the parent has certain expectations of the type of education and the quality and quantity of knowledge his or her child is to acquire. The teacher has freedom to convey knowledge and to exercise those prerogatives which flow from being a teacher. Academic freedom bestowed by the First Amendment is part and parcel of the teacher's interests and protections in teaching. The state has an overarching social and economic interest in fully developing the abilities of its citizenry.

[*30*]

No one rule of law can be prescribed which addresses the problems which may arise from these conflicting interests. The rule which may come nearest to being generally applicable is that the courts will hold in favor of the expansion of knowledge. The party which seeks to "contract the spectrum of knowledge", Griswold v. Connecticut, 381 U.S. 479, 85 S.Ct. 1678 (1965), or restrain the full expanse of human knowledge and inquiry will generally be rebuffed by the courts.

§ 2.23   Intellectual Marketplace

The courts have held that a reluctance on the part of the teacher to investigate and experiment with new ideas is an "anathema" to the idea of education. Imposition of an intellectual straitjacket on teachers or educational leaders would, according to Chief Justice Earl Warren, "imperil the future of our nation." Education is intended to be a marketplace of ideas through which society is best served when there is wide exposure to truths and an unlimited exchange of ideas. The classroom is, thus, viewed as an intellectual marketplace protected by law.

§ 2.24   Evolution and Creation Science

Whether Charles Darwin was an atheist has always bothered many people including legislators, parents, and some school administrators. Those who rigidly adhere to the strict constructionist Biblical account of creation maintain particular umbrage toward school systems which teach science from an evolutionary premise. These feelings have been so strong that many years ago a few states enacted anti-evolution laws making it a criminal offense for a teacher to teach the Darwin theory of evolution. It was this issue on which the famous "Scopes monkey trial" of Dayton, Tennessee was brought. This highly publicized confrontation between the great politician Williams Jennings Bryan and the equally outstanding lawyer Clarence Darrow ultimately resulted in the conviction (a small fine) of Scopes for teaching the theory of evolution. In the process, however, the Tennessee statute was held in such disdain that the issue lay dormant for over 30 years without a real test of the statute's constitutional validity.

Finally, in 1968 in an Arkansas case, the United States Supreme Court ruled that a 1928 anti-evolution statute, making it unlawful for a teacher in a state-supported institution to teach the theory, was unconstitutional. By 1968 only two states, Arkansas and Mississippi had such "monkey laws" on their books. The Court found the law violated the First Amendment because it proscribed a respected scientific theory from the classroom for no other reason but that it was in conflict with a particular religious doctrine in the Book of Genesis. Even though the Arkansas statute was less candid than the original Tennessee "monkey law," in that the Arkansas statute did not explicitly state that the reason for the statute was that it denied the story of the divine creation of man, the Court found that state sanction of the Christian doctrine of creation was, nevertheless, implicit in the Arkansas law and therefore unconstitutional. Epperson v. State of Arkansas, 393 U.S. 97, 89 S.Ct. 266 (1968).

[*32*]

A mixture of religious beliefs and political conditions in the late 1970's led to a revival of the evolution question in public schools. It was widely maintained that the increase in crime and immorality in the United States was caused by the teaching of evolution in the schools. On March 19, 1981, the Governor of Arkansas signed into law a bill which required balanced treatment for creation-science and evolution-science in the public schools.

The terms "creation science" and "scientific creationism" were adopted by fundamentalist religious groups as descriptive of their study of the origins of man and the causes of creation. Fundamentalists claimed their theories of the creation were as scientific as Darwin's theory of evolution. By maintaining that the Biblical theory of creation was scientific, the State of Arkansas justified creation science's equal treatment with evolution in the classroom. Fundamentalists, further, asserted that Darwin's theory of evolution was actually a kind of obverse religion, secular humanism, which taught children to be immoral and anti-theistic.

The essentials of creation-science, as provided by the statute, were (1) a sudden creation of the universe, energy, and life from nothing, (2) the insufficiency of mutation and natural selection in bringing about of all living kinds from a single living organism, (3) that changes in life occurred only within fixed limits of originally created kinds of plants and animals, (4) separate ancestry for man and apes, (5) the creation of earth's geology by catastrophism, including a world-wide flood, and (6) a recent inception (about 5,000 years) of life on earth.

In defense of the statute, the state argued from three points of view: first, that literal interpretation of the creation from Genesis does not, *per se*, mean that creation-science is religious, second; the statute's reference to creation from nothing does not necessarily imply that there is a creator who has power, intelligence, and a sense of design; and third, that simply teaching about the concept of a creator is not a religious exercise.

The federal court, McLean v. Arkansas Board of Education, 529 F.Supp. 1255 (E.D.Ark.1982), found no merit in the state's arguments. According to the court, the conception of a creator of the world is a conception of God. The idea of sudden creation from nothing, or *creatis ex nihilo*, is an inherently religious concept and the fact that creation-science is inspired by the Book of Genesis left no doubt that the law was designed to advance particular religious beliefs.

The judge went on to define science, saying, "(1) it is guided by natural law, (2) it has to be explanatory by reference to natural law, (3) it is testable against the empirical world, (4) its conclusions are tentative, i.e., are not necessarily the final work; and (5) it is falsifiable. Under this definition creation-science is not a science, but, instead is a religious doctrine which was, in this case, imposed on the youth by state law.

§ 2.25   Liberty to Teach and Learn

The power of the state to compel attendance at school and to require all students to take instruction in the English language has been long recognized. Yet, the courts have not condoned the states' overreaching their authority to prohibit the teaching of any other language. In a landmark case, rendered in 1923, Meyer v. Nebraska, 262 U.S. 390, 43 S.Ct. 625, a statute forbidding the teaching of foreign languages to students who had not completed the eighth grade in public, parochial, or private schools was challenged by an instructor in a parochial school who was retained by parents to give their child instruction in the German language. The statute was promulgated in 1919 when the thoughts of the nation's legislators were still much influenced by World War I.

Constitutional basis for the plaintiff's action was found in the Due Process Clause of the Fourteenth Amendment which provides that "No state . . . shall deprive any person of life, liberty or property without due process of law." In resolving the issue for the teacher the Court said that the state's power was limited where it infringed on the liberty interests of the teacher and the pupil. In so ruling the Court gave broad definition to the word liberty saying "the term . . . denotes not merely freedom from bodily restraint but also the right of the individual to contract, to engage in any of the common occupations of life, to acquire useful knowledge, to marry, establish a home and to bring up children, to worship God according to the dictates of his own conscience, and generally to enjoy those privileges long recognized at common law as essential to the orderly pursuit of happiness of free men."

Where state statute infringes on an individual's liberty, the legislative action may be stricken by the courts. In *Meyer*, the Court said that education of the young is regarded as a high calling, useful, honorable, and, indeed, essential to the public welfare. Becoming knowledgeable about the German language could not be regarded as harmful, meriting state proscription. The Court concluded that the teacher's right to teach and the right of parents to engage the teacher to instruct their children were within the liberty of the amendment.

§ 2.26   English Language Instruction

State law or school board rule can require that the basic language of instruction in all schools be English. The state, though, cannot instruct in the English tongue exclusively, denying interpretation and bilingual instruction to students who cannot converse in English.

This issue was dealt with by the United States Supreme Court in a San Francisco case, Lau v. Nichols, 414 U.S. 563, 94 S.Ct. 786 (1974), in which non-English-speaking Chinese students maintained that failure to provide methods of bridging the language gap was violative of the Civil Rights Act of 1964, 42 U.S.C.A. § 2000d. The 1964 Act bans discrimination "on the ground of race, color, or national origin" in "any program or activity receiving federal financial assistance." The San Francisco school district receives large amounts of federal funds. Pursuant to the Civil Rights Act, the Department of Health, Education and

Welfare had issued guidelines which specified that "Where inability to speak and understand the English language excludes national origin—minority group children from effective participation in the educational program offered by a school district, the district must take affirmative steps to rectify the language deficiency . . ." (35 Fed.Reg. 11595).

With the federal law and guidelines as the legal basis, the Supreme Court held for the plaintiff Chinese children, and in so doing observed that there can be no equality of treatment where the students do not understand English. The Court concluded that "Basic English skills are at the very core of what these public schools teach. Imposition of a requirement that, before a child can effectively participate in the educational program, he must already have acquired those basic skills is to make a mockery of public education. We know that those who do not understand English are certain to find their classroom experiences wholly incomprehensible and in no way meaningful."

§ 2.27 Dirty Words

A teacher can quote a "dirty word" in class and require students to read and discuss publications where such words are used. In a case where a teacher was dismissed because he gave his class copies of an article published in the *Atlantic Monthly* magazine in which the vulgar term for an incestuous son was used, Keefe v. Geanakos, 418 F.2d 359 (1st. Cir. 1969) and the teacher explained the word's origin to the class, its context, and why the author had used it the teacher

[*37*]

was subsequently suspended. The teacher sued to recover his position maintaining that the article was a valuable discussion of "dissent, protest, radicalism, and revolt" and was in no way pornographic. The Court agreed with the teacher in finding that the article was thoughtful and thought-provoking and to delete the offending word would have made it impossible to understand the article or the point of view of the author.

While the Court agreed that some measure of public regulation of classroom speech is inherent in every provision for public education, to deny the teacher use of such words when used in an educational context would be to demean the academic process. Whether language is offensive or inappropriate is dependent on the circumstances in the particular situation. The circumstances which must be considered include the learning taking place, the reason for use of the words, and the educational level of the students involved.

Teachers may, however, go beyond their legal bounds in use of offensive terminology. Courts have pointed out that a teacher's academic freedom does not extend to protection of conduct which is "both offensive and unnecessary to the accomplishment of educational objectives . . . such questions are matters of degree involving judgment on such factors as the age and sophistication of the students, relevance of the educational purpose, and context and manner of presentations." Brubaker v. Board of Education, School District 149, Cook County, Illinois, 502 F.2d 973 (7th Cir. 1974).

§ 2.28 Removal of Material From Curriculum

School authorities, as the principal policy makers, have comprehensive powers and broad discretion in discharging their duties to provide public education. As the Court stated in *Epperson v. Arkansas*: "By and large, public education in our nation is committed to the control of state and local authorities. Courts do not and cannot intervene in the resolution of conflicts which arise in the daily operation of school systems and which do not directly and sharply implicate basic constitutional values."

School boards, however, do not have an absolute right to remove material from the curriculum. Local authorities are prevented by the First Amendment from casting a "pall of orthodoxy" over classroom instruction. Keyishian v. Board of Regents, 385 U.S. 589, 87 S.Ct. 675 (1967). To justify removal of material from the curriculum and thereby reduce the scope of information flowing to students, the school board must be able to establish that its action is supported by a substantial and reasonable governmental interest.

Where a school board removed a motion picture, and gave as its reason that the film had too much violence for a high school classroom, the court held that the statements were made by the board without sufficient evidence as to any legitimate reason. The legitimacy of the board's action was questioned by the court because it found that the board had acted without "cognizable" and "credible" evidence that the film was detrimental to the students. In fact, the court found that the basic objections to the film as expressed by parents were religious in nature or had religious overtones and that the film had been eliminated because of its ideological content.   In further examining the evidence, the court found that although the board claimed to have removed the film because of its violent content, the board had not conducted a systematic review of violence in other teaching materials and had established no standards for such a review.   Pratt v. Independent School District No. 831, Forest Lake, Minnesota, 670 F.2d 771 (8th Cir. 1982).

§ 2.3 CENSORSHIP OF LIBRARY BOOKS

School boards possess significant discretion in the determination of the content of their school libraries, but that discretion may be abused if exercised in a political or narrowly partisan manner.   Earlier precedents regarding the authority of the school board to remove books from the school library were split.   The United States Court of Appeals for the Second Circuit had held in 1972 that the school board had the discretion to remove books from the library simply because they were without merit either as works of art or science.   President's Council, Dist. 25 v. Community School Board, 457 F.2d 289 (2d Cir. 1972).   The Court observed that administration of a school library "involves a constant process of selection and winnowing based not only on educational needs but financial and architectural realities.   To suggest that the shelving or unshelving of books presents a constitutional issue, particularly where there is no showing of a curtailment of freedom of speech or thought, is a proposition we cannot accept."

In a later case from another federal appellate court a ruling was rendered indicating school boards do not have authority, unfettered by the First Amendment, to remove books from the school library simply because they find them to be objectionable in content. Minarcini v. Strongsville City School District, 541 F.2d 577 (6th Cir. 1976). This court said that a school board could not "place conditions on the use of the library which were related solely to the social or political tastes of school board members." Further, the court observed that the public school library is a valuable adjunct to classroom discussion, that the First Amendment's protection of academic freedom would protect both the student's right not only to participate in classroom discussion but also to find and read a book on the subject of discussion. Censorship of the school library would, thus, place a serious burden upon academic freedom as protected by the freedom of speech provision of the First Amendment.

The library censorship issue was decided by the United States Supreme Court in 1982 in a case in which the school board had removed nine books from the school library. Board of Education, Island Trees Union Free School District No. 26 v. Pico, 457 U.S. 853, 102 S.Ct. 2799 (1982). The board's justification for removal of the books was that they were irrelevant, vulgar, immoral, and in bad taste, making them educationally unsuitable for junior and senior high school students.

At the outset of its discussion the Supreme Court noted that "local school boards must be permitted 'to establish and apply their curriculum in such a way as to transmit community values,' and that 'there is a legitimate and substantial community interest in promoting respect for authority and traditional values be they social, moral, or political.' " The Court, however, went on to point out that school boards could not in exercise of their broad discretion "strangle the free mind" and limit youth in acquiring important information which will allow them to become responsible citizens. The Court reemphasized that "the State may not, consistently with the First Amendment, contract the spectrum of available knowledge." In this context the student has the right to receive information and ideas and this right is the logical corollary of the rights of free speech and press. Too, the Court observed that a school library is the principal locus at which the student can exercise the freedom to inquire, study, and evaluate. In Lamont v. Postmaster General, the Supreme Court had previously held that "the dissemination of ideas can accomplish nothing if otherwise willing addressees are not free to receive and consider them." 381 U.S. 301, 85 S.Ct. 1493 (1965).

According to the Court, the critical issue to be considered in *Pico* was, the motivation behind a school board's actions. If the school board members intended the book removal to suppress certain ideas with which they disagreed, then the action was unconstitutional; on the other hand, if the board removed the books because they were "pervasively vulgar" or obscene or solely because they were "educationally" unsuitable, then no right was violated. The evidence in *Pico* showed that the board did not employ regular and unbiased procedures in reviewing the books as to their educational suitability and that, in fact, the books had been removed solely because they had been placed on a list of objectionable books by a conservative organization of parents who had prevailed on the school board for the removal.

In ruling against the school board, the Court admonished that its decision was limited to the removal of books from the library and in no way affected a school board's discretion in adding books to the school library.

§ 2.4 LACK OF SCHOLARSHIP

School boards and teachers have great discretion in determining what level of academic attainment will be required of students. School boards set general course requirements and teachers evaluate the students in achieving the objectives. Seldom will courts intervene to overturn a teacher's academic evaluation of a student. Only where the school board or the teacher acts in bad faith or is arbitrary or capricious will their actions be overturned. Students may be placed in alternative classes or retained at a particular grade level depending on their academic performance. (See Student Testing, Chapter 14 for further discussion.)

§ 2.5 PROMOTION

Schools are empowered to establish the required level of student performance. Reading attainment may be one criterion for promotion of students from grade-to-grade. In a case where two students were denied promotion because they failed to complete the requisite level of performance on the Ginn Reading Series, the court denied the students relief saying that decisions by educational authorities which are based on academic performance are within the particular province of educators. Sandlin v. Johnson, 643 F.2d 1027 (4th Cir. 1981). Such academic requirements are invalid only if they illegally classify students in a way which is prohibited by statute or by the state or federal constitutions.

In a higher education decision which has implications for elementary and secondary schools, the United States Supreme Court refused to reinstate a medical student who failed to adequately complete the internship phase of the training program. The Court said "We decline to further enlarge the judicial presence in the academic community and thereby risk deterioration of many beneficial aspects of the faculty-student relationship." Board of Curators of University of Missouri v. Horowitz, 435 U.S. 78, 98 S.Ct. 948 (1978).

§ 2.6 DIPLOMA

School boards are empowered to set academic standards required to obtain a diploma. Such requirements, however, cannot be unreasonable and the diploma cannot be withheld except for valid reasons rationally related to the state's interests in public education. By establishing and maintaining a public school system, the state creates an expectation on the part of the student that upon successful completion of required courses a diploma will be awarded. This expectation constitutes a "property interest" on the part of the student which cannot be arbitrarily taken away.

As a property interest, the diploma cannot be taken away except where the state's interest exceeds that of the individual and the denial comes about only after the student has had an opportunity to be heard through formal procedural due process. To deny the high school diploma because students failed to pass a Florida high school functional literacy examination was held to deny property interests to the student without due process of law. The court found that a test administered at the eleventh grade level covered material which had not been taught to students in the public schools of Florida, thus denial of a diploma based on a newly applied standard, after students had completed all other requirements for graduation, was unfair and violated due process. Debra P. v. Turlington, 644 F.2d 397 (5th Cir. 1981). (For further explanation of the *Debra P.* case with later adjudication, 564 F.Supp. 177 (D.Fla.1983), see Student Testing, Chapter 14.)

Nothing in federal or state law, however, stands in the way of school boards making reasonable rules to effectuate a legitimate educational purpose. A successful score on a minimal competency test can be required of all students before they may receive a diploma. Those who do not succeed in passing the test may receive only a certificate of program completion. Where severely mentally retarded and autistic students could not pass a minimum competency test, the court held that the school district was not required to issue them diplomas. Schools are required by the federal Education for All Handicapped Children Act (20 U.S.C.A. § 1401ff) to make reasonable modifications in

[45]

tests to minimize the detrimental effects of a student's handicap; however, the law does not require that the test be modified to offset a student's mental deficiency or lack of knowledge. What is required, for example, is that a blind child be given the test orally or in braille or a deaf child be given visual instead of oral exams in measuring their qualifications to receive a diploma. Brookhart v. Illinois State Board of Education, 534 F.Supp. 725 (D.Ill.1982).

§ 2.7　HOMEWORK

It is generally assumed that teachers and/or school boards may require students to devote a certain amount of out-of-school time to their studies. In fact, many believe that too little homework is required in schools today. A legal question may, though, arise where a parent objects to homework as an encroachment on parental prerogative and, too, it may be contended that the child should not be held accountable at school for work done at home.

Only a few early cases have been rendered giving guidance on this issue, but the limited precedent which is available indicates that it is an appropriate exercise of school authority to require homework so long as the requirements are reasonable and are directly related to the student's achievement at school. Teachers may punish students for refusing to do homework assignments. Mangum v. Keith, 147 Ga. 603, 95 S.E. 1 (1918). Rules, though, may not be so constrictive as to deprive parental control over the activities of their children. Thus, a school rule setting aside specific hours each night, say between 7 and 9 p.m., during which time the student must be home studying is unreasonable. On the other hand, a rule requiring a student to take math problems home, work them and return them completed to school the next day is a reasonable rule. Too much direction from the school regarding the time and place that the homework is to be performed is apparently the legal determinant. Required homework may be reasonable even though a parent contends that the student time is taken from home chores. Bolding v. State, 23 Tex.App. 172, 4 S.W. 579 (1887).

§ 2.8 SEX EDUCATION

During the last two decades boards of education have increasingly introduced sex education courses into the public school curriculum. While in most cases the implementation has gone smoothly, in some instances parents have challenged the efforts as encroachments on religious liberty and privacy. In each instance the courts have rejected the parental claims maintaining generally that such requirements are within the police power of the state.

The rationale for providing sex education is based on the state's interest in the health and welfare of its children. This has been sufficient reason for courts to hold in favor of boards of education establishing such courses. Aubrey v. School District of Philadelphia, 63 Pa.Cmwlth. 330, 437 A.2d 1306 (1981).

Mandatory sex education courses have been upheld where students and parents maintained that required sex education courses violated their religious beliefs.

A federal district court held in a Maryland case that the interest of the state in "healthy, well-rounded growth of young people" is properly enforced through required sex education courses regardless of the parents' objections based on religious scruples. Cornwell v. State Board of Education, 314 F.Supp. 340 (D.Md.1969), affirmed 428 F.2d 471 (4th Cir. 1970), cert. denied 400 U.S. 942, 91 S.Ct. 240. The prevailing view appears to be that sex education can be constitutionally defended as a required course of study.

A minority view of some courts is that the compulsory nature of sex education courses may, possibly, make them questionable as an invasion of privacy or an encroachment on the free exercise of religion. The Supreme Court of Hawaii upheld a sex education program promulgated by the state education agency, but in so doing appeared to base its approval on the fact that the program was not compulsory. Medeiros v. Kiyosaki, 52 Hawaii 436, 478 P.2d 314 (1970). No court has ruled, though, that sex education courses are unconstitutional and boards of education appear to be within their rightful authority when they require sex education, and there is little doubt that boards are acting constitutionally when the sex education courses are noncompulsory or have an "excusal" arrangement whereby parents may request that their children not be involved. A state board of education regulation requiring that local school districts develop and implement a family-life education course which included teaching about human sexuality did not violate a student's rights of freedom of religion where the regulation provided for the student to be excused from specific portions of the course which the student or parents found objectionable. Smith v. Ricci, 89 N.J. 514, 446 A.2d 501 (1982).

CHAPTER 3

RIGHT TO AN EDUCATION AND PROCEDURAL DUE PROCESS

§ 3.1 INTRODUCTION

To deny attendance at school has always been a method of controlling disruptive student conduct which enhances the integrity of the academic climate. Although the practice has fallen in some disrepute among educators in recent years, it remains in common usage in public schools and is utilized extensively in nonpublic schools.

§ 3.2 RIGHT TO EDUCATION

Until relatively recently, decisions to suspend or expel pupils were made on the convenient assumption that to attend public schools was a privilege which could be taken away at the discretion of the school authorities. Students who offended, or were thought to have offended, school rules could be summarily dismissed from school with no redress or opportunity to present their side of the story.

§ 3.21 Equal Protection Right

In 1954 in the famous Brown v. Board of Education, 347 U.S. 483, 74 S.Ct. 686 (1954), the United States Supreme Court indicated the importance of education when it required all public schools to desegregate. (See Chapter 9.)

In very strong words which apparently confirmed that education was a constitutional right protected by the Equal Protection Clause, the Court said that: "[t]oday, education is perhaps the most important function of state and local governments. . . . It is the very foundation of good citizenship. . . . In these days, it is doubtful that any child may reasonably be expected to succeed in life if he is denied the opportunity of an education." In saying this the Court invoked the Equal Protection Clause and held that all black children had a right to attend public schools with white children. Quite naturally, most persons concluded from this that education was a constitutionally protected right of every person. However, a shadow of doubt was cast on this conclusion in 1964 when the Court observed in another desegregation case that a state could possibly close down its public schools if, in the process, it did not discriminate against any particular class of students. Griffin v. County of School Board of Prince Edward County, 377 U.S. 218, 84 S.Ct. 1226 (1964). Thus a state could, presumably, close all its public schools without denying the students of the state any constitutional right.

The view that the Equal Protection Clause did not vest students with a constitutional right to attend public schools was later confirmed by the United States Supreme Court in San Antonio Independent School District v. Rodriguez, 411 U.S. 1, 93 S.Ct. 1278 (1973). Here the Supreme Court flatly concluded that education is not a fundamental constitutional right protected by Equal Protection. The Court said: "Education, of course, is not among the rights afforded explicit protection under our Federal Constitution. Nor do we find any basis for saying it is implicitly so protected." In Plyler v. Doe, 457 U.S. 202, 102 S.Ct. 2382 (1983), the Supreme Court reaffirmed that education is not a fundamental right.

Thus, the right of a child to an education or some quantum of education is not contemplated by equal protection. The Court in distinguishing its apparent sanction of education as a right in *Brown* said that the protection extended there was because of the fundamentality of race was a constitutional issue, not because of education. If, for example, a state wanted to close down all its public schools, according to the Court, students could not invoke the Equal Protection Clause to require them to stay open.

§ 3.3 SUBSTANTIVE DUE PROCESS

In 1923 the Supreme Court created a nexus between acquisition of knowledge and an individual's liberty interest under the Due Process Clause of the Fourteenth Amendment. The clause states "No state . . . shall deprive any person of life, liberty or property without due process of law." According to the Court, the word liberty has a substantive aspect which invests each person with a protected interest in acquisition and conveyance of knowledge. Meyer v. Nebraska, 262 U.S. 390, 43 S.Ct. 625 (1923). From 1923 until 1961 there was no further development of education as a due process interest. Generally, the *Meyer* precedent was construed very narrowly, having little implication for education rights, generally.

An important case, though, emerged in 1961 which indicated that denial of an education was of such seriousness as to invoke constitutional due process. In Dixon v. Alabama State Board of Education, 294 F.2d 150 (5th Cir. 1961), a federal court held that attendance at a college was so essential that it could not be denied without a hearing and attendant due process procedures. Without specifically saying so, this court implied that education was of such importance that it may be implied within the substance of the terms liberty or property under the Due Process Clause.

In spite of the impact of *Dixon*, the relationship between education and due process was not clearly defined until 1975 in Goss v. Lopez, 419 U.S. 565, 95 S.Ct. 729 (1975), at which time the Supreme Court pointed out that denial of education for even a short period of time could not be construed as inconsequential. In explaining that the individual's interest in education fell within the substantive scope of "liberty and property," the Court said: "[n]either the property interest in education benefits temporarily denied nor the liberty interest in reputation, which is also implicated, is so insubstantial that suspensions may constitutionally be imposed by any procedure one school chooses, no matter how arbitrary."

§ 3.31 Property

According to the Court, "property" encompasses those individual interests which are created by state statutes and rules entitling all citizens to a certain benefit. When a state creates a public system of education to which all children are entitled to attend, each child is vested with a property interest therein.

§ 3.32   Liberty

Due process also forbids arbitrary deprivation of liberty or denial of those interests which are implied by the term. A person's liberty includes his or her "good name, reputation, honor, or integrity." For government to take a person's liberty away requires due process of law. In *Goss*, where the Court found that procedural due process had not been afforded, the recording of the suspensions in student permanent files effectively attached a stigma infringing on the students' liberty interests. The Court said: "If sustained and recorded, those charges could seriously damage the students' standing with their fellow pupils and their teachers as well as interfere with later opportunities for higher education and employment."

§ 3.4   PROCEDURAL DUE PROCESS

To take away a liberty or property interest requires procedural due process. Courts have become cognizant of the dangers of allowing too much discretion to reside in the hands of school officials, and have acted to limit this power, by establishing standards to ensure regard for fundamental fairness. Intervention by the courts is justified on the basis of the ancient concept of "natural justice" and "due process of law" under the United States Constitution. Judicial developments have had an important impact on public education in the United States.

§ 3.5 NATURAL JUSTICE AND DUE PROCESS

Due process finds its roots in the words of Clause 39 of *Magna Charta*, 1215, which expressed that: "No freeman shall be seized, or imprisoned or dispossessed, or outlawed, or in any way destroyed; nor will we condemn him, nor will we commit him to prison, excepting by the legal judgment of his peers, or by the law of the land." This provision according to Blackstone "protected every individual of the nation in the free enjoyment of his life, his liberty and his property, unless declared to be forfeited by the judgment of his peers or the law of the land." W. Blackstone, *The Great Charter and Charter of the Forest (1759). Clause 38 added to the protection by requiring credible witnesses to be produced against the accused before he could be convicted. See Ray Stringham, Magna Charta Foundation of Freedom* 63–65 (1966). Effectively, these provisions protected a citizen against arbitrary action by the King or his agents and guaranteed a minimal level of procedural due process.

Due process emerges from the concept of natural justice. Natural justice presupposes certain rules of judicial procedure established through legal precedent which compel government and its agents to treat individuals with minimal standards of fairness. In the United States the term due process does precisely the same. Essentially the concepts of natural justice and their progeny, due process, encompass two elements:

(a) The rule against bias: No man shall be a judge in his own cause, or *nemo judex in causa sua*, and

(b) The right to a hearing: No man shall be condemned unheard, or *audi alteram partem.*

The rule against bias is the first and most fundamental principle. Accordingly, it is of prime importance that justice should not only be done but should manifestly and undoubtedly be seen to be done.

Audi alteram partem requires that the accused know the case against him and have an opportunity to state his own case. Each party must have the chance to present his version of the facts and to make submissions relevant to his case. Fairness is the hallmark of this process and though the extent of process required is sometimes in question, the basic principle that "no one should be condemned unheard" prevails.

The Fifth and Fourteenth Amendments of the United States Constitution provide that neither the federal government nor a state shall "deprive any person of life, liberty or property, without due process of law." Originally, these provisions were interpreted to apply to judicial proceedings only, and not to quasi-judicial proceedings conducted by governmental ministers or by educational agencies. In early precedents, United States educators, by virtue of standing *in loco parentis*, were not required to adhere to any particular standards of fair play when sitting in judgment over actions of students. Only since the landmark case of Dixon v. Alabama, supra, has this changed. *Dixon* manifestly established that procedural due process applied to schools and other governmental agencies and deviations from the minimal fairness required therein may void any disciplinary action taken.

§ 3.6 IMPARTIALITY: NEMO JUDEX IN CAUSA SUA

Impartiality is the essence of fair judicial treatment. Justinian stated the rule in his Institutes and numerous old English cases establish the precedent. *Institutes of Justinian*, Book 4, Title 5, Law 1 (R. W. Lee translation 1956). In 1614, in Day v. Salvadge, it was held that protection against bias was so fundamental that even the English Parliament could not enact a law contrary to the principle. Hobart 85, 87 (1614). The court said that "even an Act of Parliament made against natural equity, as to make a man judge in his own cause, is void in itself."

A judge must come to the case with an open mind without previous knowledge of the facts or preconceived notions of the outcome. No connection can exist between the judge and one of the parties involved so as to create a conflict of judicial interest.

Bias in the school setting may not always be so readily recognizable. Seldom do students or teachers sit in judgment over their own cases. If they did obvious bias would be present. Bias may be charged, though, where an administrator or officer sits in review of challenged policies which he formulated, or in review of executive action which he carried out. Further, it may be that school officers may be forced to sit as tribunals at different levels, possibly reviewing their own decisions on appeal.

A fair trial by an impartial tribunal is a basic tenet of due process, In re Murchison, 349 U.S. 133, 75 S.Ct. 623 (1955), just as it is with natural justice, and this applies to administrative agencies as well as to the court. Gibson v. Berryhill, 411 U.S. 564, 93 S.Ct. 1689 (1973). The United States Supreme Court rejected a teacher union claim that bias of the school board invalidated board action to dismiss teachers. As a party to the dispute, the school board was alleged to have a prejudicial interest in the proceedings. Hortonville Joint School District No. 1 v. Hortonville Education Association, 426 U.S. 482, 96 S.Ct. 2308 (1976).

In this case, the school teachers as a result of impasse over contract negotiations with the school board decided, illegally, to go out on strike. The school board instituted dismissal actions against the teachers and conducted a hearing prior to their dismissal. On appeal before the Supreme Court, the Attorney for the teachers claimed *inter alia* that the board was not sufficiently impartial and free from bias to exercise judgment over the striking teachers. Plaintiff teachers argued that individual board members had a personal or official stake in the decision. Because of the strike, and the difficult negotiations, the teachers alleged that board members harbored personal bitterness toward the teachers. No actual proof of this was presented other than the fact that the board had dismissed the teachers in the first place.

The Supreme Court in holding against the teachers said that mere familiarity with the facts of the case by an agency in performance of its statutory responsibility does not disqualify the decision maker. "Nor is the decision maker disqualified simply because he has taken a position, even in public, on a policy issue related to the dispute, in the absence of a showing that he is not 'capable of judging a particular controversy fairly on the basis of its own circumstances.' " Only to show that a public board is "involved" in events preceding a decision is "not enough to overcome the presumption of honesty and integrity in policymakers with decisionmaking power."

In *Hortonville*, the board members were clearly parties to the dispute and were quite obviously sitting in judgment in a dispute over that in which they had an official interest. Even in light of this, the Supreme Court found that bias must be shown to exist, in fact, and not merely by virtue of the board members being judges in their own cause. A school board having executive, quasi-legislative and quasi-judicial functions must, according to the United States Supreme Court, frequently sit in judgment over certain of its own decisions, but this, in and of itself, did not create a presumption of bias. Simply to show that an administrative agency has a dual role, without more, does not constitute a true process violation.

§ 3.7 FAIRNESS: AUDI ALTERAM PARTEM

The right to be heard as a basic principle of fairness has long been accepted as a tenet of Anglo-American law. Although the right to be heard is a spontaneously acceptable idea, it is not settled as to what it entails or where it applies. Demara Turf Club v. Phang, 26 M.L.R. 412, Sup.Ct. of British Guiana (1963). Does it require a notice for a hearing, if so what should the notice include? Is there a right to an oral hearing? Can the accused confront witnesses and cross-examine? Can the accused demand legal counsel? Can the hearing be conducted by one body and the decision be rendered by another?   Is there a right to remain silent?   All of these questions define the parameters of due process.

§ 3.8   ELEMENTS OF PROCEDURAL DUE PROCESS

A hearing is useless if the defendant does not know the charges against him and does not have time to prepare a defense.   Where a party is completely unaware of the institution of proceedings, fairness cannot be achieved.   Consequently, it is rudimentary that notice is required.

§ 3.81   Notice

Fundamental fairness requires that notice give the specific ground or grounds on which the accused is being charged and the nature of the evidence against him.   Due v. Florida Agricultural and Mechanical University, 233 F.Supp. 396 (D.Fla.1963).   According to *Dixon*, supra, the landmark case, no rigid procedural guidelines are required, but notice should contain a statement of specific charges and grounds which if proven could lead to the appropriate disciplinary action.

A notice of charges so vague "that men of common intelligence must necessarily guess at its meaning and differ as to its application" violates the first principle of due process.   Dickson v. Sitterson, 280 F.Supp. 486 (M.D.N.C.1968), affirmed 415 F.2d 228 (5th Cir. 1969).   Vagueness is primarily objectionable because it tends toward arbitrary and discriminatory enforcement and fails to provide explicit standards for those who apply them. Grayned v. City of Rockford, 408 U.S. 104, 92 S.Ct. 2294 (1972). Justice Black observed in Epperson v. Arkansas, 393 U.S. 97, 89 S.Ct. 266 (1968), that: "It is an established rule that a statute which leaves an ordinary man so doubtful about its meaning that he cannot know when he has violated it denies him the first essential of due process . . ." Quite obviously then, if a vague charge is brought against a student or the charge is based on a vague rule or statute, elementary fairness cannot be served.

§ 3.82 Opportunity to be Heard

The courts have generally held that an accused student must have the opportunity to present evidence in his own behalf. S. v. Board of Education, 20 Cal.App. 3d 83, 97 Cal.Rptr. 422 (1971). The courts have more or less implicitly assumed that such hearings will be oral in nature. The Superior Court of New Jersey has held that witnesses adverse to the accused student must be present and be compelled to testify. Tibbs v. Board of Education, 114 N.J.Super. 287, 276 A.2d 165 (1971). Of course, this assumes that school boards have subpoena power which is true in New Jersey and a few other states, but is not uniformly the case in all states. If witnesses may be compelled to appear, then almost certainly one could conclude that the accused himself has a right to appear and testify. In 1914 the United States Supreme Court said that: "[T]he fundamental requisite of due process of law is the opportunity to be heard." Grannis v. Ordean, 234 U.S. 385, 34 S.Ct. 779. Here, the court was referring to actual physical appearance and oral testimony. In its most important due process case involving students, the Supreme Court found that an oral hearing was possibly the only way which school officials in some situations could dismiss a student while allowing for fundamental fairness. Goss v. Lopez, 419 U.S. 565, 95 S.Ct. 729 (1975). To say that the student could only convey his side of the story in writing would quite obviously fly in the face of procedural due process.

While due process is a flexible doctrine, it cannot be construed to be so lax as to deny a student an oral hearing, particularly where the facts are in dispute or where they may be subject to more than one interpretation.

§ 3.83   Access to Evidence

Due process requires that every individual have an opportunity to know the evidence against him. The general rule requiring evidence be released to the accused is directly in keeping with the due process standard of *Dixon*. Dixon v. Alabama Board of Education, supra. See also Goss v. Lopez, supra, Esteban v. Central Missouri State College, 415 F.2d 1077 (8th Cir. 1969), cert. denied 398 U.S. 965, 90 S.Ct. 2169 (1970), Soglin v. Kauffman, 418 F.2d 163 (7th Cir. 1969), and Sullivan v. Houston Independent School District, 475 F.2d 1071 (5th Cir. 1973), cert. denied 414 U.S. 1032, 94 S.Ct. 461. The Court put it succinctly: "The student should be given the name of the witnesses against him and an oral or written report on the facts to which each witness testifies." In *Mills*, a federal court in Washington, D.C. required the school board to inform parents of their right to examine the child's school records before a hearing, including tests, reports, medical, psychological and educational information. Mills v. Board of Education of District of Columbia, 348 F.Supp. 866 (D.D.C.1972).

§ 3.84 Cross-Examination

Cross-examination of witnesses is fundamental to the criminal trial, but, in administrative hearings, particularly in the educational setting, its status is less definitive. In Esteban v. Central Missouri State College, supra, the United States Eighth Circuit Court of Appeals set out procedural safeguards for student disciplinary actions but it excluded cross-examination as a general requirement. *Mills*, supra, contrarily, specifically required that schools provide the parent or guardian the opportunity to confront and cross-examine witnesses.

The United States Supreme Court in *Goss* did not go so far as to require the confrontation and cross-examination of witnesses for short-term suspensions. The Court said "[w]e stop short of construing the Due Process Clause to require . . . that hearings . . . [or] suspensions must afford the student the opportunity . . . to confront and cross-examine witnesses . . . ." The issue in *Goss* was short-term suspensions but the court left open, that for more serious offenses, a more formal procedure might be required. It has always been recognized that the more important the rights at stake, the more formal the procedural safeguards. S. v. Board of Education, 20 Cal.App.3d 83, 97 Cal.Rptr. 422 (1971).

Therefore, for a more serious offense, i.e., expulsion, to maintain fundamental fairness, cross-examination may be required. The right of cross-examination may be required for an administrative hearing if the testimony of one witness is the critical factor in determining the outcome of the hearing.

A problem with requiring witnesses to be present is that all school boards do not have subpoena power. With no subpoena power, the student and school officials may ask the witnesses to attend but cannot compel them to do so.

§ 3.85   Hearsay

The courts have generally held that hearsay evidence is admissible in a formal school disciplinary hearing. In the leading case on this issue, a school principal, read before the school board statements made by teachers regarding a student's conduct. Boykins v. Fairfield Board of Education, 492 F.2d 697 (5th Cir. 1974), cert. denied 420 U.S. 962, 95 S.Ct. 1350 (1975). The board in using this evidence ultimately suspended eight students for a week and expelled eight for their part in a school boycott. The students maintained that the information was hearsay and could not be used as a basis for dismissal. The Court disagreed saying: "There is a seductive quality to the argument—advanced here to justify the importation of technical rules of evidence into administrative hearings conducted by laymen—that, since a free public education is a thing of great value, comparable to that of welfare sustenance or the curtailed liberty of a parolee, the safeguards applicable to these should apply

[*64*]

to it . . . . In this view we stand but a step away from the application of the *strictissimi juris* due process requirements of criminal trials to high school disciplinary processes. And if to high school, why not to elementary school? It will not do. . . . Basic fairness and integrity of the fact-finding process are the guiding stars. Important as they are, the rights at stake in a school disciplinary hearing may be fairly determined upon the 'hearsay' evidence of school administrators charged with the duty of investigating the incidents. We decline to place upon a board of laymen the duty of observing and applying the common-law rules of evidence." *Boykins,* supra.

Similarly, hearsay has been allowed in hearings where students have committed serious offenses. Tasby v. Estes, 643 F.2d 1103 (5th Cir. 1981), and has been allowed by implication in a case involving expulsion. Linwood v. Board of Education, 463 F.2d 763 (7th Cir. 1972), cert. denied 409 U.S. 1027, 93 S.Ct. 475, and Whiteside v. Kay, 446 F.Supp. 716 (W.D.La.1978).

Some courts have, however, not allowed hearsay. A Nebraska court did not allow hearsay in an expulsion hearing, Fielder v. Board of Education, 346 F.Supp. 722 (D.Neb.1972), and a Connecticut court refused to allow hearsay in a hearing involving a thirty-day suspension. DeJesus v. Penberthy, 344 F.Supp. 70 (D.Conn.1972).

Goss did not address the hearsay question directly, the only guidance it provided was the general admonishment that "[l]onger suspensions or expulsions for the remainder of the school term, or permanently, may require more formal procedures." Too, the Supreme

[*65*]

Court emphasized in Board of Curators of University of Missouri v. Horowitz that due process should provide a "meaningful hedge against erroneous action." 435 U.S. 78, 98 S.Ct. 948 (1978). This language leaves substantial discretion to the school board in determining the extent of formality to be used in a hearing.

The Supreme Court's intent in *Goss* and *Horowitz* has been interpreted by a Wisconsin court as allowing hearsay statements from teachers or staff members in an expulsion hearing before the school board. Racine Unified School District v. Thompson, 107 Wis.2d 657, 321 N.W.2d 334 (App.1982). This appears to represent the prevailing view of the courts.

§ 3.86 Legal Counsel

Presence of legal counsel is not a fundamental element of fairness but it may well be invoked by the courts if the issues are legally complex or the interests of the accused are of great magnitude. Legal counsel was not required by the United States Supreme Court in *Goss* for suspensions of less than ten days, but as with cross-examination, the Court implied that where more severe penalties could be invoked against a student, counsel may be required. Goss v. Lopez, supra.

Counsel, then, may probably be denied by tribunals adjudicating relatively minor student disciplinary cases, but, where major detriment may result for the accused, counsel may be elevated to a more important aspect of fairness. On balance, however, representation by legal counsel cannot be said to be, at this time, a fundamental or basic element of due process in the school setting.

§ 3.87   Appropriate Tribunal

Whether the tribunal or hearing committee is an appropriate one depends on at least three issues, (a) the make-up of membership, (b) the *ultra vires* doctrine, and (c) due process. Courts are not concerned with whether a tribunal has representation of administrators, teachers or students; the only legal concern is that no conflict of interest or bias exists.

An administrative agency cannot delegate away its quasi-judicial or discretionary functions provided it statutorily by a state legislature. Games v. County Board of School Trustees, 13 Ill.2d 78, 147 N.E.2d 306 (1958); See also State ex rel. School District No. 29 v. Cooney, 102 Mont. 521, 59 P.2d 48 (1936). Likewise, a local school board cannot delegate its discretionary powers to a subordinate. This does not mean that an administrative committee cannot delegate to a subcommittee the responsibility to collect information, facts, and evidence to be presented to the full official committee for consideration and judgment.

It would be *ultra vires*, though, for the statutorily constituted school board to delegate to a subordinate committee or individual, the power to actually hand down a decision in a matter which statute required it, alone, to exercise. Similarly, it would contravene due process for a subcommittee to render a decision from a hearing it conducted and then have the superior or full committee to reverse the lower decision in the absence of full and complete hearing documentation. Due process requires, unequivocally, that the decision cannot be made by anyone other than the appropriate tribunal.

In general then it may be said that he who hears the case must also decide it. It is a breach of due process for a member of a judicial tribunal to participate in a decision if he has not heard the evidence presented in the case. Rulings by administrative bodies have been frequently quashed because decisions were given affecting individual rights where oral presentations were made before hearing officers other than those who actually rendered the decision. Bias and ignorance alike preclude fair judgment upon the merits of a case.

§ 3.88 Self-Incrimination

In the United States the Fifth Amendment protects the individual against self-incrimination in a criminal proceeding. The Fifth Amendment states in part: ". . . nor shall [*any person*] be compelled in any criminal case to be a witness against himself. . . ." This right extends to college students in disciplinary proceedings, but if the student chooses to remain silent the disciplinary action against him may proceed unimpaired. Where elementary and secondary pupils are concerned, the courts give very little guidance. The dilemma is, or course, that at the lower levels the school stands *in loco parentis* and as such can presumably punish a child for not confessing to breaking a school rule, or he can be found insubordinate by the principal for his refusal to speak out regarding rule violations.

The inconclusiveness of the self-incrimination question is demonstrated by several cases. In one case, the court held that student witnesses could not be compelled to testify against the accused since it "might be regarded as detrimental to the best interests of the school." State v. Hyman, 180 Tenn. 99, 171 S.W.2d 822 (1943). Also, where a girl allegedly cheated on a history examination and later, under substantial pressure from the school principal, confessed, the court found that the confession was invalid and denied due process since it was not gained through the process of a full-blown hearing. Goldwyn v. Allen, 54 Misc.2d 94, 281 N.Y.S.2d 899 (1967). On the other hand, a California court found no merit to a college student's contention that procedural due process was denied because a hearing committee did not recognize the privilege against self-incriminaton. Goldberg v. Regents of University of California, 248 Cal.App.2d 867, 57 Cal.Rptr. 463 (1967).

At present a school official can apparently compel the accused to testify even though his utterances may subject him to expulsion or other punishment.

A complicating factor is added where the charge against the student may also be of such nature as to violate criminal statute. A substantial question arises as to whether the student's testimony before a school tribunal can be used against him in a criminal prosecution. Wright has maintained that in this circumstance the student cannot be compelled to testify and should be able, without fear of reprisal, to validly "take the Fifth." Charles Alan Wright, The Constitution on the Campus, 5 Vanderbilt Law Review 1027 (1969). This opinion is at odds with the Supreme Court of Vermont which refused to enjoin a school disciplinary hearing until after a criminal trial against the student who argued that evidence given in the school hearing would incriminate him.   Nzuve v. Castleton State College, 133 Vt. 225, 335 A.2d 321 (1975).   See also Furutani v. Ewigleben, 297 F.Supp. 1163 (N.D.Cal.1969).   This court held that discipline imposed by the academic community need not await the outcome of other proceedings, saying: "Educational institutions have both a need and a right to formulate their own standards and to enforce them; such enforcement is only coincidentally related to criminal charges and the defense against them."

At this time, the general rule of law appears to preclude student access to the Fifth Amendment privilege against self-incrimination in a school hearing.   Due process does not require it and the school administrator is unaffected by its strictures.

§ 3.9   IMPACT OF PROCEDURAL DUE PROCESS

With the evolution of procedural due process as a potent force in the quasi-judicial administrative processes, school boards and school officials are required to formulate guidelines which will protect students.   Due process balances the child's interest against corresponding and sometimes contrary school interests.   At very least, due process requires school officials to provide the child with a hearing which is impartial and free of bias, and, secondly, to guarantee the student that fairness will prevail.   Minimal due process requires that the administrator give the student adequate notice of what is proposed, allow the student to make representations on his own behalf, and/or appear at a hearing or inquiry, and to effec-

[70]

tively prepare his case and answer allegations presented.

Courts have maintained that "The touchstones in this area are fairness and reasonableness." Due v. Florida Agricultural and Mechanical University, 233 F.Supp. 396 (N.D.Fla.1963); See also Jones v. State Board of Education, 279 F.Supp. 190 (D.Tenn.1968), affirmed 407 F.2d 834 (6th Cir. 1969). The precise boundaries of fairness must be kept reasonably flexible to ensure freedom for school districts to operate. The United States Supreme Court has reminded us that: "Due process is an elusive concept its exact boundaries are undefinable, and its content varies according to specific factual contexts . . . . Whether the Constitution requires that a particular right obtain in a specific proceeding depends upon a complexity of factors. The nature of the alleged right involved, the nature of the proceeding, and the possible burden on that proceeding, are all considerations which must be taken into account." Hannah v. Larche, 363 U.S. 420, 80 S.Ct. 1502 (1960). But, flexibility cannot be an excuse for denial of proper procedure. Minimal fairness in the words of *Dixon* requires that (a) notice should be given containing a statement of the specific charges and grounds, (b) a hearing should be conducted affording the administrator or board with opportunity to hear both sides in considerable detail, (c) the student should be given the names of the witnesses against him, and an oral or written report on the facts, (d) the student should be given the opportunity to present his own defense against the charges and to produce either oral testimony or written affidavits in his own behalf, (e) if the hearing is not before the Board empowered to make the decision, the results and findings of the hearing should be presented in a report open to the student's inspection. Dixon v. Alabama State Board of Education, supra.

Beyond these rudiments of "fair play" various judicial precedents add specificity reducing the school administrator's boundaries of discretion. The following guidelines are suggestive of such boundaries.

§ 3.91   Guidelines: Due Process

I. Bias

1. The judge must come to the hearing with an open mind without preconceived notions of the ultimate outcome.

2. No connection can exist between the parties involved and the administrator except through his *ex officio* position as an officer of the school. No decisionmaker should be disqualified simply because of a position he has taken on a matter of public policy.

3. Intercommittee membership, although not illegal, should be avoided where possible in order to prevent any impression of bias. Committee membership should not be permitted to even approach offending the "real likelihood" of bias standards.

II. Fairness

1. Every student has a right to be heard when punishment for an offense is severe enough to deprive him of schooling, even for a few days.

2. Notice should be given conveying the specific ground or grounds with which the student is being

[72]

charged citing rules or regulations which have been broken. Notice must not be vague or ambiguous.

3. Notice should be delivered to the student, in writing, in sufficient time to ensure ample opportunity to prepare a defense to the allegations.

4. It goes without saying that the burden of proof should bear on the school and not the student.

5. The student should be given the opportunity to testify and present evidence and witnesses in his or her own behalf.

6. The tribunal should make its decision only on the information presented at the hearing.

7. With the possible exception of evidence which could be harmful to the child or the parent, all evidence should be made available to the accused child, parent, and legal counsel. In re Gault, supra.

8. To confront and cross-examine witnesses is apparently not basic to due process, however, cross-examination may be required for more serious offenses or to maintain fundamental fairness.

9. To have legal counsel present is not looked upon by the courts as being essential to fairness. The rule appears to be that the "right to have legal counsel present is a function of the complexity of the case" and the potential loss to the student.

10. Due process requires that the administrator with the quasi-judicial responsibility for rendering a judgment must both hear the case and make the decision. Delegation of decision-making authority is *ultra vires*. An administrator or a board, neverthe-

less, may delegate the collection of evidence, to a subordinate so long as the final decision is made by the lawful authority based on the evidence presented.

11.   Students appear to have no right to remain silent to avoid self-incrimination in a school hearing. This is true even where the student claims that evidence given may tend to incriminate him in a later criminal proceeding on the same charge.

12.   Hearsay may be admissible in either suspension or expulsion hearings.

CHAPTER 4

FREEDOM OF SPEECH AND EXPRESSION

§ 4.1 INTRODUCTION

Courts presume that rules and regulations are valid unless there is a clear abuse of power and discretion on the part of the school.

A rule or regulation may be challenged on several grounds, the most common being that the rule is (1) *ultra vires*, beyond the board's legal authority, and (2) vague or overly broad, or that it violates one of several constitutional prohibitions such as freedom of expression, religion, privacy, due process, or equal protection.

To raise the *vires* issue simply means that the student maintains that the regulation is beyond the legal power vested in the school board by state law. A rule of a residential public high school that required all students to wear khaki uniforms while at school and while visiting public places within five miles of school was held not to be *ultra vires* when the students are in the custody of the school, but the rule became *ultra vires* as school officials sought to apply it to children on holidays or weekends when in the custody of their parents. The question becomes how far does the school's authority extend before it encroaches on the parent's and student's personal prerogatives.

Two different common law principles may render school disciplinary actions invalid, (1) ambiguity or vagueness or rules, and (2) arbitrary or capricious application of rules. The two principles are akin to each other because ambiguous or vague rules may give such broad latitude that administration of the rules may be based on the personal whim or fancy of either the administrator or teacher. Vagueness and overbreadth, a lack of specificity delegates excessive authority in application of rules. These common law principles which govern all governmental agencies have, in recent years, been incorporated into constitutional law, as the rights and freedoms of students have become more clearly defined. For example, vagueness of a rule and arbitrary administration thereof may well invoke questions of both substantive and procedural due process under the Fourteenth Amendment of the Constitution of the United States.

School rules and regulations will not stand if they deny individual rights or freedoms which are protected by the federal or state constitutions. This does not mean that rights and freedoms are without limitation. It does mean, however, that school authorities must have a very good reason to deny a student his or her rights and freedoms. If a school rule is to prevail there must be a rational relationship between the rule and the purpose for which it is designed. In some instances where fundamental interests such as religion or race are concerned, the courts have held that the school authorities must have a compelling reason to support rules promulgated to control or categorize students.

§ 4.2 BALANCING THE INTERESTS

At one time it was believed that to attend school was a privilege and that virtually any school rule or regulation constraining a student's conduct was valid. Today, the privilege doctrine is discredited and it is uniformly held that students do not "shed their constitutional interests when they enter a schoolhouse door." Having constitutional rights does not mean that a student's conduct can go unregulated. All members of society are subject to reasonable restraints, without which a society cannot adequately function. An environment for learning requires that student conduct be regulated. It is obvious that a student cannot be permitted the personal freedom to come and go at will or to ignore rules regarding silence in a library. In order to balance the constitutional rights of pupils against the necessity for order, peace and quiet, the courts have promulgated the "balance of interests" test. The interests of the school are weighed against the student's loss of a particular freedom or right. This balancing test is the heart of the United States Supreme Court's decision in Tinker v. Des Moines Independent School District, 393 U.S. 503, 89 S.Ct. 733 (1969). *Tinker* established that school rules and regulations should be based on a determination of the school's legitimate interests. If the purpose for a rule or regulation is unclear or nonexistent, then there should be no rule. Teachers and administrators must examine their policies to determine their legitimacy.

[77]

§ 4.3   FORECAST OF DISRUPTION

In *Tinker*, the Supreme Court explained the balance of interests in terms of potential for disruption of the school. If a student's exercise of free speech or expression justifies a "reasonable forecast of substantial disruption," then it can be curtailed.

In *Tinker*, certain students and their parents decided to publicize their objections to hostilities in Vietnam, and to indicate their support for a truce by wearing black armbands to school. School principals in Des Moines became aware of the plan to wear armbands and two days before the protest passed a rule prohibiting students from wearing an armband to school. Students who refused to remove their armbands would be suspended from school. Students did wear armbands and were subsequently suspended.

After holding that armbands constituted a manifestation of free speech falling under the ambit of the First Amendment, the court stated: "School officials do not possess absolute authority over their students. Students in school, as well as out, are 'persons' under our Constitution. They are possessed of fundamental rights which the State must respect, just as they themselves must respect their obligations to the State. In our system, students may not be regarded as closed-circuit recipients of only that which the State chooses to communicate. They may not be confined to the expression of those sentiments that are officially approved. In the absence of a specific showing of constitutionally valid reasons to regulate their speech, students are entitled to freedom of expression of their views." With this as the *constitutional* basis of students' rights, the court then sought to determine if the wearing of a black cloth around the arm could in fact interrupt school activities or intrude on the lives of other students. The Court, in holding for the students, found that the record demonstrated no facts which could have been reasonably construed by school officials as evidencing a "forecast of substantial disruption" or of constituting "material interference" with school activities.

The Supreme Court's words were carefully chosen. For a student activity to be proscribed, the school officials must be able to reasonably forecast disruption, and the disruption must be more than minimal, it must be substantial. Too, the disruption must be physical, and be deleterious to the intellectual environment of the school program.

Reasonableness of forecast must be more than mere vague apprehension of disruption, or an "undifferentiated fear or apprehension." There must be evidence to support the expectation of substantial disruption.

§ 4.31 Limitations on Students' Rights

After reading *Tinker*, one may ask what controls, if any, can reasonably be placed on students' conduct? Even though *Tinker* did not explicitly state when and under what circumstances controls could be placed on students, it certainly did not imply that students have unlimited freedom to say, do, or express themselves in any manner which they may desire.

§ 4.32   Wearing Insignias

A closely analogous factual situation to *Tinker* involved the wearing of buttons at Shaw High School in Cleveland.   In this case, Guzick v. Drebus, 431 F.2d 594 (6th Cir. 1970), the court followed the *Tinker* test yet reached an opposite result.   Here, some black students sought to wear a particular button to school which demonstrated their support for a Vietnam truce. Under a long-standing *informal* school rule forbidding the wearing of buttons or any other type of insignia, a student was suspended.   The court, in upholding the school rule, distinguished *Tinker* and clarified the rule of law.   Freedom of speech and expression can be restrained if the rule is reasonably based on long-standing knowledge of the likely conduct of students in such circumstances with similar disruptive stimulus. Where a school has had problems with social strife and gang conflict, a rule against the wearing of insignia or emblems which fragment students into groups, divisions, or fraternities, may be viewed as reasonably forecasting material and substantial school disruption. Too, it was shown by the evidence that the rule prohibiting wearing of insignia and emblems had been applied in an even-handed manner, with school officials uniformly denying students to wear "White is Right" or "Black Power" buttons, headdress, or other types of clothing which expressed inflammatory messages. Such was not the case in *Tinker*, where no rule had existed against armbands until two days before the protest.

To summarize, (1) school officials may make and enforce reasonable rules which control student conduct even though the restraints encroach on a perceived constitutional right of freedom of speech or expression. (2) Symbolic speech and expression are protected as in the case of armbands or buttons. (3) Curtailment of students' rights must be based on reasonable rules, formal or informal. To be reasonable a rule must be promulgated to accomplish some appropriate educational objective. (4) Denial of a right must be based on a "reasonable forecast of material and substantial disruption," and the rule must be applied uniformly in all like circumstances.

§ 4.4 SIT–INS

The precedent prescribed in *Tinker* has been consistently followed in other federal court decisions. For example, prohibition of student sit-ins and nonattendance at classes have been upheld by the courts because they were obviously disruptive of the schools.

§ 4.5 FLAGS

School prohibitions of the Confederate flag have been upheld where racial tension was exacerbated and the use of the flag manifested a desire to maintain segregated schools. Smith v. St. Tammany Parish School Board, 448 F.2d 414 (5th Cir. 1971). Yet, in a northern state where no *de jure* segregation had previously existed, the courts have declined to force school districts to remove the Confederate flag as the school flag. Banks v. Muncie Community School, 433 F.2d 292 (7th Cir. 1970).

§ 4.6 PERSONAL APPEARANCE

Under the general principle that school authorities may make reasonable rules and regulations controlling student conduct, school authorities may regulate student dress and personal appearance. It has been said that it is in the interest of the school to divert the students' attention from the hemline to the blackboard, or from beards to books. Whether or not a particular mode of dress or appearance detracts from the learning environment has a great deal to do with the acceptable standards of a particular community. That which is not acceptable in a rural midwestern town may be quite normal in a major eastern metropolis. If dress or personal appearance is so different and noticeable that it takes away from the ongoing educational program, the school authorities have a valid interest in intervening.

Some early courts held that it is a proper function of the school to require students to wear uniforms to school, and to prohibit the wearing of cosmetics, certain types of hosiery, low-necked dresses, or any style of clothing which may tend, according to community norms, to be immodest; but today it is doubtful that such rules would prevail in many communities. Pugsley v. Sellemery, 158 Ark. 247, 50 S.W. 538 (1923).

Yet, reasonableness of regulations must be judged as applied to the particular facts of each case. In *Stromberg*, an apparently questionable rule prohibiting the wearing of heel plates in school was held to be reasonable because of noise and possible damage to the school's hardwood floors. Stromberg v. French, 60 N.D. 750, 236 N.W. 477 (1931).

§ 4.61 Dress Codes

Dress codes have been stricken by the courts when it has been shown that the rules were too broad, vague, ambiguous (see above), or did not relate to any legitimate educational purpose. A school board dress regulation is valid only to the extent necessary to protect the safety of the wearer, male or female, or to prevent disruption or distraction which interferes with the education of other students. A flat prohibition against girls wearing slacks to school has been held invalid because such a rule relates only to style and taste, and cannot be justified on the basis of safety, order, or discipline. Scott v. Board of Education, Union Free School District #17, Hicksville, 61 Misc.2d 333, 305 N.Y.S.2d 601 (1969).

Schools may adopt easily understood, specifically stated, dress standards which effectively proscribe immodest attire, unsafe or indecent clothing. A school rule which forbids the wearing of tight skirts or shorts six inches above the knee has been upheld, but a rule which proscribes the wearing of "bizarre" or immodest clothing, including knickers, jump suits, frayed trousers, and skirts six inches below the knee, has been held invalid. Wallace v. Ford, 346 F.Supp. 156 (E.D.Ark.1972).

In some jurisdictions personal appearance is deemed to be a fundamental constitutional interest. Where this is the law, the school system bears the burden of proof to show compelling reasons why the code is necessary.

In Bishop v. Colaw, 450 F.2d 1069 (8th Cir. 1971), a federal appeals court stated that one's freedom to govern his or her own personal appearance ranks high on the spectrum of societal values and is protected by the Due Process Clause of the Fourteenth Amendment, yet, personal freedoms are not absolute and they must yield when their exercise intrudes on the freedoms of others. School authorities may establish rules which protect the freedom of all students to learn in an educational setting, free from disruption. The burden rests on the school authorities to give valid reasons for the denial of such a personal freedom. The courts will balance the individual student's interests against the school's interest to maintain a proper learning environment.

§ 4.62   Hair Codes

Recently, the number of haircut cases has declined, but a decade ago courts were deluged with student long hair questions. Historically, the style of hair has been a contentious issue between schoolmasters and students. Students with generally more radical behavior have tended to deviate from what the teachers thought was acceptable in hair styles. The law is not well settled, in fact, the federal courts of appeals are split on the issue. The First, Third, Fourth, Seventh, and Eighth Circuits have held that students have a constitutionally protected right to choose their own hair style, while the Fifth, Sixth, Ninth, and Tenth Circuits have held that personal appearance is not a fundamental interest and that schools may reasonably regulate hair styles.

In those states where the students have prevailed, the courts have elevated personal appearance to a fundamental interest, and have placed the burden on school boards to show why the school's interest is of such magnitude as to restrain this basic freedom. Several United States constitutional provisions have been used in these cases, the First Amendment's guarantee of free expression, the Fourth Amendment's guarantee of the right to privacy, and the Fourteenth Amendment's guarantee of due process and equal protection. Each has been used to successfully strike down various hair codes. In jurisdictions where personal appearance is elevated to a fundamental interest, school systems must present evidence to show that long hair creates "substantial and material disruption" in the school, or causes health or safety hazards, or, in some other way impinges on the educational program and other students' freedoms. Such evidence is usually very difficult to obtain and in these jurisdictions the students usually prevail.

In the circuits where personal appearance has not been held to be a fundamental interest, the school systems need only show that hair code is rationally related to a legitimate educational purpose. For example, in the Fifth Circuit, school grooming codes are presumed to be *prima facie* constitutional. The burden is placed on the student to state a cause of action designed to show that the code is discriminatory and is arbitrarily or capriciously enforced. If a student can show that the rule is so vague that it is applied to some students but not to others, the rule is likely to fall.

[*85*]

There is no United States Supreme Court precedent applicable to the fifty states and it is impossible to reconcile the conflicting decisions of the federal courts of appeals. The best advice for teachers and school boards is to ascertain the rule of law for their own jurisdiction and follow the precedents of the courts therein.

§ 4.7   MEMBERSHIP IN STUDENT SOCIETIES

School systems and states have, in many instances, found it to be educationally necessary to prohibit student fraternities, sororities and secret societies on public school campuses. It is reasoned that these organizations create undesirable divisions among students, and, in so doing, greatly harm the morale of the school. Where states have enacted laws against such groups, the courts have uniformly upheld them. Such statutes have either prohibited such organizations outright, or have required school boards to expel students who are members. Students have usually challenged these statutes as a denial of equal protection under the Fourteenth Amendment, but have not succeeded in their efforts to invalidate such statutes.

In one case, the court upheld a school board regulation made pursuant to statute which proscribed fraternities, sororities, and secret societies, including charity clubs, but excluding the Boy Scouts, Hi-Y, and a few other clubs, to be held within the discretion of the school board. Passel v. Fort Worth Independent School District, 453 S.W.2d 888 (1970), cert. denied 402 U.S. 968, 91 S.Ct. 1667 (1971). Such a regulation did not constitute discrimination against members of charity clubs who claimed their Fourteenth Amendment equal protection rights were violated.

The courts have also held that, in statutory prohibitions against societies, the word "secret" extends to exclusive social clubs whose memberships are determined by its own members. Societies or organizations, regardless of what they call themselves, may be prohibited under the aegis of secret societies if their membership is not open to all students. Robinson v. Sacramento City Unified School District, 245 Cal.App.2d 278, 53 Cal.Rptr. 781 (1966).

Just as these statutory and regulatory prohibitions do not violate equal protection, neither do they collide with the United States Constitution's First Amendment freedoms guaranteeing freedom of assembly or Fourteenth Amendment due process interests. As far as freedom of assembly is concerned, the courts have clearly maintained that adults have a complete and unrestrained right to form and maintain private, secret, or nonsecret clubs, whether for snobbish or more legitimate social reasons, but the public schools are a different setting entirely. Here the school systems have a definite interest in weighing the good of such clubs against their more inimical aspects. Where the school board, in the exercise of its judgment, feels that the harm outweighs the good, then the clubs, regardless of what they are called, can be banned. The students' rights in the school setting are subject to limitation.

It should also be noted that adult rights are not unlimited and cannot be because people do not exist in a political and social vacuum, and their acts may be, at times, harmful to others. In explaining the distinction

[87]

between adults and students, secret clubs and societies, the California court, in *Robinson,* stated the rule of law in this manner: "Here the school board is not dealing with adults, but with adolescents in their formative years. And it is not dealing with activities which occur only within the home, and which, therefore, might be said to relate exclusively to parental jurisdiction and control. It is dealing under express statutory mandate with activities which reach into the school and which reasonably may be said to interfere with the educational process, with the morale of high school student bodies as a whole, and which also may reasonably be said not to foster democracy but to frustrate democracy." Such prohibitions, of course, in no way prohibit clubs or organizations whose memberships, activities, and function are decided by academic or athletic merit, such as French clubs, Latin clubs, letterperson clubs, etc.

§ 4.8 STUDENT PREGNANCY

Pregnancy of unmarried students presents certain educational problems which may be detrimental to both the girl involved and to the school. Earlier, the school rid itself of the issue by simply requiring that unmarried pregnant girls be suspended or even expelled from school. Such a rule was in many cases a relief to the pregnant student since it absolved them from compulsory attendance and allowed them to stay home unnoticed by other students. Usually, though, pregnancy of an unmarried student meant that her educational program was at an end. This was the unfortunate situation until the early 1970's, when more enlightened school administrators began to wonder about the consequences of such exclusions. Gradually schools began to enact rules which allowed girls a choice of attending a separate night course, having home instruction during pregnancy, or attending separate classes at school especially designed for pregnant students.

The legal issue involved here is whether a student who has a right to attend school can be excluded for a reason such as pregnancy. The weight of the more recent authority is that pregnancy is not a valid reason to exclude a girl from an education. To do so is to violate the Equal Protection Clause of the Fourteenth Amendment. Perry v. Grenada Municipal Separate School District, 300 F.Supp. 748 (N.D.Miss.1969).

A correlative issue is whether the pregnant student can be required to leave the regular school program and participate in a special school program, or take only homebound instruction. Although there is conflict among the various court jurisdictions, Title IX (see: Chapter 11) prohibits requiring a female to attend an alternative program. This Act provides that the female may choose an alternative program if she desires. The majority of court cases have been adjudicated on constitutional grounds and not on the statutory grounds of Title IX. A federal district court in Georgia has held that a school rule which requires pregnant students or unwed mothers to attend night school does not violate the students' fundamental constitutional right of procreation. Houston v. Posser, 361 F.Supp. 295 (N.D.Ga.1973). In this case, an unmarried fifteen-year-old mother sought reentry into the regular daytime public school program but was denied. The court held that education was not a fundamental constitutional interest and thereby the school board had to show only a "rational basis" for its rule, instead of a "compelling state interest." It was rational, the court held, for the school to exclude students from the regular program who marry or become parents because they are more precocious than other students, and mixing the two groups will lead to disruption. The court noted that the girl was not denied an education, but was instead forced to attend a fully accredited night school.

This decision, though, is drawn into question by another federal district court decision in Massachusetts, which held that a pregnant student could not be denied attendance in the regular school program even though the school district had made a provision for the girl to have elaborate and expensive home-bound instruction. In denying enforcement of the school rule, the court held that the full scope of educational benefits could not be attained without attending school with other students. To force the student to hide away at home while receiving instruction violated her constitutional right to attend school. Ordway v. Hargraves, 323 F.Supp. 1155 (D.Mass.1971). Where the federal district court in Georgia had accepted that attendance of pregnant students in the regular school program may cause disruption, the court here rejected a similar argument by the school. No evidence was presented to show that the pregnant condition of a student would occasion disruption or would otherwise interfere with the school program.

Some boards have justified home-bound instruction for pregnant students for the students' health and protection. Such rules have been accepted by some courts. State v. Chamberlain, 175 N.E.2d 539 (Ohio 1962). If the court requires that the reason for the rule be merely rational and not compelling, the rule will likely withstand challenges to its constitutionality under equal protection.

On the other hand, if a student can convince a court that such a rule creates an "irrebuttable presumption" automatically incapacitating the student from regular school activities, then there may be a violation of the Due Process Clause of the Fourteenth Amendment. In LaFleur v. Cleveland Board of Education, 414 U.S. 632, 94 S.Ct. 791 (1974) (see: Chapter 18), the United States Supreme Court held that a school teacher could not be automatically suspended from employment because of pregnancy. The court ruled that the right to procreate was fundamental, and infringement by the state had to be supported by a "compelling state interest."

§ 4.9 IMMORALITY

Immorality is a broad term, encompassing wickedness, lying, cheating, stealing, sexual impurity, or unchastity. Immorality is not necessarily confined to sexual matters, instead, it may be acts which are *contre bonos mores*, that which is considered to be inconsistent with the moral rectitude of the community. Synonyms are corrupt, indecent, depraved, dissolute, while its antonyms are decent, upright, good, and right. A student who so flagrantly violates the norms

[*91*]

of the school and community as to be immoral under these definitions can be dismissed from school. Also, the selling of drugs or liquor to other students, fraud or plagiarism, sexual promiscuity and lascivious conduct may all constitute immorality.

Pregnancy of an unwed student is not necessarily immoral, but how the pregnancy occurs may be. Sexual intercourse at school may certainly be considered immoral conduct. For a minor to undress for another student or for an adult for the purpose of satisfying sexual desires is immoral conduct violating not only school rules but may offend delinquency statutes as well. Holton v. State, 602 P.2d 1228 (Alaska 1979). Such activities on the part of students, in violation of school rules, may be punishable by dismissal from school.

§ 4.10 MARRIAGE

In early cases, courts were inclined to uphold school rules denying participation in school extracurricular activities by married students. In these cases, participation in extracurricular activities was considered to be a privilege which could be denied a married student. Today, because the courts do not view education as being merely a privilege, educational activities offered to one student must be offered to all students regardless of whether the student is married. As with all rules, there are some exceptions. For example, the United States Court of Appeals for the Tenth Circuit has held that school attendance could not be denied without necessary procedural safeguards, but that similar constitutional protections did not apply to each component of the educational process, indicating that participation in extracurricular activities may be denied without due process. Albach v. Odle, 531 F.2d 983 (10th Cir. 1976). The weight of authority, though, appears to support the position that both students' rights of marital privacy, Moran v. School District No. 7, 350 F.Supp. 1180 (D.Mont.1972), and equal protection, Hollon v. Mathis Independent School District, 491 F.2d 92 (5th Cir. 1974), are violated by prohibiting participation in extracurricular activities.

§ 4.11 DRUGS, TOBACCO, AND ALCOHOL

School authorities may prohibit drugs, alcohol, and guns (or other weapons) on school grounds or in off-campus activities which bear on the conduct of the school. Most states have statutes against the possession of drugs on school grounds, but in the absence of such laws, school boards may promulgate their own regulations. Students may be expelled from school for violation of drug regulations, but may not be expelled for simply having been charged in court with possession of drugs. Harvard v. Clark, 59 Misc.2d 327, 299 N.Y.S.2d 65 (1969).

Schools may, too, control or prohibit the use and possession of tobacco and alcoholic beverages in school. Dismissal has been held to be appropriate punishment even though spiking of punch at school was so light as to be barely chemically detectible. So long as procedural due process is properly carried out, dismissals have been upheld. Wood v. Strickland, 420 U.S. 308, 95 S.Ct. 992 (1975).

§ 4.12 WEAPONS

Of course, students cannot bring firearms or other dangerous weapons to school. Teachers have a responsibility to act, within reason and physical capability, to protect students from injury due to weapons. It is a legal presumption that teachers have not only the right, but the obligation, to remove dangerous objects and weapons from the possession of students. A teacher may use physical force in carrying out this responsibility. Metcalf v. State, 21 Tex.App. 1774, 17 S.W. 142 (1886).

CHAPTER 5

RELIGIOUS ACTIVITIES IN PUBLIC SCHOOLS

§ 5.1 INTRODUCTION

The teaching function is very important to virtually all religions. Doctrines and dogmas of religious groups are spread and church membership is increased by teaching to youth and nonbelievers. It is natural that as sectarian beliefs are advanced they will come in conflict with secular purposes of the state. Very early in this country education was conducted almost exclusively by the churches for the purposes of advancing their religious beliefs, and where the state provided tax funds to support schools one of the justifications was to teach the citizenry to read the Bible. In fact, the first governmental effort to establish tax-supported schools in this country was in 1647 when the colony of Massachusetts, by statutes provided for general taxation in local communities for the purpose of keeping men knowledgeable of the Scriptures in order that they might not fall into the grip of the "old deluder, Satan."

The concept of public education "divorced from denominational control was foreign to the colonial mind." Leo Pfeffer, *Church, State and Freedom*, Boston: Beacon Press, 1967, p. 321. Later Justice Frankfurter in the *McCollum* case was to explain that: "Traditionally, organized education in the Western world was Church education. It could hardly be otherwise when the education of children was primarily the study of the Word and the ways of God. Even in Protestant countries, where there was a less close identification of Church and State, the basis of education was largely the Bible, and its chief purpose inculcation of piety. To the extent that the State intervened, it used its authority to further the aims of the Church."

"The emigrants who came to these shores brought this view of education with them. Colonial schools certainly started with a religious orientation." People ex rel. McCollum v. Board of Education, 333 U.S. 203, 68 S.Ct. 461 (1948).

"The pervasiveness of the early religious influence on public schools is illustrated by the primer which was used to teach most public school pupils to read in New England in the latter part of the seventeenth century. The book entitled *The New England Primer* taught the alphabet using letters and pictures with Biblical connotations, for example: "A—in *Adam*'s fall we sinned or P—*Peter* denies His Lord and cries." Because of these origins, religious involvement in public education has been difficult to curb.

Over the decades many conflicts have developed between the clergy and the proponents of public education. When Horace Mann led the way in the 1830s to creating the first state system of public schools in Massachusetts, his chief opposition came from clergymen who sought to prevent him from creating Godless institutions. Mann had insisted that the public schools should have no sectarian religious motivations and that the state should "abstain from subjugating the capacities of children to any legal standard of religious faith."

Later, contrary to Mann's beliefs as the public schools became better developed, religious activities were permitted in most states, including prayer, Bible reading, and other religious exercises. By the twentieth century, all but a few states had regular morning religious services. The practices were generally acquiesced to by the state courts and were, except in a few states, held to be consistent with state constitutions.

The public school system envisioned by Mann which was established throughout this country was an innovation unlike any other country's preceding it. This system of public education was founded on three basic assumptions: "First, that the legislature has the power to tax all—even the childless and those whose children attend private schools—in order to provide free public education for all; second, that the legislature has the power to require every parent to provide for his children a basic education in secular subjects; third, that the education provided by the state in the free schools must be secular." Pfeffer, supra, p. 327.

Each of these basic premises of public education continues to be attacked today. Parents of private school children maintain they are entitled to tax credits because of what they consider (erroneously) to be double taxation. Parents contest compulsory attendance laws, state regulation of private schools, and home instruction (see Chapter 1); and continuing efforts are made to teach religious doctrines in the pub-

[*97*]

lic schools ranging from religious exercises to teaching creation-science (see Chapter 2).

§ 5.2 FREE EXERCISE AND ESTABLISHMENT

The controversy between advocates of religious sectarianism versus secularism in the schools is a part of a larger conflict which tends to permeate most governments and societies, the unending struggle between Church and State. Today, a casual glance at a newspaper reminds one that the Middle East, with Christian against Muslim, Muslim against Muslim, and Jew against both, is a raging torrent of religious bigotry and persecution. Ireland, Poland, and El Salvador are all current conflicts with critical religious overtones. Today's religious conflicts are merely descendants of the great religious quarrels of Europe which resulted in millions of deaths from wars and persecutions.

The European experience of embattled Church and State was fresh on the minds of founding fathers in America when the First Amendment was drafted. The basic antecedents to the religion clauses of the First Amendment were found in James Madison's *Memorial and Remonstrance Against Religious Assessments* and Thomas Jefferson's *Act for Establishing Religious Freedom*. Both were documents written in response to attempts to establish religion in Virginia and to encroach on individual religious liberty. Madison admonished that all persons had a right to "free exercise of their religion according to the dictates of their conscience;" and Jefferson asserted that it was time to do away with the "impious presumption of legislators and rulers, civil and ecclesiastical who . . .

have assumed dominion over the faith of others"; and that a person's "civil rights should have no dependence on [his] religious opinions."

§ 5.3 WALL OF SEPARATION

When finally promulgated and ratified in 1791, the religion provisions of the First Amendment provided: "Congress shall make no law respecting an establishment of religion, or prohibiting the free exercise thereof; . . ."

John Adams interpreted these two clauses to mean that "Congress will never meddle in religion . . ."; and Jefferson explained the intent was to create a "wall of separation between Church and State." It had been from Jefferson's urging, while serving in France in 1787, that Madison proceeded to champion the promulgation and ratification of the Bill of Rights.

Interpretations of the meaning of the First Amendment have carried forward to today. Time and again the United States Supreme Court has delineated the boundaries between Church and State only to have legislatures and school boards open new cracks and fissures requiring further interpretation. To Justice William O. Douglas there was little debate over the intent of the Amendment. He said ". . . [T]here cannot be the slightest doubt that the First Amendment reflects the philosophy that Church and State should be separated." And so far as interference with the "free exercise" of religion and an "establishment of religion are concerned, the separation must be complete and unequivocal." Zorach v. Clauson, 343 U.S. 306, 72 S.Ct. 679 (1952).

§ 5.4 CONSTITUTIONAL STANDARD

In the large number of religion and public school cases which have come before the United States Supreme Court over the years, the one principle of law which appears to be consistent throughout is that the state must be "neutral" toward religion. As stated in *Zorach*, the government should show "no partiality to any one [religious] group" and should let "each [group] flourish according to the zeal of its adherents and the appeal of its dogma." This neutrality of government means, according to Justice Black's opinion in *Everson*, that: "The establishment of religion clause of the First Amendment means at least this: 'Neither a state nor the Federal Government can set up a church. Neither can pass laws which aid one religion, aid all religions or prefer one religion over another . . . . No tax in any amount, large or small, can be levied to support any religious activities or institutions, whatever they may be called, or whatever form they may adopt to teach or practice religion.' "

§ 5.41 Three-Pronged Test

This required neutrality is, however, difficult to define. Prior to 1970, the Supreme Court sought to determine state neutrality with a two-part test which required that: (1) the action of the state not be intended to aid one religion or all religions and (2) the principle or primary effect of the program be one that "neither advances nor inhibits religion." In 1970 the Supreme Court added a third prong to the test, that the state must not foster "an excessive government entanglement with religion." Walz v. Tax Commission, 397 U.S. 664, 90 S.Ct. 1409 (1970).

In 1971 the Supreme Court combined these three standards and applied them in striking down salary supplements to teachers in parochial schools and purchase of educational services from parochial schools in Lemon v. Kurtzman, 403 U.S. 602, 91 S.Ct. 2105 (1971). Now, when each Church and State case is litigated, the courts must relate the factual situation to the three-pronged test: (1) purpose, (2) effect, and (3) excessive entanglement.

§ 5.5   RELIGIOUS ACTIVITIES

§ 5.51   Released Time

Many different schemes have been devised for using the public schools as a supportive device for teaching religion. A common practice, by the turn of the century, in many school districts, was for a portion of the school day to be set aside for religious instruction in the public school building. This went on without serious challenge until the *McCollum* case in 1948 in People ex rel. McCollum v. Board of Education, 333 U.S. 203, 68 S.Ct. 461, in which the United States Supreme Court held unconstitutional a released time situation in which Protestant teachers, Catholic priests, and a Jewish rabbi came into the public schools each week to teach religion. Students who wanted to attend were *released* from their regular classes and those students who did not went to another location in the building to pursue their secular subjects. Attendance reports were kept and absences were reported back to the sec-

[*101*]

ular teachers. The school district defended the practice maintaining that the students were not compelled to attend the religious classes and that one religion was not favored over another.

The Court in striking down the practice said that state tax-supported facilities could not be used to disseminate religious doctrines whether it aided only one or all religions. Too, the Court noted that the state's compulsory attendance law provided a valuable aid to religion in that it brought the children to a central location at which the churches could capture the students' attention. According to the Court, there existed too close a cooperation consisting of the following features: weight and influence of the public school is cast behind a program for religious instruction; public school teachers provide the attendance accounting and police process, keeping track of students who are released; the normal classroom activities come to a halt; the public school provides a crutch for the churches to support religious training. For these reasons the practice was held to violate the First Amendment.

Following *McCollum*, the City of New York devised another released time program whereby students were released from public schools, during the school day, to attend religious services off school grounds. A period was set aside each week when students could leave the public school to go to a church or church school to attend religious services. The program was entirely optional, the school authorities were neutral, and teachers did no more than release the students when so requested by parents. In upholding this plan the Supreme Court said that the state could accommodate religion without aiding religion and that it would "press the concept of separation of Church and State" to condemn the New York law. For government to fail to accommodate this type of released time plan would constitute a callousness toward religion which is not required by the First Amendment.

Can, though, public schools release students to leave public school grounds to take courses for credit in parochial schools? This issue was litigated in a Utah case when the Logan Public School District established a released time program with parochial schools. The program provided for the release of students to a seminary; while at the seminary students received credit for classes in the Old and New Testament. The grades for these classes were recorded on the student's permanent record. A Utah State Board of Education policy allowed credit for release time programs, such as Bible History, as long as the electives were not mainly denominational. The court ruled the released time program *per se* is constitutional; but receiving credit is unconstitutional because it would require public school officials to assess the religious content of the classes. This assessment would require a judgment on what is and what is not religious and therefore would exceed the permissible bounds of accommodation and become entanglement, a violation of the Establishment Clause. Lanner v. Wimmer, 662 F.2d 1349 (10th Cir. 1981).

§ 5.52   Prayer and Bible Reading

Prior to 1962 some states required the beginning of each school day with a prayer and the reading of verses from the Bible. The New York State Board of Regents composed a prayer which they recommended be used in the public schools. The prayer was: "Almighty God, we acknowledge our dependence upon Thee, and we beg Thy blessings upon us, our parents, teachers, and our Country." The Supreme Court determined the prayer was a violation of the Establishment Clause. "[W]e think that the constitutional prohibition against laws respecting an establishment of religion must at least mean that in this country, it is no part of the business of government to compose official prayers for any group of the American people to recite as a part of a religious program carried on by government." Engel v. Vitale, 370 U.S. 421, 82 S.Ct. 1261 (1962).

Then in 1963 came the famous companion cases, School District of Abington Township v. Schempp and Murray v. Curlett, 374 U.S. 203, 83 S.Ct. 1560 (1963). Pursuant to state statutes in Pennsylvania and Maryland local school districts had prayer and Bible reading at the beginning of each day. Children who did not want to stay in the room were excused while the exercises proceeded. The reading of the Bible and Lord's Prayer was challenged as a violation of the First Amendment. The Court determined that the exercises and the law requiring them violated the Establishment Clause of the First Amendment. But the Court went on to say, "It certainly may be said that the Bible is worthy of study for its literary and historic qualities. Nothing we have said here indicates that such study of the Bible or of religion, when presented objectively as a part of a secular program of education, may not

[*104*]

be effected consistently with the First Amendment. But the exercises here do not fall into those categories." Therefore, the Bible may be used in appropriate study of history, civilization, ethics, and comparative religion; but those Bible study classes must be taught in a manner that is secular and does not promote religion. If the classes are not objectively taught, then they are unconstitutional. Wiley v. Franklin, 497 F.Supp. 390 (E.D.Tenn.1980). See Stone v. Graham, 449 U.S. 39, 101 S.Ct. 192 (1980).

In order to get prayer back into the public schools, a few legislatures have passed statutes similar to New Mexico's which states, "[e]ach school board may authorize a period of silence not to exceed one minute at the beginning of the school day. This period may be used for contemplation, meditation or prayer, provided that silence is maintained and no activities are undertaken." The New Mexico statute was declared unconstitutional in Duffy v. Las Cruces Public Schools, 557 F.Supp. 1013 (D.N.M.1983). See also: May v. Cooperman, 572 F.Supp. 1561 (D.C.N.J.1983). Although the legislature stated that the statute was secular, the court said, ". . . the legislative avowals of secular purpose are clearly self serving . . . [and] the presence of the word 'prayer' . . . is compelling evidence that there was no secular purpose sought to be achieved." The New Mexico statute was essentially copied from a Massachusetts statute except New Mexico added the word "contemplation." New Mexico lawmakers assumed their statute would be constitutional since a federal district court had declared the

Massachusetts statute constitutional. Gaines v. Anderson, 421 F.Supp. 337 (D.Mass.1976).

In a more recent case a federal district court upheld two Alabama statutes permitting voluntary recitation of prayers led by teachers. Jaffree v. Board of School Commissioners of Mobile County, 554 F.Supp. 1104 (S.D.Ala.1983). Later Justice Powell stayed this district court decision, stating; "conducting prayers as part of a school program is unconstitutional . . . ." Jaffree v. Board of School Commissioners of Mobile County, ___ U.S. ___, 103 S.Ct. 842 (1983). On appeal to the United States Court of Appeals, Eleventh Circuit, the federal district court's decision was reversed. Jaffree v. Wallace, 705 F.2d 1526 (11th Cir.1983), rehearing denied 713 F.2d 614.

State legislatures or school boards may have a moment of silence at the beginning of each school day but any statute or policy that refers to prayer or religious exercises will generally be declared unconstitutional. In Karen B. v. Treen, 653 F.2d 897 (5th Cir. 1981), affirmed 455 U.S. 913, 102 S.Ct. 1267 (1982), the Fifth United States Circuit Court of Appeals struck down a statute authorizing voluntary student or teacher initiated prayer at the beginning of the school day.

§ 5.53 Voluntary Student Religious Meetings

Some students have requested the opportunity to meet at school on a voluntary basis and study the Bible and have religious exercises. These activities have been requested to take place before or after school and occasionally during periods designated for clubs. Some school administrators have acquiesced to these activities, and some school boards have established policies allowing such activities. The students claim this is a basic right of free exercise. One such case was Lubbock Civil Liberties Union v. Lubbock Independent School District, 669 F.2d 1038 (5th Cir. 1982) where the school board passed a policy stating; "The school board permits students to gather at the school with supervision either before or after regular hours on the same basis as other groups as determined by the school administration to meet for any educational, moral, religious or ethical purpose so long as attendance at such meeting is voluntary." The court determined that the policy violated all parts of the tripartite test, because it did not have a secular purpose, it promoted religion and it caused excessive entanglement.

The court rejected the free exercise argument of the students since it would be credible only if there was a total foreclosure of a student's right to worship. But the court noted, "[t]he students attend school only several hours a day, five days a week, nine months during the year. The other hours are effectively open for their attendance at religious activities at places other than state-supported schools."

The school district relied on Widmar v. Vincent, 454 U.S. 263, 102 S.Ct. 269 (1981) where the Supreme Court declared a university policy which denied students access to buildings for voluntary religious programs, a violation of free speech. This decision was based on the campus being a public forum and religious groups having a right of equal access. The *Lubbock* court rejected the public forum argument as did the Second Circuit in Brandon v. Board of Education of Guilderland School District, 635 F.2d 971 (2d Cir. 1980), cert. denied 454 U.S. 1123, 102 S.Ct. 970 (1981). In *Brandon* the court upheld the school's refusal to allow prayer meetings before and after school as not a violation of free exercise. *Lubbock* cited *Brandon* in rejecting the public forum argument when the court said, "First, a high school is not a 'public forum' where religious views can be freely aired. The expression of religious points of view, and even the performance of religious rituals, is permissible in parks and streets when subject to reasonable time, place and manner regulations. . . . The facilities of a university have also been identified as a 'public forum,' where religious speech and association cannot be prohibited . . . while students have First Amendment rights to political speech in public schools . . . sensitive Establishment Clause considerations limit their right to air religious doctrines." See Bender v. Williamsport Area School District, 563 F.Supp. 697 (M.D.Penn.1983).

In another case the student council requested and received permission to recite prayers and read verses from the Bible at high school assemblies. The Ninth United States Circuit Court of Appeals ruled that the act was unconstitutional violating the Establishment Clause and could not be saved by the fact the prayers and readings were recited by volunteers. Collins v. Chandler Unified School District, 644 F.2d 759 (9th Cir. 1981).

§ 5.54   Posting Ten Commandments

The Kentucky legislature passed a statute requiring the posting of the Ten Commandments on the wall of each classroom in the state. The posters were to be purchased with private donations. At the bottom of each poster the statute required the printing of the following statement: "The secular application of the Ten Commandments is clearly seen in its adoption as the fundamental legal code of Western Civilization and the Common Law of the United States."

The United States Supreme Court ruled that the disclaimer at the bottom did not change the pre-eminent purpose of the Ten Commandments which was plainly religious. Therefore, the statute violated the Establishment Clause of the First Amendment. Stone v. Graham, 449 U.S. 39, 101 S.Ct. 192 (1980).

§ 5.6   USE OF PUBLIC FUNDS

§ 5.61   Shared Time

Shared time, which has also been called "dual enrollment," is an arrangement between public school boards and private schools by which they share private or public school facilities. This concept is primarily found where a private school does not have a specific offering and, a student takes the class for credit at a public school. These types of programs have been upheld to be constitutional, but public school districts are not required to establish such programs. It is within the prerogative of the public school board whether or not to establish a shared time program.

In a shared time case, where a sixth-grader from a Christian academy was denied enrollment in a public junior high school band class, and the private school provided no band class and the public school only allowed full-time students to participate in public programs, the student alleged a denial of equal protection.

The court determined that although the legislature allowed "shared time" programs, whether to implement them or not is at the discretion of a local board. Simply because services are offered by a public school does not mean private school children have the right to receive equal services. Since no constitutional issue was involved and establishing a shared time program is at the discretion of a local board, the court felt the plaintiff's remedy was "to elect a school board which will change the district's policy." Snyder v. Charlotte Public Schools District, 123 Mich.App. 56, 333 N.W.2d 542 (1983). In Luetkemeyer v. Kaufmann, 364 F.Supp. 376 (W.D.Mo.1973), affirmed 419 U.S. 888, 95 S.Ct. 167 (1974), the Court held the providing of transportation to public school children and not to nonpublic students did not deny equal protection nor due process. Also, the providing of bus transportation to public school students and not to private school students for field trips was not an equal protection violation. Cook v. Griffin, 47 A.D.2d 23, 364 N.Y.S.2d 632 (1975).

§ 5.62   Purchase of Instructional Services

In 1971 the United States Supreme Court declared Rhode Island and Pennsylvania statutes allowing the purchase of services from private schools, mainly church schools, unconstitutional because of excessive entanglement between the church schools and the state. Lemon v. Kurtzman, 403 U.S. 602, 91 S.Ct. 2105 (1971). The Rhode Island legislature passed an act which allowed state officials to supplement the salaries of private school teachers up to fifteen percent of their annual salary. The teacher could only teach secular subjects and use materials that were available in public schools. Also, the teacher must agree in writing not to teach a course in religion so long as he or she received a salary supplement. Secular subjects were defined as mathematics, modern foreign languages, physical science, and physical education. The state could also pay for textbooks and instructional materials if approved by state officials. Since the state required to closely monitor what went on in the classrooms, the court held that there was excessive entanglement.

The state of Michigan authorized local school boards to establish "shared time" programs with private schools and to lease from the private school real and personal property as needed. Public schools could lease classroom space for six dollars per class per week for elementary and ten dollars per class per week for secondary schools. Teachers would be employed by the public schools and teach in the previously leased space.

The Grand Rapids Public Schools established the "shared time" program with private schools. Most of the teachers hired for the program were former private school teachers who simply remained in their private school. The federal district court found a few minor aspects of the program different from that declared unconstitutional in Lemon v. Kurtzman, supra, but stated, the program "is fundamentally and substantially comparable to that of the nonpublic schools involved in Lemon v. Kurtzman." Therefore, the Michigan shared time program was declared unconstitutional because the primary effect was to advance religion. The law also created excessive entanglement. Americans United for Separation, etc. v. School District, 546 F.Supp. 1071 (W.D.Mich.1982).

§ 5.63   Textbooks

In 1928 the Louisiana legislature passed an act which allowed the purchasing and supply of textbooks for school children throughout the state, which included private school children. The United States Supreme Court upheld the act as not violative of the Fourteenth Amendment based on the "Child Benefit Theory." Cochran v. Louisiana State Board of Education, 281 U.S. 370, 50 S.Ct. 335 (1930).

The state of New York passed legislation which allowed the lending of textbooks to parochial school children free of charge. The United States Supreme Court in Board of Education of Central School District No. 1 v. Allen, 392 U.S. 236, 88 S.Ct. 1923 (1968), determined that the Act was constitutional and did not violate the Establishment Clause of the First Amendment. Therefore the loaning of textbooks to private school children does not conflict with the Federal Constitution. Loans have been subsequently upheld in Meek v. Pittenger, 421 U.S. 349, 95 S.Ct. 1753 (1975) and Wolman v. Walter, 433 U.S. 229, 97 S.Ct. 2593

(1977). Although a state legislative act providing textbooks to private school children may not violate the
Federal Constitution, it may very well violate the
state's constitution. A number of states have more
restrictive separation of Church and State provisions
in their constitutions than the Federal Constitution.
See: In re Advisory Opinion re Constitutionality of
1974, 394 Mich. 41, 228 N.W.2d 772 (1975); California
Teachers Association v. Wilson Riles, 29 Cal.3d 794,
176 Cal.Rptr. 300, 632 P.2d 953 (1981).

§ 5.64 Tuition and Tax Benefits

In May of 1972 the Governor of New York signed
legislation providing fiscal support to private schools.
One section of the legislation was divided into two
parts: (1) a tuition grant program and (2) a tax benefit
program. The tuition grant program provided $50 to
$100 (but no more than fifty percent of tuition actually
paid) to low-income families who enrolled their children in private schools.

The second section, the tax benefit program, allowed
the parents of private school children to deduct from
their adjusted gross incomes a specified amount. The
amount was based on a sliding scale. The more income earned, the less tuition could be deducted. The
program had a $25,000 adjusted gross income as a ceil-
ing. The Supreme Court stated, "[o]ur examination of
New York's aid provisions, in light of all relevant considerations, compels the judgment that each, as written, has a primary effect that advances religion and
offends the constitutional prohibition against laws rejecting an establishment of religion." Committee for

Public Education and Religious Liberty v. Nyquist, 413 U.S. 756, 93 S.Ct. 2955 (1973). The Supreme Court in a companion case to *Nyquist* declared a Pennsylvania statute which reimbursed parents $75 to $150 per child unconstitutional. "We hold that Pennsylvania's tuition grant scheme violates the constitutional mandate against the 'sponsorship' or 'financial support' of religion or religious institutions." Sloan v. Lemon, 413 U.S. 825, 93 S.Ct. 2982 (1973).

In 1983 the United States Supreme Court in a tax deduction case Mueller v. Allen, ____ U.S. ____, 103 S.Ct. 3062 (1983) upheld tax deductions for tuition, textbooks, and transportation. The Court distinguished *Mueller* from *Nyquist* because Mueller allowed parents of children in both public and private schools to take tax deductions. The Court said that *Mueller* was "vitally different" from *Nyquist*. In *Nyquist* ". . . public assistance amounting to tuition grants, [was] provided only to parents of children in non-public schools. This fact had considerable bearing on our decision striking down the New York statute . . ." Under the Minnesota law all parents may take tax deductions whether their children attend public schools or private sectarian or nonsectarian private schools.

The tripartite test was used to determine the constitutionality of the Minnesota program. The court ruled the statute had a secular purpose of insuring the state of a well-educated citizenry. Also, the primary effect was not to advance religion since parents of both public and private students participated in the deduction.

[*114*]

There, also, was no excessive entanglement since any entanglement would be minor and not excessive.

§ 5.65   Transportation

The state of New Jersey authorized reimbursement of bus transportation expenses to parents of children of private school children. The practice was challenged as a violation of the New Jersey Constitution and the Federal Constitution. The New Jersey Court decided the provision violated neither the state nor Federal Constitution. The case was appealed to the United States Supreme Court contending a violation of the Federal Constitution. The Court ruled that there was no violation of the First Amendment. Since the statute was based on the child benefit theory, the court said ". . . we cannot say that the First Amendment prohibits New Jersey from spending tax-raised funds to pay the bus fares of Parochial School pupils as a part of a general program under which it pays the fares of pupils attending public and other schools." Everson v. Board of Education, 330 U.S. 1, 67 S.Ct. 504 (1947).

The *Everson* case established that the Federal Constitution is not offended if transportation aid is provided to private school children. Some states, because of the restrictive nature of the separation of Church and State clauses of their state constitutions, have prohibited transportation aid. But, approximately thirty states provide aid in a variety of ways, such as, tuition reimbursement, direct grants to private schools, allowing private school children to ride public school buses, and providing transportation but allowing payment through another government agency.

Although private school transportation has been permitted in some states, because of health and safety factors of going to and from school, providing aid for field trips has been declared unconstitutional. Ohio attempted to allocate funds to private schools for field trip activities. The Supreme Court declared the reimbursement for field trips unconstitutional, because there was no way for public school authorities to adequately insure that the trip would have a secular purpose without close supervision of the nonpublic trips, and this close supervision would foster excessive entanglement. Wolman v. Walter, 433 U.S. 229, 97 S.Ct. 2593 (1977).

§ 5.66   Standardized Testing and Scoring

The state of Ohio passed legislation ". . . [t]o supply, for use by pupils attending nonpublic schools within the district, such standardized tests and scoring services as were in use in the public schools of the state." The United States Supreme Court in Wolman v. Walter, supra, ruled it was constitutional because the state had a legitimate interest in insuring youth have an adequate secular education. Since the standardized tests were obviously secular and the purpose was to benefit the state and the child, the statute was not violative of the First Amendment. Therefore, if it does not violate the state constitution, financial assistance may be given to private schools by paying for standardized tests and the subsequent scoring of those tests.

§ 5.67   Reimbursement for Teacher-Made Test

The state of New York passed a statute which provided reimbursement to church-sponsored schools for the expenses incurred by the schools when teachers prepared tests for their classes.   The Supreme Court ruled this statute violated the Constitution because there were "no means available, to assure that internally prepared tests were free of religious instruction."   Another significant element of the statute was that no means were established to audit the state-granted expenditures.   The legislature had provided no requirement for audits for fear of violating the excessive entanglement test.   Levitt v. Committee for Public Education, 413 U.S. 472, 93 S.Ct. 2814 (1972).

After the *Levitt* decision, New York legislated payment for teacher-made tests but required an audit.   In Committee for Public Education v. Regan, 444 U.S. 646, 100 S.Ct. 840 (1980), the Supreme Court ruled the reimbursement for teacher-made tests now met all constitutional standards because the funds were audited by the state.

§ 5.68   Diagnostic and Therapeutic Service

The state of Ohio passed legislation, "[t]o provide speech and hearing diagnostic services to pupils attending nonpublic schools within the district.   Such service shall be provided in the nonpublic school attended by the pupil receiving the service" and also "[t]o provide diagnostic psychological services to pupils attending nonpublic schools within the district. Such services shall be provided in the school attended

[*117*]

by the pupil receiving the service." Although these services were to be performed on nonpublic school property, the service had to be provided by public school employees except where physicians were involved. In Wolman v. Walter, supra, the United States Supreme Court stated, "[w]e conclude that providing diagnostic services on the nonpublic school premises will not create an impermissible risk of the fostering of ideological views. It follows that there is no need for excessive surveillance, and there will not be impermissible entanglement. We therefore hold [the statute] constitutional."

The state of Ohio also enacted legislation authorizing the expenditure of funds to provide certain therapeutic services, guidance, and remedial service, to students in private schools. All services were to be performed on public premises by public school or health department employees. The Court ruled the services were to help the child and not the religious institution. Because the services were performed off the nonpublic school premises, they were found not to advance religion or create excessive entanglement. Wolman v. Walter, supra.

§ 5.69   Instructional Materials and Equipment

State legislatures have attempted to provide instructional materials and equipment to private schools. Pennsylvania passed legislation authorizing the loaning of instructional materials and equipment to nonpublic schools, which were defined as periodicals, photographs, maps, charts, sound recordings, films, projectors, and laboratory equipment. The act appears neutral since instructional materials and equipment are secular; but the court declared the act would result in ". . . direct and substantial advancement of religious activities, . . . and thus constitute an impermissible establishment of religion." Since the equipment could be used for sectarian education within the school, there was no feasible monitoring system that would not violate the excessive entanglement standard. Meek v. Pittenger, 421 U.S. 350, 95 S.Ct. 1753 (1975). Ohio attempted to circumvent the Meek decision, by loaning equipment to the parent or pupil who would then let the private school use it. The Supreme Court said, "[d]espite the technical change in legal bailee, the program in substance is the same as before [Meek] . . .", therefore, violating the Establishment Clause. Wolman v. Walter, supra.

CHAPTER 6

STUDENT PUBLICATIONS

§ 6.1 INTRODUCTION

School authorities are governmental officials and their attempts to restrain or suppress student publications is looked upon with careful scrutiny by the courts. Freedom of the press is a cornerstone of the basic freedoms found in a democracy. In the Pentagon papers case, the United States Supreme Court stated the importance of freedom of the press: "In the First Amendment the Founding Fathers gave the free press the protection it must have to fulfill its essential role in our democracy. The press was to serve the governed, not the governors. The Government's power to censor the press was abolished so that the press would remain forever free to censure the Government." New York Times Co. v. United States, 403 U.S. 713, 91 S.Ct. 2140 (1971).

Accordingly, it would be unthinkable for government agencies to have the legal authority to censor the press; yet, school districts are government agencies and as such have been given special leeway to exercise limited controls over student publications. This authority derives from the historical special legal relationship between the school and the student. This relationship, the *in loco parentis* doctrine, establishes a tolerance by which the courts view student publications.

§ 6.2 TYPES OF PUBLICATIONS

Limitations apply to independent, privately published student publications or to school-sponsored student publications as distinguished from those communications edited, controlled, and published as official organs of the school, itself. Sometimes, though, conflicts arise over whether a publication is controlled by the school or the students. Prior restraint of publication of a school-affiliated literary magazine where a student is the editor-in-chief will not be allowed. Koppell v. Levine, 347 F.Supp. 456 (E.D.N.Y.1972). Certainly, the school can control the content of school newspapers where a teacher or the principal edits the newspaper and directly control its contents. Such would not be considered to be merely a school-sponsored or an independent student newspaper. The legal disputes in question have arisen over attempts by school authorities to control independent student publications or school-sponsored publications which are controlled and/or edited by students.

§ 6.3 PRIOR RESTRAINT

Prior restraint cannot be exercised by school officials over independent student publications except through very specific procedures and for well-defined reasons. Off-campus publications which are brought to school and distributed come under the same constitutional standards as independent student newspapers published on campus. Prior restraint, itself, is highly objectionable to the courts and attempts to control publication through the use of vague or overly broad regulations have been held to be unconstitutional. To the courts, prior restraint is much more threatening to our democratic freedom than post-publication sanctions; accordingly, some courts have held that prior restraint is by its very nature unconstitutional. In 1972, the United States Court of Appeals for the Seventh Circuit held that school officials could not exercise prior restraint over student publications or prevent their distribution. They could, however, regulate the manner of distribution and could punish students after distribution if the material was obscene, libelous, or disruptive. Fujishima v. Board of Education, 460 F.2d 1355 (7th Cir. 1972).

In Gambino v. Fairfax County School Board, 429 F.Supp. 731 (E.D.Va.1977), affirmed 564 F.2d 157 (4th Cir. 1977), the Fourth Circuit refused to allow a school board to place prior restraints on an article in the school newspaper. The article concerned information about contraceptives, and school board policy prohibited teaching about contraceptives in the curriculum. The Fourth Circuit said the school board has total control over the curricula but not the student newspaper. The student newspaper was declared a public forum and not an extension of the curriculum. Therefore, being a public forum, no prior restraints would be permitted. This novel concept would appear to establish that no action could be taken by school officials in regard to student newspapers. But this may not be the case since the same circuit, the Fourth, allowed a school administrator to prohibit the distribution of a student newspaper for advertising marijuana and hashish pipes on the grounds that he was protecting the health and safety of students. Williams v. Spencer, 622 F.2d 1200 (4th Cir. 1980). See also: Baughman v. Freienmuth, 478 F.2d 1345 (4th Cir. 1973).

§ 6.31   Health and Safety

In 1980 the Fourth Circuit Court of Appeals ruled that school officials could halt the distribution of a student publication which "encourages actions which endanger the health and safety of students." Students were prohibited from distributing an underground newspaper which advertised the sale of drug paraphernalia. The court stated: "The First Amendment rights of students must yield to the superior interest of the school in seeing that materials that encourage actions which endanger the health or safety of students are not distributed on school property." Williams v. Spencer, supra.

Mental health or psychological harm was a major issue in preventing the distribution of a sex survey by students in Trachtman v. Anker, 563 F.2d 512 (2d Cir. 1977). The editor-in-chief of the student newspaper wanted to distribute a twenty-five question anonymous survey which was designed to elicit preference, knowledge, attitudes, and experience concerning contraception, homosexuality and masturbation. School officials sought to prohibit the material because it "would invade the rights of other students by subjecting them to psychological pressures," which could be psychologically damaging. Testimony was presented by psychologists and psychiatrists to support the school's contention of psychological harm. The court ruled that freedom of expression or press does not go so far as to allow material to be distributed which is reasonably believed to cause harm to the mental or physical health of others.

§ 6.32   Political Issues

Neither prior restraint nor post-publication sanctions will be permitted if the control is exercised to limit discussion of political issues. School authorities' attempts to prevent distribution of antiwar leaflets, or articles protesting antimarijuana laws, have been held unconstitutional. Criticism of school officials has been upheld so long as it is not obscene, libelous, or disruptive of the school. In fact, it is only through the application of well-defined rules and regulations proscribing obscene, libelous, and disruptive publications that school authorities can limit publication at all.

§ 6.33   Obscenity

Obscenity is not constitutionally protected for either adults or for students. Obscenity is not vulgarity. Vulgarity is normally legally acceptable. The United States Supreme Court has upheld publication of a cartoon showing a policeman raping the Statue of Liberty, saying that it was vulgar but not obscene. Papish v. Board of Curators of University of Missouri, 410 U.S. 667, 93 S.Ct. 1197 (1973). The four-letter word slang term for sexual intercourse, taken alone, is not obscene, it is merely vulgar. Obscenity requires eroticism. Where a man wore a jacket displaying the slang term for sexual intercourse on his back, the United States Supreme Court held that it was not obscene because it was not erotic. Cohen v. California, 403 U.S. 15, 91 S.Ct. 1780 (1971). Obscenity standards as applied to adults are different from those applicable to minors. The standard for adults is set out in the United States Supreme Court case of Miller v. California, 413 U.S. 15, 93 S.Ct. 2607 (1973), rehearing denied 414 U.S. 881, 94 S.Ct. 26, as: "(1) Whether the average person, applying contemporary community standards, would find that the work taken as a whole appeals to the prurient interest; (2) whether the work depicts or describes, in a patently offensive way, sexual conduct specifically described by the applicable state law; and (3) whether the work, taken as a whole, lacks serious literary, artistic, political, or scientific value." In this regard, "prurient interest" means to excite lustful thoughts, morbid interest in sex, arouse impure sexual desires, an inclination toward lewdness, or that which is provocative of an unhealthy or antisocial attitude toward sex. Where publications fall under the proscription as defined in *Miller*, government agencies can ban their distribution even to adults.

Student publications distributed in schools may be obscene where they would not ordinarily be in public distribution to adults. John E. Nichols, "Vulgarity and Obscenity in the Student Press," *Journal of Law and Education*, Vol. 10, No. 2, April 1981, pp. 207–218. The standard for minors appears to come from a United States Supreme Court case in which the court found that materials may be obscene for minors, yet not for adults, if they depict or describe sexual conduct which "(i) Predominately appeals to the prurient, shameful, or morbid interest of minors, and (ii) is patently offensive to prevailing standards in the adult community as a whole with respect to what is suitable material for minors, and (iii) is utterly without redeeming social importance for minors." Ginsberg v. New York, 390 U.S. 629, 88 S.Ct. 1274 (1968). The words central to obscenity in the school setting are whether the "adult community as a whole" finds the material patently offensive for distribution to minors. Certainly, community standards and norms vary substantially but, in most instances, adults do desire to protect their children from the gamut of sexually oriented materials. If this is the case, the school may enact a regulation validly circumscribing the community standards.

§ 6.34   Libelous Material

Libel is printed or written defamation of a person published without justification and with malice. (See Chapter 13, Defamation.) Publication of misrepresentations, known to be false, which subject a person to public ridicule or shame is libel. If rules and regulations are specific and their application is uniform, school officials may be justified in exercising prior restraint if material to be published by students is "libelous *per se*," but may not be if the material is only "libelous *per quod*." The distinction between "libel *per se*" and "libel *per quod*" is actionable only if special damages are pleaded and proved by the plaintiff. A school principal or teacher may, possibly, be justified in stopping publication of an obvious libel, where such restraint would not be permissible if it were merely potentially libel or libel *per quod*. Libel *per quod* depends on the attendant reaction of persons involved and subsequent proof that the publication became libelous only after considered in connection with innuendo, colloquy, and other explanatory circumstances.

The United States Supreme Court has established that a newspaper cannot libel "public figures" such as governors, legislators, famous actors, etc., unless the material is published with actual malice; that is, with knowledge that it was false or with reckless disregard of its truth or falsity. (See Chapter 13.) New York Times Co. v. Sullivan, 376 U.S. 254, 84 S.Ct. 710 (1964). Students, teachers, and school officials are not likely to be considered to be public figures by most courts. Certainly, fellow students are not public figures regardless of whether they have been vice-president or president of student government; therefore, defamatory articles in student newspapers about fellow students are not privileged to the same degree as an article in the *New York Times* written about a public figure. Thus, articles in student newspapers written about fellow students may be considered to be libel *per se* and, thereby, may, depending on content, be restrained by school authorities. Frasca v. Andrews, 463 F.Supp. 1043 (E.D.N.Y.1979).

§ 6.35 Disruption

Another rationale which may be used by school authorities to justify prior restraint is a reasonable forecast of material interference and/or substantial disruption. The Tinker v. Des Moines, supra, test is whether school authorities might "reasonably forecast substantial disruption or material interference with school activities." It has been uniformly advanced by the courts that students be given wide "latitude for free expression and debate consonant with the maintenance of order." Healy v. James, 408 U.S. 169, 92 S.Ct. 2338 (1972). It is difficult, if not virtually impossible, for school authorities to show that a publication will create material interference or substantial disruption. An article criticizing school authorities cannot be curtailed under the assumption that the publication would undermine teacher or administrator control of students. A few "earthy" words in a student publication are not sufficient to forecast material interference or substantial disruption. Jacobs v. Board of School Commissioners, 490 F.2d 601 (7th Cir. 1973), vacated as moot 420 U.S. 128, 95 S.Ct. 848 (1975). A school official cannot reasonably forecast interference or disruption unless it can be shown that a similar publication did, in fact, cause interference and disruption at the school on an earlier occasion. Even then, the cause/effect relationship between publication and the disturbance would be virtually impossible to substantiate.

§ 6.4 PRIOR RESTRAINT CRITERIA

The prevailing rule of law regarding school-sponsored student publications or independent student publications is that prior restraint will not be valid unless based on standards which contain "precise criteria sufficiently spelling out what is forbidden so that a reasonably intelligent student will know what he may write and what he may not write." Baughman v. Freienmuth, 478 F.2d 1345 (4th Cir. 1973). To exercise valid prior restraint, the school must provide specific standards which enable students to comprehend their rights and responsibilities and give school officials an objective standard to determine what constitutes obscenity, libel, material interference, or substantial disruption or a reasonable forecast thereof. This requirement by the courts is justified on the grounds that narrowly drawn regulations provide the student and the administration with objective standards by which to measure the students' conduct, and, it limits the discretion of the school official so as to reduce the likelihood of arbitrary or capricious denial of a constitutional freedom.

The constitutional requirements for exercise of prior restraint are summarized by the United States Court of Appeals for the Fourth Circuit in Baughman v. Freienmuth, supra, as follows:

(a) Secondary school children are within the protection of the first amendment, although their rights are not coextensive with those of adults.

(b) Secondary school authorities may exercise reasonable prior restraint upon the exercise of students' first amendment rights.

(c) Such prior restraints must contain precise criteria sufficiently spelling out what is forbidden so that a reasonably intelligent student will know what he may write and what he may not write.

(d) A prior restraint system, even though precisely defining what may not be written, is nevertheless invalid unless it provides for:

(1) A definition of "distribution" and its application to different kinds of material;

[*129*]

(2) Prompt approval or disapproval of what is submitted;

(3) Specification of the effect of failure to act promptly; and,

(4) An adequate and prompt appeals procedure.

Bear in mind that the aforementioned standards for prior restraint of student publications appear to be the prevailing view of the courts. One should be cautioned, however, that some courts have maintained that prior restraint *per se* is impermissible. This view appears to have gained momentum in recent years. See: Leon Letwin, "Administrative Censorship of the Independent Student Press," South Carolina Law Review, Vol. 28, No. 5, March 1977, pp. 565–585.

CHAPTER 7

SEARCH AND SEIZURE

§ 7.1 INTRODUCTION

Teachers and principals have always found it necessary to search students and remove from their possession items which may be harmful to them or to others. Several years ago most searches were found to be necessary to remove slingshots or pocketknives from a student's possession, or to detect and retrieve the fruits of minor thievery. Such searches remained almost entirely an affair internal to the school and seldom, if ever, involved outside authorities. Today, however, the prevalence of drugs, handguns, bombs, and/or bomb threats have broadened the importance of school search and seizure to include offenses which may subject the student to criminal prosecution. Such conditions have brought on a series of court decisions which attempt to define the role of school authorities and the constitutional rights of students.

§ 7.2 FOURTH AMENDMENT

School authorities have both the moral and legal responsibility to maintain order and decorum in the schools and to protect students from harming themselves or others. At the same time, students have constitutional protections which cannot be unreasonably denied. ". . . when a child enters the school he is required to attend, there is not the same reasonable expectation of privacy that he would have in other situations. Even though the school officials are state agents, their position *in loco parentis*, in the eyes of the minor student, puts them in a position of authority similar to a parent. In a school, each student's security depends upon a certain amount of restraint upon the activities of the students. Whether for security or disciplinary purposes, this restraint is assumed and expected by all students. Faced with such authority in a setting requiring control of his behavior, the child cannot reasonably expect to have the same amount of privacy as he would outside of the school." Interest of L.L., 90 Wis.2d 585, 280 N.W.2d 343 (App.1979).

The balance between school prerogatives and students' rights with regard to search and seizure is to be found in the interpretation of the Fourth Amendment to the Constitution of the United States, which provides that "The right of people to be secure in their persons, houses, papers, and effects, against unreasonable searches and seizures shall not be violated and no warrants shall issue, but upon probable cause . . . ."

The Fourth Amendment imposes the judgment of a magistrate or a judge between the citizen and the police. Police may not search unless they present evidence to a judge that something illegal is secreted in a specific place. The judge determines if the evidence presented constitutes "probable cause" for a search and, if so, a warrant may be issued. Thus, police must have probable cause to justify a search. School authorities are not required to have probable cause before they can search, but instead are held to a less restrictive standard of "reasonable suspicion." School teachers and administrators when engaged in school discipline matters, such as searching students, do so to maintain order and decorum in the school and to protect the health and safety of the students. Their duties are not to enforce criminal statutes as is required of police officers. D.R.C. v. State of Alaska, 646 P.2d 252 (Alaska 1982).

§ 7.21 Reasonable Suspicion

The courts, being fully aware that the educational processes would be greatly impaired if school teachers and administrators were held to the same strict standards as the police, have held that students' rights are not fully coextensive with individuals in society. Courts do not require warrants for student searches by school authorities. It is assumed that searches in school are calculated to maintain school discipline and are not initiated to provide evidence for criminal prosecution. Thus, school authorities are held to a lesser standard to justify a student search, that of *reasonable suspicion*.

This lower standard is generally justified by courts on the principle of *in loco parentis*, the school standing in place of the parent. The *in loco parentis* authority is not unlimited and must be weighed against the student's right to privacy. School authorities must have reasonable suspicion to invoke their privilege to search and cannot do so at whim or fancy or in an arbitrary or capricious manner. A New York court has explained: "The *in loco parentis* doctrine is so compelling in light of public necessity and as a social concept antedating the Fourth Amendment, that any

[*133*]

action, including a search, taken thereunder upon *reasonable suspicion* should be accepted as necessary and reasonable." [Emphasis added] State v. Baccino, 282 A.2d 869 (Del.Super.1971).

Two conditions are required for search by school authorities: (1) the search must be conducted within the scope of the school's educational function and (2) the search must be reasonable under the particular facts of the case.

A Florida court has held that a teacher did not have reasonable suspicion merely because boys looked suspicious and they "appeared to look away from her, to look at something else," when she passed them in the school corridor. The court in this case, however, observed that school officials are not required to have reasonable suspicion to merely detain students. A subsequent search after the students were detained could be undertaken based on reasonable suspicion which might be substantiated by students' actions after detention. "The validity of any subsequent search must be determined on the basis of conditions then existing." W.J.S. v. State of Florida, 409 So.2d 1209 (Fla.App.1982).

Reasonable suspicion must be reasonably specific. A sweeping, undifferentiated, and indiscriminate search of all students cannot be defended on the grounds of reasonable suspicion. "The blanket search or dragnet is, except in the most unusual and compelling circumstances, anathema to the protection accorded citizens under the fourth amendment. The state may not constitutionally use its authority to fish for evidence of wrongdoing." Jones v. Latexo Independent School District, 499 F.Supp. 223 (E.D.Tex.1980).

Where school officials ignore the need to determine individualized suspicion prior to a search, the intrusion cannot be justified on grounds of reasonable suspicion. To require all students to empty their pockets, to remove clothing, or to search all automobiles in the school parking lot would likely fall under the classification of an invalid dragnet.

School officials may, however, patrol the school parking lot and if anything suspicious is in view when they look in auto windows, a legal search may be launched. In a case where a teacher's aide in supervising the school parking lot saw a "bong" (waterpipe) in a car and a search ensued revealing marijuana, the court held the search legal. In this circumstance, when a suspicious object of drug paraphernalia was in "open view," school officials were justified in opening the car to retrieve it. State of Florida v. D.T.W., 425 So.2d 1383 (Fla.App.1983).

§ 7.22 Right of Privacy

The courts have ruled that students have a right to privacy which is protected by the Fourth Amendment and that this right cannot be invaded unless the intrusion can be justified in terms of the school's legitimate interests. The right of privacy is not absolute but is subject to reasonable school regulation within the bounds of reasonable suspicion.

The right of privacy, itself, is predicated on two factors being present: first, whether the person in question "exhibited an actual (subjective) expectation of privacy," and, second, whether the "expectation of privacy be one that society is prepared to recognize as 'reasonable.' " The Supreme Court has said that: "The Fourth Amendment protects people, not places. What a person knowingly exposes to the public, even in his own home or office, is not a subject of Fourth Amendment protection. . . . But what he seeks to preserve as private, even in an area accessible to the public, may be constitutionally protected." Katz v. United States, 389 U.S. 347, 88 S.Ct. 507 (1967).

A one-way mirror in a boys' restroom in a high school used to observe students buying marijuana did not violate students' right of privacy. Stern v. New Haven Community Schools, 529 F.Supp. 31 (E.D. Mich.1981). The court reasoned that the community had a significant interest in school discipline and protection of students from drugs. Accordingly, the court found that the school's *in loco parentis* responsibility obligated school officials to maintain the health and safety of all students. The test according to the court is one of balancing the school interests in the surveillance against the plaintiff's interest in privacy. Here the balance was in favor of the school.

§ 7.23   Reasonableness

Whether a search is reasonable must be decided on the conditions of each case. School authorities must have some verifiable evidence which implies that something harmful is hidden by a student.

To determine reasonableness, the court will weigh the danger of items for which the search is conducted against the students' right of privacy. The courts recognize that school officials have a duty and responsibility to provide a safe environment in which students can learn and develop. Reasonableness of a search will ultimately be determined by factors such as the student's age, record of past conduct, and the seriousness of the problem that the school officials are trying to solve. If school officials have obtained valid information that drugs are hidden in the school or evidence shows that previous incidents suggest that drugs may be hidden at the school, then a search may be adjudged to have been undertaken on reasonable grounds.

Court decisions in several states have established criteria for determining reasonable grounds for a search by school officials: (1) the child's age, history, and school record, (2) the prevalence and seriousness of the problem in the school to which the search was directed, (3) the exigency requiring the search without delay, (4) the probative value and reliability of the information used as a justification for the search, and (5) the teacher's prior experience with the student. The teacher's training and prior knowledge of the student's behavior may further provide a reasonable basis for an immediate search.

§ 7.3 CANINE SEARCHES

Courts disagree over whether dogs may be used to establish reasonable suspicion for school officials to conduct searches. The issue is whether dogs can be used to establish reasonable suspicion by blanket sniffing of every child in a school room. A Texas court has held that to do so violates the student's privacy because such indiscriminate searching ignores the need to individualize suspicion prior to the intrusion.

To use dogs in this manner is tantamount to fishing for cause to establish reasonable suspicion; using a search to establish rationale for a search is to violate the Fourth Amendment. Jones v. Latexo Independent School District, supra.

This court held that sniffer dogs perceived odors undetectable to human beings much the same way that electronic listening devices pick up sounds not audible to the human ear. According to this court, such devices cannot be used by the police or school officials to fish for evidence to establish probable cause or reasonable suspicion.

On the other hand, the U.S. Court of Appeals for the Seventh Circuit has affirmed a lower court's ruling which upheld the use of sniffer dogs to establish reasonable suspicion. This court held that the dogs could be used to detect drugs even though the school officials had no information indicating that drugs were in the possession of any specific students. The court was of the opinion that the school official's responsibility of caring for the health and welfare of the students was of such weight as to justify the use of canines. Doe v. Renfrow, 475 F.Supp. 1012 (N.D.Ind.1979), modified 635 F.2d 582 (7th Cir. 1980), cert. denied 451 U.S. 1022, 101 S.Ct. 3015 (1981) (Justice Brennan dissenting).

The U.S. Court of Appeals for the Fifth Circuit has maintained that dogs may be used to establish reasonable suspicion. According to the court, if a dog alerts a hundred times and there is no contraband found ninety times, then the dog may not be deemed to arouse reasonable suspicion. On the other hand, a high level of accuracy by a dog might be used to develop a record of reliability which could be used as evidence justifying reasonable suspicion. Accordingly, each court must examine the record of reliability of the particular dog. Horton v. Goose Creek Independent School District, 693 F.2d 524 (5th Cir. 1982).

In spite of this case, the courts are split on the issue of search dogs; however, the use of dogs appears to be a legally questionable activity. Beyond the law, use of dogs in schools is obviously abhorrent to any recognized professional educational method or practice.

§ 7.4 EXCLUSIONARY RULE

Even though a school does not undertake a search to discover unlawful items, the evidence obtained may be used against a student in a criminal prosecution. But if school officials act beyond their authority and conduct or participate in an illegal search with police, then the exclusionary rule will apply if the state tries to use the fruits of the search to prosecute. This exclusionary rule was first enunciated by the United States Supreme Court in Weeks v. United States, 232 U.S. 383, 34 S.Ct. 341 (1914).

Being cognizant of this rule and, similarly, being aware that school officials do not need to obtain search warrants, in order to search, the police will many times prevail on the school principal to institute a search for them. Sometimes it is difficult to determine whether the police were secondarily helping the principal conduct a search or whether the police were the primary agents instigating the search to obtain information for criminal prosecution.

§ 7.5   LIABILITY FOR ILLEGAL SEARCH

One may wonder what the consequences are of an illegal search of students by teachers or school administrators. What redress is available for the student? As discussed above, if the search is illegal, its fruits will be excluded from prosecution of the student should a criminal trial ensue. Beyond this, the student may conceivably bring an action under the Civil Rights Section 1983, 42 U.S.C.A. (See: Chapter 12, Civil Liability.) As discussed elsewhere in this book, a student may seek damages if school officials maliciously deny his or her constitutional rights. It is important to note that if school officials deny constitutional rights, but do so in good faith fulfillment of their responsibilities and not in ignorance and disregard for established indisputable principles of law, then no liability will occur. This immunity is accorded only within bounds of reason. The United States Court of Appeals for the Seventh Circuit has held that simple common sense would indicate that a thirteen-year-old's constitutional rights are invaded by a nude search required by school officials in seeking to discover hidden drugs. The court said: "We suggest as strongly as possible that the conduct herein described exceeded the 'bounds of reason' by two and a half country miles. It is not enough for us to declare that the little girl involved was indeed deprived of her con-

stitutional and basic human rights. We must also permit her to seek damages from those who caused this
humiliation . . .." Doe v. Renfrow, supra.

§ 7.6 POLICE INVOLVEMENT

Because school officials may on the basis of reasonable suspicion search students without a search warrant, police will on occasion seek school assistance in
searching students. The stronger probable cause
standard to which police must adhere makes it more
advantageous and opportune for police to merely convince a school principal that a search is needed. If
this is done, the court must decide whether the principal was, in fact, conducting the search based on his
own initiation or whether the search was really conducted for the police.

Since such a fine line may exist as to which party is
the primary searcher, the courts have resolved the
question by holding that police officers must have a
warrant to conduct a valid search of students in active
conjunction with a school official. A Florida court has
explained: ". . . where a law enforcement officer
directs, participates or acquiesces in a search conducted by school officials, the officer must have probable
cause for that search, even though the school officials
acting alone are treated as state officials subject to a
lesser constitutional standard for conducting searches
in light of the *in loco parentis* doctrine." M.J. v.
State of Florida, 1st. Dist. Case No. 55–120, May 18,
1981.

Where a search is conducted with the cooperation
and participation of the police, school officials may be

seeking items which violate school rules but police are normally in quest of illegal contraband which can be used as evidence in a criminal prosecution. In such instances a police search cannot dwell "under the banner of *'in loco parentis.'*" Picha v. Wieglos, 410 F.Supp. 1214 (N.D.Ill.1976).

§ 7.7 CONSENT

School authorities do not need the consent of the student in order to conduct a search. By virtue of their *in loco parentis* relationship with the student, and with reasonable suspicion, teachers, principals and other school officials may search. On the other hand, if the police participate in the search, they must have a warrant or obtain the student's consent. Consent, though, must be given freely and willingly without undue coercion. Accordingly, the police cannot ask a school official to influence the student's decision to permit a search. Students are under the control of the school and will in most instances respond positively to school authority, such authority cannot be used by police to acquire the student's consent.

§ 7.8 SEARCHES OF PERSON

School officials acting with reasonable suspicion can demand that a student empty his or her pockets or purse for inspection. Tarter v. Raybuck, 556 F.Supp. 625 (N.D. Ohio 1983). If the student refuses to empty his or her pockets or purse, the school official can compel compliance. Where a vice-principal and a student had a tug-of-war of the student's coat and the student lost, the court held that such force on the part of

[*142*]

school officials was within their *in loco parentis* authority. State v. Baccino, 282 A.2d 869 (Del.Super. 1971). Although the courts have allowed school officials to search students, they have disallowed strip searches. Unanimously the courts have determined strip search to be an invasion of privacy. Doe v. Renfrow, supra.

Use of force in searching students had been upheld even where the search was conducted off school grounds. In one instance, the discipline coordinator in a school noticed a bulge in a student's pocket, and further observed the student nervously putting his hand in and taking it out of the pocket. When confronted the student bolted for the door, ran off school grounds; whereupon, the coordinator gave chase and caught the student, finding narcotics, drug paraphernalia, syringe, eyedropper, etc. When the student sought to exclude this evidence in a criminal proceeding, the court held against the student. The court said that the *in loco parentis* authority allowed the school official to search the student on school grounds and such powers did not "end abruptly at the school door." People v. Jackson, 65 Misc.2d 909, 319 N.Y.S.2d 731 (1971).

§ 7.9 LOCKERS AND DESKS

School lockers do not have the attributes of privacy that a person's pockets, automobile or home may have. The courts have said many times that the Fourth Amendment protects persons not places, and as such privacy is determined by the assumption by persons that their possessions are safe from governmental intrusion. School lockers and school desks are not students' own, personal hideaways, exclusive of everyone, including school officials. Lockers are not in the nature of a dwelling, motor vehicle, or private locker rented on private premises. Most courts, in fact, view school lockers and desks as having co-owners, the student and the school. Although the student may have control of his school locker as against fellow students, his possession cannot be viewed as absolute against the school.

Indeed, courts appear to feel that inspection of lockers is a responsibility of school administrators which is inherent in the proper exercise of control and management of the school.

Since lockers and desks are under the control of the school and are assigned to students with predetermined conditions that they will not secret illegal items therein, it is well established that the school principal can give consent to police to search them. This is, of course, quite different from searches of the person which require that the student himself consent if police are to validly search and have no warrant. One constitutional theory is that when two people are in possession and control of property, that either can give consent to search and if anything illegal is found by police, it can be used to prosecute either or both parties. Thus, a school official who has control of school property can give police permission to search and any illegal substances found therein may be admissible evidence in a criminal prosecution.

The school's control over such spaces as lockers and desks is clearly justified by a New York court, "Indeed, it is doubtful if a school would be properly discharging its duty of supervision over students, if it failed to retain control over the lockers. Not only have the school authorities a right to inspect but this right becomes a duty when suspicion arises that something of an illegal nature may be secreted there." People v. Overton, 20 N.Y.2d 360, 283 N.Y.S.2d 22, 229 N.E.2d 596 (1967), affirmed on reargument, 24 N.Y.2d 522, 301 N.Y.S.2d 479, 249 N.E.2d 366 (1969).

§ 7.10 AUTOMOBILE SEARCH

Few cases are available to define the law governing searches of students' automobiles in school parking lots. The precedents which do lend light to the subject suggest that there is no difference in the school official's prerogative in searching autos or in conducting body searches. Reasonable suspicion is required before such a search can be undertaken. One case which provides some limited guidance emanates from a search of a student's vehicle by private school officials. In this instance the automobile was found to contain cannabis and a can of beer. The court observed that the *in loco parentis* authority of the school made such searches permissible. Keene v. Rodgers, 316 F.Supp. 217 (D.C.Me.1970). Aside from the *in loco parentis* thrust, this case has limited value because a private school is not restrained by the Fourth Amendment. Constitutional guarantees of privacy do not extend to protection of a private person from search of another person or a private institution.

Presumably, the privacy protection of an auto is no greater than that of the person. Pockets and vehicles have been viewed the same. In Jones v. Latexo, supra, the Texas case, a dragnet searching of pockets and vehicles by a sniffer dog was held unconstitutional not because of the place that was searched, but because the school officials did not have verifiable grounds to support reasonable suspicion that something illegal was secreted in either place.

The law relating to body searches appears to apply equally to automobiles; school officials may search if they have reasonable cause to believe that something is hidden in an automobile which will harm the health and safety of the students and/or constitute a detriment to the conduct of the school.

CHAPTER 8

STUDENT DISCIPLINE

§ 8.1 INTRODUCTION

Courts have long recognized that if schools are to be properly conducted, teachers and principals must be given authority to maintain an orderly and responsible learning environment. This requires that students live and study in a relationship of mutual accord with other students and with the school faculty. Disruption of the school social setting will almost certainly have deleterious effects on the quality of the educational program. Recognizing this the courts have uniformly held that student conduct is under the control of the professional school personnel.

Parents, by law, acquiesce in this control over their children when they place the child in the charge of the school. Thus, the teacher and principal are said to stand *in loco parentis*, in the place of the parent, in the performance and exercise of those functions necessary to operate the schools.

§ 8.2 IN LOCO PARENTIS

To stand *in loco parentis* means that the teacher has the authority and the duty to guide, correct, and punish the child in the accomplishment of educational objectives. The teacher is the substitute for the parent while the child is in school and for those endeavors which bear directly on the school. The teacher does not have unlimited control over the student and, of course, neither does the parent for that matter. Child abuse is prohibited whether it is committed by the parent or the teacher. To stand in the place of the parent, though, means that the teacher can control the conduct of the student in various ways, including corporal punishment. Blackstone, the great jurist, in summarizing the law of England in 1788 wrote that "The master is *in loco parentis*, and has such a portion of the powers of the parent committed to his charge as may be necessary to answer the purposes for which he is employed." Authority to control students is not necessarily vested in the teacher through affirmative school board policy; it, instead, is derived from the common law relationship between teacher and pupil. In other words, a teacher is assumed to stand *in loco parentis* unless state law or school board policy takes that authority away. It has historically been held by the courts that there exists, on the part of students, the obligations of civil deportment, obedience to reasonable commands, and a respect for rights of other pupils. Students must submit to these requirements and teachers have an inherent duty to see to it that good order is carried out. These obligations on the part of both students and teachers constitute the common law of the school.

Implicit in the *in loco parentis* authority is the power of the state to control student conduct for the welfare of the school. Statutes or regulations may place limits on the teacher's authority to discipline students. Where statute or rule limits the teacher's discretion, the teacher must act accordingly. Similarly, where rules establish boundaries to the school authority limiting control of pupil conduct to activities on school grounds in school hours, the teacher cannot unilaterally expand his or her prerogatives.

Most states do not have statutes governing corporal punishment. In the absence of statutes the common law rule of moderate and reasonable punishment prevails. About 21 states have statutes which reinforce the common law rule by authorizing moderate use of corporal punishment. Some of these states have defined the limits of reasonableness to which the teachers are required to adhere. A few states have prohibited corporal punishment and California requires parental permission before corporal punishment can be administered.

§ 8.21   Reasonable Rules

If students break reasonable school rules, they may be held accountable. The broken rule, though, must be a reasonable one. Courts are relatively vague as to what constitutes reasonableness, but have generally held that a rule must, first, be motivated by reason and humanity premised on accomplishment of some desirable educational result and, second, the teacher must act in good faith in enforcing the rule. By standing *in loco parentis* teachers have a legal presumption in favor of the correctness of their actions. To forego this presumption a teacher must have been motivated by malice and with disregard for the pupil's welfare.

§ 8.3   CORPORAL PUNISHMENT

Corporal punishment has been widely accepted as a medium for disciplining school children for hundreds of years. Samuel Johnson, the great lexicographer, in lamenting the decline in corporal punishment in the English schools of the eighteenth century, once said, "There is now less flogging in our great schools than formerly, but then less is learned there; so that what the boys get at one end they lose at the other." Teachers today may legally, in most jurisdictions, inflict reasonable corporal punishment for the purpose of maintaining the discipline and efficiency of the school. This right is restricted to the limits of the school's jurisdiction and is not a general right of chastisement that is found with parental authority.

Punishment administered must be moderate with a proper instrument taking into account the age, sex, size and overall physical strength of the child. Within these broad limits a teacher must balance the gravity and heinousness of the offense with the extent of the punishment to be meted out. Because teachers are usually present when student mischief transpires and normally know the manner, look, tone, gestures, language, setting and general circumstances of the offense, courts will allow teachers considerable latitude in their exercise of discretion. Yet, punishment which is cruel and excessive will not be tolerated by the courts. Cruel and excessive punishment is evidence of malice which will forego the teacher's *in loco parentis* privilege.

Malice may be evidenced by showing that the instrument used to administer the punishment was improper. An important consideration, here, is whether the instrument is the type normally used and commonly accepted in the community or in other schools. For

[*150*]

example, switches and paddles are acceptable types of instruments. Use of rawhide belts have been upheld as appropriate where rawhide was used in other schools in the vicinity. Size, shape, and weight of the instrument are undoubtedly considerations.

§ 8.31   Assault and Battery

Corporal punishment may invoke the charge against the teacher of assault and battery. Actions may be brought either in criminal law or in tort. If the criminal action is successful against a teacher, the teacher may be subject to a fine or imprisonment. In a tort action the unsuccessful defendant will suffer monetary damages. Torts are discussed in more detail in a later chapter of this book. (See Chapter 12).

Actions against teachers for criminal assault and battery are relatively infrequent. A New York court said whether such an action is successful depends on the circumstances and the severity of the punishment. Some of the factors to be considered are: the prior conduct of the student, whether there was malice on the part of the teacher, the motivation for punishment, pupil's size and strength and the effect of the pupil's conduct on other pupils in the school. People ex rel. Hogan v. Newton, 185 Misc. 405, 56 N.Y.S.2d 779 (1945).

Prior conduct of the pupil is a very important factor for the court to consider. Punishment may be more severe if the student has a long history of rule infractions. In a case where a teacher was convicted at trial of criminal assault and battery for whipping a pupil who had dropped a book from the school auditorium balcony, the state appeals court reversed the decision because the student's prior misbehavior had not been taken into account in considering the reasonableness of the punishment. People v. Mummert, 183 Misc. 243, 50 N.Y.S.2d 699 (1944).

§ 8.32　Excessiveness of Punishment

Punishment has been held to be excessive where a teacher beat a boy for difference of opinion over a trivial matter which arose on the playground. The court pointed out that pupils were accountable to teachers for their behavior, but that severe whippings for insignificant matters would not be tolerated by the courts. Hardy v. James, 5 Ky. 36 (1872). In another case, a teacher, using a paddle made of flooring, whipped a boy twice in one day for not repeating a riddle from the newspaper and for throwing a paper wad in class. In noting the bruises that had been inflicted, the court held that the punishment was excessive. Berry v. Arnold School District, 199 Ark. 1118, 137 S.W.2d 256 (1940). In another instance where a school principal in dragging a small boy to the school office threw him down the stairs and sat on him, the court found the force used to be beyond reason. Calway v. Williamson, 130 Conn. 575, 36 A.2d 377 (1944).

§ 8.33　Cruel and Unusual Punishment

The only United States Supreme Court case directed to corporal punishment is Ingraham v. Wright, 430 U.S. 651, 97 S.Ct. 1401 (1977). It involved an action by students who claimed that corporal punishment constituted "cruel and unusual" punishment as proscribed by the Eighth Amendment of the United States Constitution. In this case, the school principal and an assistant had whipped two students with a paddle, about 20 licks, so severely that one suffered a hematoma requiring medical attention. The Court, while admitting that the punishment was possibly too severe, nevertheless, denied the students relief under the Eighth and the Fourteenth Amendments.

In commenting generally on corporal punishment, the Court said that even though professional and public opinion is sharply divided on the practice, the Court could discern no trend toward its elimination, that at common law a single principle has governed the use of corporal punishment: "Teachers may impose reasonable but not excessive force to discipline a child. . . . The prevalent rule in this country today privileges such force as a teacher or administrator reasonably believes to be necessary for [the child's] proper control, training and education."

Further, the Court noted that to the extent that the force used by the teacher is unreasonable or excessive, virtually all states provide the student with possible criminal law remedy and additionally a possible claim for damages may lie in a tort action.

With regard to tort, the Court said that among the important considerations are the "seriousness of the offense, the attitude and past behavior of the child, the nature and severity of the punishment, the age and strength of the child, and the availability of less severe but equally effective means of discipline." Noting that the law could provide redress to the student in both criminal law and in tort, the Court refused to extend the Eighth Amendment to effectively prohibit use of corporal punishment in the schools.

In considering the question the Court gave a thorough analysis of the intent of the "cruel and unusual" provision of the Eighth Amendment finding that the prohibition was meant to apply to criminal cases where, historically, persons were punished by being maimed in various ways, including having their ears or hands cut off, or having been drawn and quartered before being put to death or crucified. Such historical antecedents to the Eighth Amendment led the Court to conclude that public school spankings were not envisioned as falling within the Amendment's proscriptions. The Court concluded by saying "The openness of the public school and its supervision by the community afford significant safeguards against the kinds of abuses from which the Eighth Amendment protects the prisioner. In virtually every community where corporal punishment is permitted in the schools, these safeguards are reinforced by the legal constraints of common law. . . . We conclude that when public school teachers or administrators impose disciplinary corporal punishment, the Eighth Amendment is inapplicable."

With regard to plaintiff's claim that procedural due process must be given each student before punishment, the Court disagreed. Even though the Court found that physical punishment fell within the scope of "liberty" as a substantive due process interest, the need to have notice and a hearing prior to spanking was obviated by the longstanding common law tradition which gives the teacher a privilege to administer moderate punishment.

Thus, corporal punishment in the schools does not invoke federal constitutional protections against cruel and unusual punishment of the student. As observed above, if the punishment is too severe, immoderate, unreasonable or administered with malice, students have a choice of two remedies. First, the student can bring a criminal action against the teacher for assault and battery or, secondly, the student can seek damages in tort. (See Chapter 12).

§ 8.34 Substantive Rights

The courts have not clearly decided whether corporal punishment denies substantive due process under the Fourteenth Amendment. That punishment denies a liberty or property interest of the child has been contended by parents since the *Ingraham* case was rendered. This view is premised on *Ingraham* wherein the lower court, Fifth Circuit, it was observed that, "Paddling of recalcitrant children has long been an accepted method of promoting good behavior and instilling notions of responsibility and decorum into the mischievous heads of school children. We do not here overrule it." 525 F.2d 909, 917 (5th Cir. 1976) *en banc* affirmed on other grounds 430 U.S. 651, 97 S.Ct. 1401 (1977).

In quoting this case, a federal district court in Alabama held in 1983 that a simple spanking administered at school could not violate substantive due process even though there were minor bruises to the buttocks of the child. Hale v. Pringle, 562 F.Supp. 598 (M.D. Ala.1983).

On the other hand, the United States Court of Appeals in the Fourth Circuit has said that whether substantive due process is violated depends on the circumstances under which the punishment is administered. A cause of action may be created if the punishment is excessive. This court said that the standard of whether a violation occurred is " . . . whether the force applied caused injury so severe, was so disproportionate to the need presented, and was so inspired by malice or sadism rather than a merely careless or unwise excess of zeal that it amounted to a brutal and inhumane abuse of official power literally shocking to the conscience." Hall v. Tawney, 621 F.2d 607 (4th Cir. 1980).

Presumably, the excessiveness of the punishment would be beyond that required to maintain a successful action against the teacher in tort or criminal law. The United States Supreme Court, however, did not indicate in *Ingraham* that a separate substantive constitutional right existed, therefore, this viewpoint must be considered as a minority view.

§ 8.4 Out–Of–School Activities

The teacher has no general right of discipline over students after school hours and off school grounds, but this rule has its limitations. The school has the responsibility to discipline students going to and from school; such authority extends to any student misconduct which has a direct or immediate tendency to harm or subvert the proper performance of the educational function. When children fight and misbehave in treatment of each other such is likely to carry over to their performance in school. A classic case is where the one boy intimidates another by announcing that he will "meet him after school" to settle affairs. In these instances the welfare of the child and the school are intertwined.

In this regard, Mechem has summarized the rule of law as follows: "The authority of the teacher is not confined to the school room or grounds, but he may prohibit and punish all acts of his pupils which are detrimental to the good order and best interests of the school, whether such acts are committed in school hours or while the pupil is on his way to or from school or after he was returned home." Mechem on Public Officers, § 730.

The most explicit case demonstrating this point of law is O'Rourke v. Walker, 102 Conn. 130, 128 A. 25 (1925), an old Connecticut case, wherein a principal administered moderate corporal punishment to two young boys for abusing and annoying two small girls while on their way home from school, after school hours. The mother of one of the boys sued the school principal maintaining that he had no legal right to administer punishment for any misconduct of the pupil which did not occur in school hours, or for misbehavior which did not take place in the school building or on the school grounds. The lower court concluded and the appellate court affirmed: "(1) that the conduct of the plaintiff boys had a tendency to demoralize the other pupils of the school and to interfere with the proper conduct of the same; (2) that the acts of the plaintiff were detrimental to the good order and best interests of the school; (3) that the defendant, as the principal of said school, in the absence of rules established by the school board or other proper authority, had a right to make and enforce all necessary and proper rules for the regulation of the school and pupils during school hours and afterwards; (4) that said punishment administered by the defendant was reasonable and proper."

The court observed that to rule otherwise would create a serious loss of discipline in the school and could result in possible harm to innocent pupils in attendance. Home is not considered to be a sanctuary for pupils which automatically removes the school's authority. In dictum, the Court posed the following hypothetical situation: "Supposing that some strong-armed juvenile bully attending school lived upon the next block and sought for a brief moment the asylum of his home, and thence sallied forth and beat, abused and terrorized his fellow pupils as they passed by returning home, then, by the claim urged by plaintiff, he would be immune from punishment by the school authorities, while, if he began his assaults before he had passed within the bounds of his own front yard, he would be liable to proper punishment for any harm done. Now the harm done to the morale of the school is the same. The injured and frightened pupils are dismayed and discouraged in going to and coming from the school, and demoralized while in attendance. . . . The harm to the school has been done, and its proper conduct and operation seriously harmed by such acts."

[*158*]

Placed in this light one can easily see why the courts allow the schools authority to have rather broad scope. Much can happen to students which will bear on their school performance and in such cases the school has an interest. This is not to imply that the school has general control over student affairs outside of school when the conduct relates only remotely to the morale and decorum of the school, but it does say that the school has the authority to act if misconduct of students has a *direct* bearing on the well-being of the school.

Nor is the control of external conduct limited to abuse of other students. If a student denigrates the school by abusing a teacher off school grounds, see: Fenton v. Stear, 423 F.Supp. 767 (W.D.Pa.1976), then an official school response may be in order. The misbehavior of the student must not have a merely remote and indirect tendency to injure the school, but must have a direct and immediate tendency to do so. The injury to the school must be in the nature of subversion of the teacher's authority which may result in disorder and insubordination. Such misbehavior may come in the form of verbal abuse in the presence of other pupils after school hours or on weekends, Fenton, supra. The classic case setting out this common law principle is the case of "old Jack Seaver." Lander v. Seaver, 32 Vt. 114, 76 Am.Dec. 156 (1859). In this instance a student had returned home from school and while driving the family cow past the schoolmaster's house was heard, in the presence of other students, to disrespectfully refer to the master as "old Jack Seaver." The next morning Mr. Seaver whipped the

[*159*]

offending boy. In denying relief to the boy in an action for assault and battery against Mr. Seaver, the court held that such misconduct was done in an effort to insult and demean the master in the eyes of other students. Such acts the court found, would undoubtedly have a deleterious effect on the ability of the teacher to supervise and direct the learning of the children when they returned to school—a direct and immediate tendency to injure the school.

According to a Nebraska court, the extent of school authority goes beyond school boundaries and may supersede parental authority in certain circumstances. "General education and control of pupils who attend public schools are in the hands of school boards, superintendents, principals, and teachers. This control extends to health, proper surroundings, necessary discipline, promotion of morality and other wholesome influences, while parental authority is temporarily superseded." Richardson v. Braham, 125 Neb. 142, 249 N.W. 557 (1933).

School authority, however, may not be exercised to encroach on parental prerogatives of the students' freedom outside the school where the welfare of other students or the conduct of the school is not diminished. As with all rules affecting student conduct, those governing the students' activities off school grounds must be reasonably related to an appropriate school purpose and the enforcement of the rules must be uniformly applied to all students in similar circumstances.

CHAPTER 9

RACIAL SEGREGATION

§ 9.1 INTRODUCTION

Governments have the inherent authority to reasonably classify persons for legitimate purposes. Reasonableness of classification and legitimate purposes are, however, difficult to define. But the history of slavery and racial discrimination in the United States and its moral and ethical consequences make classifications by race an anathema to American society. The American tradition of relying on mass public education as the means by which persons gained social and economic mobility naturally resulted in the public schools being a primary battleground on which the racial discrimination issue was to be contested. The most relevant court decisions involving the racial discrimination in American history have been educationally related.

§ 9.2 SEPARATE–BUT–EQUAL

The pernicious doctrine of separate-but-equal emanated from a dispute before 1850 when the Supreme Court of Massachusetts legalized the concept in permitting racial segregation in the public schools of Boston. Roberts v. City of Boston, 59 Mass. (5 Cush.) 198 (1850). In this case a Negro child was compelled by school board rule to attend an elementary school designated for black children even though other elementary schools were closer to her home. The child's lawyer, Charles Sumner, the famous abolitionist, maintained that separate schools "exclusively devoted to one class must differ essentially, in its spirit and character, from that public school known to the law, where all classes meet together in equality." He argued that persons who were otherwise equal before the law should not be made unequal by discriminatory devices such as segregated schools. The Massachusetts court disagreed with Sumner, and in so doing, created the separate-but-equal doctrine and justified it by saying that the great principle of equality before the law did not warrant the assumption that all persons are clothed with the same civil and political powers and that such powers, and the benefits therefrom, may vary depending on the "infinite variety of circumstances" surrounding society. The judge concluded that this infinite variety of circumstances which may justify school segregation can be found in societal standards which separate the races. Thus, according to the court, separation of races in schools was not discriminatory, so long as the school facilities were not unequal. The court did not believe that segregation of the races was *per se* unequal.

The *Roberts* case was decided under the Constitution of Massachusetts, because the United States Constitution, at that time, contained no prohibition against racial discrimination.

§ 9.21 Equal Protection Clause

It was not until 1868 when the American people enacted the Fourteenth Amendment that racial discrimination became impermissible at the federal level. The Fourteenth Amendment provided that " . . . No

[*162*]

state shall . . . deny any person within its jurisdiction the equal protection of the laws."

In spite of this amendment racial segregation persisted as courts failed to fully enforce its intent. Many states enacted Jim Crow laws which extended segregation to most aspects of public life, including separate waiting rooms in railroad stations, train cars, telephone booths, separate storage for textbooks used by black school children, separate elevators, and separate Bibles for swearing in Negro witnesses in some southern courts, and, of course, separate schools. The federal goverment's practices were as obnoxious as many of the southern states since federal laws and regulations also promoted segregation, including the maintenance of separate schools in the District of Columbia.

Segregation gained legal credence through the precedent of "separate-but-equal" which was adopted by the United States Supreme Court as applying to the Fourteenth Amendment in the infamous Plessy v. Ferguson, 163 U.S. 537, 16 S.Ct. 1138 (1896).

Justice Harlan dissented in *Plessy* maintaining that the separate accommodations contributed to creation of a racial caste system excluding blacks from association with whites. Because whites held the prestige, wealth, and power in society, the doctrine of "separate-but-equal" condemned blacks to a permanently inferior position. *Plessy*, however, was the precedent that prevailed until 1954 when the Supreme court, in Brown v. Board of Education, 347 U.S. 483, 74 S.Ct. 686 (1954), held the separate-but-equal doctrine to be inherently unconstitutional.

§ 9.22   Demise of Separate-but-Equal

The United States Supreme Court was never able to clearly enunciate what constituted "equal" in the context of "separate-but-equal." It was, though, generally understood that the entire absence of facilities would violate equal protection. As a result states made some provision, though in most cases quite modest, for black students to have some type of facility. Educational facilities at the graduate and professional school levels were, generally, not available in southern states for black students. Where this was the case, the state legislatures usually provided some type of tuition assistance for black students to attend colleges in other states. In Missouri ex rel. Gaines v. Canada, 305 U.S. 337, 59 S.Ct. 232 (1938), a Negro plaintiff who did not want to attend law school in another state challenged the State of Missouri because it had no law school for black students. Justice Hughes, writing for the majority of the United States Supreme Court, ruled that Missouri must either permit plaintiff to attend the white law school or that the state must establish a black law school. At the next session of the Missouri legislature a statute was enacted to create a law school for blacks.

It was not until twelve years after *Gaines*, however, that the Supreme Court was asked to rule on the quality of the separate facilities. The inferiority of the black institutions was obvious, but no court decision had established a standard of comparison until 1950, when the Supreme Court in Sweatt v. Painter, 339 U.S. 629, 70 S.Ct. 848 (1950), held that the black law school in Texas was so inferior to the University of Texas

Law School that it could not be contrued as a "separate-but-equal" facility. Separate-but-equal had by this time forced the Court into an untenable and unworkable position of justifying separate facilities when it was quite clear that the requirement of equal tradition, prestige and influence by definition denied the efficacy of the "separate-but-equal" doctrine, to say nothing of its moral and ethical shortcomings.

§ 9.3 THE BROWN CASE

A frontal attack was launched on the doctrine by the NAACP in the decade of between 1940 and 1950 led by Thurgood Marshall and a battery of black lawyers, law professors, historians, and sociologists who had analyzed both the legal and social ramifications of segregation. Brown v. Board of Education of Topeka, supra, was the first cited case of five cases which were carefully selected to present the complete issue of school segregation to the Supreme Court. Initial arguments were made on December 9, 1952, two and one-half years after the *Sweatt* decision, but the Court reached no decision based on these first briefs and arguments. The case was reargued on December 8, 1953, after which the *Brown* decision was rendered and the doctrine of "separate-but-equal" was nullified.

The basic legal issue propounded by the Court was whether the Fourteenth Amendment contemplated abolishment of school segregation. This was the essential question, whether the constitutional intent was to prohibit state statutory or regulatory segregation of the public schools. The Court rendered its decision saying: "We conclude that in the field of public educa-

[*165*]

tion the doctrine of 'separate-but-equal' has no place. Separate educational facilities are inherently inequal."

The potential societal effects of *Brown* were so pervasive that the Court was forced to carefully evaluate alternative enforcement measures. Suddenly, the dual system of public education in seventeen states which had been legal under "separate-but-equal" was now unconstitutional. Because of these immense ramifications, on the rendering of the *Brown* decision, the Court charged plaintiffs, defendants and friends of the Court to return and present alternatives for implementation. The plan that was finally adopted by the Court in *Brown II* in 1955, said that the lower courts should act "with all deliberate speed" in desegregating the public schools. Brown v. Board of Education, 349 U.S. 294, 75 S.Ct. 753 (1955).

Because *Brown* dealt only with state-enforced segregation no guidelines were established for the courts to follow in bringing about desegregation. *Brown* extended only to the erasure of state segregation laws and their enforcement, but did not provide guideposts for abrogation of the continuing effects of segregation.

§ 9.4 WITH ALL DELIBERATE SPEED

A plethora of lower federal court decisions dominated the actions of school boards in the South during the fifteen years after *Brown*. Almost immediately, upon remand to a lower federal court, in a companion case to *Brown*, Briggs v. Elliott, 132 F.Supp. 776 (E.D.S.C. 1955), the issue of desegregation versus integration was addressed. Here the federal judge was asked to determine whether *Brown* merely meant to abolish state sanctioned segregation or did it intend that the courts force the states to act affirmatively to integrate the schools. The judge concluded that "all that is decided, is that a state may not deny to any person on account of race the right to attend any school that it maintains. . . . The Constitution, in other words, does not require integration. It merely forbids segregation." Accordingly, for several years thereafter, this case stood as precedent for school districts which did not want to take affirmative action to mix white and black children in the same schools.

§ 9.41 Interposition

In other instances the speed of desegregation was delayed by state officials and interposing themselves and their offices between court decrees and the people. The most glaring example was probably that involving the public schools of Little Rock, Arkansas, where state officials sought to revive the Civil War doctrines of nullification and interposition to prevent integration of the Central High School in Little Rock. The constitutionality of the state officials' actions was finally decided by the United States Supreme Court when it said: "In short, the constitutional rights of children not to be discriminated against in school admission on grounds of race or color declared by this Court in the Brown case can neither be nullified openly or directly by state legislators or state executive or judicial officers, nor nullified indirectly by them through evasive schemes for segregation whether attempted 'ingeniously or ingenuously.' "   Cooper v. Aaron, 358 U.S. 1, 78 S.Ct. 1401 (1958).

One device used to circumvent the effects of *Brown* was to close the public schools and to provide vouchers for students to attend private schools. When this method of maintaining segregation was challenged, the Supreme Court held that the ill effects of such a system bore more heavily on Negro students because the white students had access to accredited private schools while the Negro children did not. Thus the Court concluded that to close public schools and contribute tax funds for students to attend segregated private schools was a violation of equal protection. Griffin v. County School Board of Prince Edward County, 377 U.S. 218, 84 S.Ct. 1226 (1964).

§ 9.42   Freedom of Choice

Whether the Equal Protection Clause required that states merely eradicate state enforced segregation or act affirmatively to integrate, the issue addressed in *Briggs*, continued as a major question. The United States Office of Education issued guidelines for desegregation of school districts in southern states which, if not followed, could result in withholding of federal funds. The guidelines, initially, called for freedom of choice plans to be submitted in order to qualify for the federal funds, but, after a time, it was concluded that freedom of choice would not bring about desegregation in many districts. It was found that black parents for many reasons, including community coercion, would not choose to send their children to schools which were formerly all white.

When the "freedom of choice" issue finally reached the United States Supreme Court, the Court concluded that if freedom of choice plans actually worked to desegregate the schools, then they were legal alternatives; but if they failed to integrate the schools, then the state and school districts must devise schemes that would mandate placement of black children in schools with white children and vice versa. According to the Court, a "freedom of choice" plan must "effectuate a transition" to a "unitary system." Green v. County School Board of New Kent County, 391 U.S. 430, 88 S.Ct. 1689 (1968).

§ 9.43 Desegregate at Once

The "all deliberate speed" standard which was attributed to Justice Felix Frankfurter proved to be unworkable. After fifteen years of attempting to implement this standard, the United States Supreme Court reconsidered the entire question in Alexander v. Holmes, 396 U.S. 19, 90 S.Ct. 29 (1969). In despair the Court concluded that the "all deliberate speed" terminology was a legalized term that allowed too much discretion and resulted in action so deliberate that schools would remain segregated in many districts of the South. The Court said ". . . continued operation of segregated schools under a standard of allowing 'all deliberate speed' for desegregation is no longer constitutionally permissible." The Court ordered all school districts in the seventeen southern states to "terminate dual school systems at once and to operate now and hereafter only unitary schools." From the date of this decree, all school districts in the south were required to become unitary without further delay.

§ 9.5 THE SWANN CASE

Even though Alexander v. Holmes County Board of Education required that every school district operating dual school programs for blacks and whites were to immediately terminate the practice and to establish unitary schools, the Supreme Court did not clearly define what unitary meant nor did it prescribe the standards to be used by school authorities to disestablish dual school systems. This the Supreme Court undertook to accomplish in Swann v. Charlotte-Mecklenburg Board of Education, 402 U.S. 1, 91 S.Ct. 1267 (1971). *Swann* addressed the issues in four contexts—the use of racial quotas, the elimination of one-race schools, racial gerrymandering of attendance zones and the use of buses for remedial purposes.

§ 9.51   Racial Quotas

Several earlier lower court decisions had used ratios of black to whites in the total school population to establish racial quotas for each school. A federal district court had established a 71–29 ratio for schools in Charlotte-Mecklenburg Cournty, North Carolina and ruled that no school could be operated with an all black or predominately black student body. The lower court also set a particular ratio as a required norm. The Supreme Court said that if it was, in fact, the lower court's intent to establish a "mathematical racial balance reflecting the pupil constituency of the system" then the approach would be disapproved and the lower court would be reversed. The Supreme Court said: "The constitutional command to desegregate schools does not mean that every school in every community must always reflect the racial composition of the school system as a whole." The Court did acknowledge, however, that "very limited use" of mathematical ratios was within the equitable remedial discretion of a district court and that "awareness of the racial composition of the whole system is likely to be a useful starting point in shaping a remedy to correct past constitutional violations."

It should be noted that more recently the United States Supreme Court upheld the use of explicit quotas setting aside 10 percent of federal contracts for minority business enterprises. Fullilove v. Klutznick, 448 U.S. 448, 100 S.Ct. 2758 (1980). This suggests that quotas will remain an important affirmative action device but are not constitutionally required.

§ 9.52   One-Race Schools

A second question necessary to define a unitary system is whether one-race schools are to be permitted at all. The Court answered this question affirmatively, but admonished that such schools required close judicial scrutiny to determine whether the assignment of pupils was a part of state-enforced segregation. Where a school district's desegregation plan permits such schools to continue, the district has the burden of showing that pupil assignments are "genuinely nondiscriminatory."

§ 9.53   Remedial Altering of Attendance Zones

Racial gerrymandering of districts as required by courts are permissible devices to overcome segregation. Pairing, clustering, and grouping may also be validly required by the lower courts. The Supreme Court said that no rigid rules could be set because of varying local conditions such as traffic patterns and availability of good highways, but that pairing and grouping of noncontiguous school zones may be feasible alternatives. Mere administrative awkwardness or inconvenience is not to be allowed to stand in the way of such remedial actions. Concerning assignment of children to the nearest or neighborhood school the Court said: "All things being equal, with no history of discrimination, it might well be desirable to assign pupils to schools nearest their homes. But all things are not equal in a system that was deliberately constructed and maintained to enforce racial segregation." Thus, where *de jure* segregation has prevailed, the school district must reassign students to bring about integration whether or not the reassignments result in breaking up neighborhood school attendance patterns.

§ 9.54   Busing

The use of busing to alleviate segregation has long been a volatile issue. Until *Swann* the Supreme Court had not directly sanctioned busing as a remedial measure to effectuate integration. In *Green*, supra, the freedon of choice case, the Court had remained vague on the issue saying merely that measures must be taken which are "workable," "effective," and "realistic." With regard to busing, the Supreme Court said in *Swann* that: "Bus transportation has been an integral part of the public education system for years and its use is not novel nor are the people unaccustomed to use of buses." Further, the Court pointed out that in Charlotte-Mecklenburg, elementary pupils' bus trips averaged about seven miles; therefore, the present wide use of buses strongly supported the use of bus transportation as on e tool for remedying school segregation. "Desegregation plans," the Court said, "cannot be limited to the walk-in school."

§ 9.6 DE FACTO AND DE JURE SEGREGATION

With the *Alexander* case, supra, it was well decided that school districts in states with legal segregation, *de jure*, before *Brown*, had an affirmative duty to integrate, but it had not been clearly decided whether schools that were *de facto* segregated because of housing patterns were required to integrate. President Nixon summarized the law in 1969 saying that "There is a fundamental distinction between so-called 'de jure' and 'de facto' segregation: de jure segregation arises by law or by the deliberate act of school officials and is unconstitutional; de facto segregation results from residential housing patterns and does not violate the Constitution."

Earlier, the United States Court of Appeals for the Seventh Circuit had said that "There is no affirmative United States constitutional duty to change innocently arrived at school attendance districts by the mere fact that shifts in population either increase of decrease the percentage of either Negro or White pupils." Bell v. School City of Gary, 324 F.2d 209 (7th Cir. 1963).

§ 9.61   Implicit Intent to Segregate

Thus, if segregation is *de facto* and no *de jure,* no affirmative duty exists to integrate. In the seventeen southern states all segregation was *de jure,* but in the North *de jure* segregation could only be present if the plaintiffs could show that states or local school boards had acted either explicitly or implicitly to bring about segregation. In explaining the requirement for northern states, the Supreme Court said in *Keyes,* a Denver case, that " . . . we have held that where plaintiffs prove that a current condition of segregated schooling exists within a school district where a dual system was compelled or authorized by statute at the time of our decision in *Brown* . . ., the state automatically assumes an affirmative duty to 'effectuate a transition to a racially nondiscriminatory school system.' " In states where dual systems of education did not exist, the plaintiffs must show that there was official purpose or intent to segregate. Keyes v. School District No. 1, Denver, 413 U.S. 189, 93 S.Ct. 2686 (1973).

§ 9.62   Interdistrict Integration

In reversing a lower court decision which had found that *de jure* segregation existed in Detroit and its suburbs, creating a constitutional requirement to integrate several of the suburban districts with the Detroit school system, the United States Supreme Court said that before boundaries of school districts can be changed to integrate it must be shown that "racially discriminatory acts of the state or local school districts, or of a single school district have been a substantial cause of interdistrict segregation." Milliken v. Bradley, 418 U.S. 717, 94 S.Ct. 3112 (1974). The Supreme Court could not find in the record of the Detroit case any evidence that would suggest discriminatory acts, explicit or implicit, by the state of Michigan or by suburban districts that would cause the districts themselves to be segregated.

§ 9.63   Northern De Jure Segregation

De jure segregation has, though, been found to exist within several school districts in northern states. For example, both the Columbus and Dayton, Ohio, school systems were held to have been segregated by discriminatory acts of public officials and, thus, an affirmative duty was required to eradicate the vestiges of such *de jure* segregation. Columbus Board of Education v. Penick, 443 U.S. 449, 99 S.Ct. 2941 (1979); Dayton Board of Education v. Brinkman, 443 U.S. 526, 99 S.Ct. 2971 (1979). To desegregate, the Court required that a "balanced" school system be attained; the Court said: "[T]he measure of the post-*Brown* conduct of a school board under an unsatisfied duty to liquidate a dual school system is the effectiveness, not the purpose of the actions in decreasing or increasing the segregation caused by the dual system." Thus, the school board must not only abandon its discriminatory practice, but it must establish policies and procedures which will integrate the schools.

§ 9.64   State Equal Protection

In 1970 the Supreme Court of California held that state school boards had a constitutional obligation to take reasonable steps to alleviate segregation in public schools whether it be classified as *de facto* or *de jure* in origin. Crawford v. Board of Education, 17 Cal.3d 280, 290, 130 Cal.Rptr. 724, 734, 551 P.2d 24, 34 (1970). Accordingly, the Equal Protection Clause of the California Constitution was more forceful in compelling desegregation than equal protection of the Fourteenth Amendment. However, in 1979 the voters of California ratified Proposition I amending the Equal Protection Clause of the California Constitution providing that state courts shall not order mandatory pupil assignment or transportation to overcome racial imbalance unless a federal court so requires under federal case law. The effect of this amendment was to limit the sweep of the Equal Protection Clause in the California Constitution while not affecting the federal requirements. Crawford v. Los Angeles Board of Education, 458 U.S. 527, 102 S.Ct. 3211 (1982). The Court said we reject the contention that "once a state chooses to do 'more' than the Fourteenth Amendment requires, it may never recede."

§ 9.65   Northern De Jure Segregation Defined

A 1971 case involving the desegregation of the San Francisco school district dealt with the distinctions between *de jure* and *de facto*. The school district having a large racial minority and a great diversity of ethnic groups had substantial racial imbalance among its schools. Johnson v. San Francisco Unified School District, 339 F.Supp. 1315 (N.D.Cal.1971). Even though this decision was later vacated, Johnson v. San Francisco Unified School District, 500 F.2d 349 (9th

Cir.1974), it is instructive because of its discussion of the North-South and *effect-intent* issues. The school board defended its school boundaries by maintaining that the court decisions forbidding segregation applied only to those states "which at an earlier time, had dual school systems," therefore, the school board was not required to adopt affirmative measures where no dual system had previously existed. The district court rejected this argument refusing to draw a distinction between segregation in the North and South. The Court said that: "It is shocking, indeed, it is nonsensical, to assume that such practices are forbidden to school authorities in Florida or North Carolina, for example, but are permitted to school authorities in California. Neither the United States Supreme Court nor any other Court has drawn a Mason-Dixon line for constitutional enforcement."

The San Francisco school board further maintained that its actions were not unconstitutional because the district officials merely drew attendance lines without regard to racial or ethnic groups. In addressing this issue, the district court further defined the *de facto* and *de jure* distinction by explaining that any action by school authorities "which creates or continues or heightens racial segregation of school children is *de jure*." On appeal, the judgment of this district court was vacated because the U.S. Supreme Court had held in *Keyes*, supra, that the differentiating factor between *de jure* and *de facto* segregation is whether the purpose or intent is to segregate, not whether the effect is to segregate. When the district court used the words "creates", "continues" or heightens" segregation, it was erroneously using the effect test. The appeals court could find no evidence to suggest that the San Francisco school officials had "intentionally discriminated against minority students by practicing a deliberate policy of racial discrimination."

An excellent example of what constitutes *de jure* segregation in a northern state is found in a Pennsylvania case in 1982, Hoots v. Commonwealth of Pennsylvania, 672 F.2d 1107 (3d Cir. 1982). Here the state had enacted a school district reorganization statute requiring each county board of school directors to prepare a plan of organization for school districts for review by the State Board of Education. The plan approved for Alegheny County called for creation of five school districts, four of which had 87 percent or more white students and a fifth district that had 63 percent black. A federal district court held the plan unconstitutional finding that action by both state and county boards had the intent to segregate the students of the school districts and, as such, "constituted an act of *de jure* discrimination in violation of the Fourteenth Amendment." According to the court, defendants could foresee the predictable effects of the reorganization and from that an inference of segregative intent could be drawn. Further, substantial evidence was presented that white parents and school officials sought to shield white students from attending school with nonwhites. Most damaging was testimony by a desegregation consultant that "race, indeed, was taken into consideration" by public officials, "in recreating school districts" and that certain neighborhoods were excluded from the white districts because they were predominately black.

§ 9.66   Single Standard

Although the prevailing view remains today that there is a legal distinction between *de facto* and *de jure* segregation, the trend is toward a single standard. The basic distinction is that in the states which had legal segregation before 1954, the burden is on the school district to overcome vestiges of past discrimination. If the effect is to segregate then it must be addressed with affirmative action to erase the racial imbalance. On the other hand, in other states plaintiffs must show that there was an official intent to segregate before remedial measures will be required by the courts. Justice Powell in a concurring opinion in *Keyes* argued that such a dual standard is not now justified. He said ". . . The net result of the Court's language, however, is the application of an effect test to the actions of southern school districts and an intent test to those in other sections, at least until an initial dejure finding for those districts can be made. Rather than straining to perpetuate any such dual standard, we should hold forthrightly that significant segregated school conditions in any section of the country are a prima facie violation of constitutional rights . . ."

Justice Douglas, in dissent in *Keyes*, agreed with Powell maintaining that there should be no legal distinction made between *de facto* and *de jure* segregation. Douglas said, "The school board is a state agency and the lines that it draws, the locations it selects for school sites, the allocations it makes of students, the budgets it prepares are state action for Fourteenth Amendment purposes . . . I think it is time to state that there is no constitutional difference between *de jure* and *de facto* segregation, for each is the product of state actions or policies . . ."

CHAPTER 10

EDUCATION OF THE HANDICAPPED

§ 10.1 INTRODUCTION

State provision for education of the handicapped has historically been far from adequate. Until the mid to late 1960's, most states did not have uniform standards for education of the handicapped and many states did not provide state financing for such purposes. Handicapped students were systematically excluded from educational programs because their learning, emotional or physical handicaps tended to disrupt the continuity of the everyday school program; or the costs of such education were beyond that which the public was willing to undertake.

Today the situation is much different, both state and federal statutes guarantee educational opportunity for the handicapped and court decisions have mandated that the civil rights of the handicapped be protected.

§ 10.2 RIGHT TO ATTEND SCHOOL

Two important cases provided the initial impetus for both state legislatures and the Congress to provide new legislation guaranteeing educational opportunity for handicapped children. The first case, *Pennsylvania Association for Retarded Children* (PARC) was brought by the parents of seventeen children who claimed that Pennsylvania laws enacted prior to 1972 were unconstitutional. Pennsylvania Association for Retarded Children v. Commonwealth, 334 F.Supp. 1257

(E.D.Pa.1971), 343 F.Supp. 279 (E.D.Pa.1972). The laws allowed for exclusion of handicapped children from public school if they were certified by psychologists as "uneducable and untrainable." The parents claimed that: (1) the law did not provide for appropriate due process measures to be taken before exclusion, such as notice to parents and a proper hearing, (2) the children were denied equal protection because they were declared to be uneducable with a rational factual basis for such determination, (3) the state constitution guaranteed education for all children and the law which excluded handicapped children was arbitrary and capricious. The federal district court held that exclusion of handicapped children was, indeed, unconstitutional, that: "having undertaken to provide a free public education to all its children, including its exceptional children, the Commonwealth of Pennsylvania may not deny any mentally retarded child access to a free public program of education and training." The court gave the parties involved an opportunity to agree on procedures acceptable to both sides. A consent decree was issued which stated in part that a "free public program of education and training appropriate to the child's capacity, within the context of a presumption that, among the alternative programs of education and training required by statute to be available, placement in a regular public school class is preferable to placement in a special public school class i.e., a class for 'handicapped' children (only) and placement in a special public school class is preferable to placement in any other type of program of education and training . . ."

To determine the education and training appropriate to the "child's capacity" required elaborate due process procedures which were set out in the decree. From the due process procedure, the school was to determine if the child could be first placed in a regular class (mainstreamed), or in the alternative placed in a self-contained or special resource room. The last and least desirable alternative was placement in homebound or other setting outside the public school.

Shortly following *PARC* the *Mills* case emerged which further accentuated the problem of educating the handicapped. Mills v. Board of Education of District of Columbia, 348 F.Supp. 866 (D.D.C.1972). Because this case arose in Washington, D.C., it gained substantial notoriety having a great impact on both state and federal legislation. In this case, parents challenged exclusionary practices which had resulted in nearly 18,000 handicapped children going without public education in 1972–73. The District of Columbia law mandated a free public education for all children between the ages of 7 and 16. Parents claimed that denial of education violated the constitutional right of due process. On the other hand, school officials argued that to educate the handicapped children would cause a great financial burden for which there was not adequate funding.

The federal district court held that the equal protection was implicit in the Due Process Clause of the Fifth Amendment applying to the District of Columbia and that through this provision a right existed to attend public schools. While the substantive aspects of due process gave these students a right to attend pub-

[*183*]

lic schools, the procedural aspects of due process gave the students a right of a fair hearing before they could be excluded or placed in alternative classes within the school system.

In answer to the school district's financial concerns, the court bluntly stated that "If sufficient funds are not available to finance all of the services and programs that are needed and desirable in the system, then the available funds must be expended equitably in such a manner that no child is entirely excluded from a publicly supported education consistent with his needs and ability to benefit therefrom. The inadequacies of the District of Columbia Public School System whether occasioned by insufficient funding or administrative inefficiency, certainly cannot be permitted to bear more heavily on the 'exceptional' or handicapped child than on the normal child." In the decree the court established due process procedures which included step-by-step detail on how notice was to be given to parents when placement of a child was contemplated, who should serve as hearing officers, and the requirements for the actual hearing. Many of these procedures were later adopted in state and federal legislation to protect the interests of the handicapped.

§ 10.3   Public Law 94–142

With the awareness created by the litigation in *PARC* and *Mills* and emergent cases in other states, the Congress moved rapidly to provide federal legislation and funding which would assist in educating the handicapped. The federal law entitled Education for All Handicapped Children Act of 1975, 20 U.S.C.A. §

§ 1401, initially applied to all children between the ages of 3 and 21. (See Appendix B.) Public school services, though, may be limited by state law which may extend to a more limited age group. In order to receive federal funds under the Act, states must abide by the Act and regulations made pursuant to it.

Most importantly, the Act assures that all handicapped children have access to "a free appropriate public education and related services designed to meet their unique needs." The appropriate educational program must be tailored to each handicapped child's educational needs. An "individualized education program" (IEP) is designed for each child and reevaluation of the plan must be conducted annually. Another provision requires that handicapped children be educated in the "least restrictive" environment appropriate to their needs. This means that handicapped children be placed in regular classes (mainstreamed) when possible. A regular class with appropriate supplemental services is preferable to special classes, special classes are preferable to separate special schools, and special schools are preferable to homebound instruction. If no public facilities are available, then private schools may be used in the alternative and public funds may be used to defray the costs.

Some of the procedural safeguards provided for in the Act are: (1) access by parents to relevant school records, (2) prior notice to parents of any proposed change in their child's educational placement, (3) opportunity for a fair and impartial hearing, including right to be represented by a lawyer or advisor, right to present evidence, to subpoena, confront and cross-examine witnesses and obtain a transcript of the hearing and written decision, (4) opportunity to appeal to court, and (5) right of child to remain in current placement during pendency of hearing proceedings.

Much litigation has emerged during the last several years which clarifies several of the provisions of the Act. Most of these cases have to do with interpretation of appropriateness of program, placement, and costs of treatment.

§ 10.31   Free Appropriate Public Education

The key to meeting the requirements of P.L. 94–142 is to determine what constitutes an appropriate education. In the most authoritative statement yet made in interpretation of P.L. 94–142, the United States Supreme Court in Hendrick Hudson District Board of Education v. Rowley, 458 U.S. 176, 102 S.Ct. 3034 (1982), ruled on the question "What is meant by the Act's requirement of a 'free appropriate public education' "? The case arose when parents of Amy Rowley, a deaf student, contested the appropriateness of the educational program provided her by the Hendrick Hudson School District. Amy had minimal residual hearing and was an excellent lipreader. Prior to her entering the school after meeting with her parents, it was decided to place her in a regular kindergarten class and she would have supplemental assistance provided with an FM hearing aid which would amplify words spoken into a wireless receiver by the teacher and other students during classroom activities. Amy successfully completed kindergarten and as was required by law a new IEP was prepared for her for her first-grade

[*186*]

year. The IEP called for her to be mainstreamed in a regular classroom, continue to use the FM equipment and additionally receive instruction from a tutor for the deaf for one hour each day and from a speech therapist for three hours a week. Her parents agreed with the IEP but insisted that, additionally. Amy should also be provided with a qualified sign-language interpreter, full time, in all her academic classes. The school district officials disagreed maintaining that the child did not need the interpreter.

In reviewing the evidence, the lower federal district court found that even though the child was performing better than the average child for her class; she understands much less of what transpires in class than if she were not deaf. Thus, she was not learning as much as she would have without her handicap. With this in mind, the lower court concluded that a "free appropriate public education" must be defined as "an opportunity to achieve her full potential commensurate with the opportunity provided other children." The federal Court of Appeals affirmed but the United States Court reversed and remanded the decision. The high Court interpreted the Act as requiring that services for handicapped be sufficient to permit the child "to benefit" from instruction, but was not intended to prescribe a substantive standard prescribing a level of education.

In taking issue with the lower court's determinations that "the goal of the Act is to provide each handicapped child with an equal educational opportunity" and to maximize each child's potential "commensurate with the opportunity provided other children," the Supreme Court maintained that the lower courts had erred and that there was evidence of "congressional intent to achieve strict equality of opportunity or services." Rather, according to the Court, the intent was to merely provide "a basic floor of opportunity consistent with equal protection."

As to how and by whom the "basic floor" is to be defined, the Court said that the Act expressly charges states with the responsibility of providing teachers, administrators, and programs and practices appropriate for education of the handicapped. The Court concluded that it was "unlikely that Congress intended the courts to overturn a State's choice of appropriate educational theories . . ." in treating the needs of handicapped children. The Act requires that state and local educational agencies in cooperation with the parents or guardian of the child would decide on the appropriateness of the educational services to be offered, but where there is disagreement the Act vests the authority for final determination in the State. The Supreme Court said "We previously have cautioned that courts lack the 'specialized knowledge and experience' necessary to resolve 'persistent and difficult questions of educational policy.' We think Congress shared that view when it passed the Act. As already demonstrated, Congress' intention was not that the Act displace the primacy of the States in the field of education, but the States receive funds to assist them in extending their educational systems to the handicapped. Therefore, once a court determines that the requirements of the Act have been met, questions of methodology are for resolution by the States." *Rowley*, supra.

Latitude of states, however, is limited by provisions of the Act which mandate preference be given to certain types of education. For example, the Act expressed and the Court in *Rowley* emphasized that "states 'to the maximum extent appropriate' must educate handicapped children 'with children who are not handicapped.' " This is the mainstreaming requirement. In this regard, following *Rowley*, the United States Court of Appeals for the Eighth Circuit held that the state of Arkansas could not require a deaf child to leave her local district school to attend the Arkansas School for the Deaf, the state residential school for deaf children. The state authorities had determined that the child could only acquire the best possible education by attending the state school. The appeals court, noting that *Rowley* did not require that the state "maximize" the educational opportunity, found that an overriding requirement of the Act was that the child should remain with other children in a regular school setting with nonhandicapped children. The court, therefore, invoked *Rowley* to overrule the state's placement of the child. Springdale School District #50 of Washington County v. Grace, 693 F.2d 41 (8th Cir. 1982).

§ 10.32   Related Services

The Education of All Handicapped Children Act, in 20 U.S.C.A. § 1401(18) defines "appropriate" education in part as providing for "special education and related services." What are "related services" and to what extent is a local school district required to provide for them? This issue was addressed in a Texas case involving a child afflicted with myelomeningocele, a birth defect more commonly known as spina bifida. As a result of this handicap, the child suffers from speech and orthopedic impediments including a neurogenic bladder which does not function normally and requires catheterization several times a day. Tatro v. State of Texas, 703 F.2d 823 (5th Cir. 1983).

The IEP for the child did not require that the school provide the catheterization, *per se*, and the school district maintained it had no legal obligation to assign personnel to do so. Administrative appeals were pursued to the state board of education which held for the school district. The parents, thereafter, sued maintaining that the words "related services" in the federal law required that the school district provide the service to the child if an "appropriate" education was to be provided. The school district countered that under Texas law catheterization can be performed only if a physician is physically present to control and supervise the procedure and by such participation the service becomes, by definition "medical treatment." School districts, according to the Education of All Handicapped Children Act, 20 U.S.C.A. § 1401(17), are not required to provide medical services to students. The appeals court brushed this contention aside pointing out that Texas law also provided that medical doctors could delegate such activities to qualified persons, not only to nurses. The school district could, therefore, legally, provide the personnel to perform the catheterization.

The school district further argued that the catheterization is not a related service because it is not required to benefit from special education. In response the court maintained that the IEP called for the child to be placed in a self-contained special education class and that attendance in this class would not be possible if catheterization services were not rendered by the school personnel. Thus, failure by the district to provide the service would prevent fulfillment of the IEP and the Act requires that the IEP be carried out by the district.

Because of the nebulous nature of the term "related services", this area of the Act will undoubtedly result in much more litigation. Presently, however, *Tatro* appears to be the leading case and sets the precedent on definition of "related services."

§ 10.33   Placement

Proper placement of the student in a particular program or school is a most important aspect of the individualized educational program (IEP). There may be several options for placement of handicapped students in programs within the public school, but there is also the recognized alternative of placement in a nonpublic school which has special education facilities. A question arises as to whether the nonpublic school options must be taken into account when the student's IEP is devised and if failure to do invalidates the IEP. The United States Court of Appeals for the Fourth Circuit has held that such consideration of private services are not required to have a valid IEP. Hessler v. State Board of Education of Maryland, 700 F.2d 134 (4th Cir.1983). The court said "While the federal and state statutory schemes clearly contemplate the use of nonpublic educational services" under the circumstances, we think it clear that such resort is limited to those instances in which public educational services appropriate for the handicapped child are not available."

Further, the court said that just because parents may be able to show that the nonpublic school program is possibly more appropriate or better than the public school program, this does not mean that the public school program is necessarily inappropriate. Following the rationale of *Rowley*, this court emphasized that there was no obligation on the part of the school district to provide a handicapped child "all services necessary to maximize his or her potential commensurate with the opportunity provided to other children."

Where it is shown that a placement in a summer school program, in addition to the regular year-long program, prevents the handicapped child from retrogressing educationally, the school district may be required to provide a summer program. The requirement of the Act that personalized instruction be provided to meet individual needs of the handicapped child may possibly require an IEP with summer school as a requisite condition. Yaris v. Special School District of St. Louis County, 558 F.Supp. 545 (E.D.Mo. 1983).

§ 10.34   Cost of Services

When handicapped children are placed in nonpublic residential schools, the costs, many times, skyrocket far beyond levels anticipated by budget minded school boards. A federal court in New Jersey has held that the local school districts cannot refuse to pay the residential costs of such facilities. To do so, according to the court, would work to advantage the economically elite and would be incompatible with the New Jersey Constitution. D.S. v. Board of Education of Town of East Brunswick, 188 N.J.Super. 592, 458 A.2d 129 (1983).

According to P.L. 94–142, the public school must keep the student in the "current educational placement" pending the result of the student's educational evaluation and the development of the IEP. This normally creates few problems, but what if the parent without agreement of the school board places the child in an expensive private school during pendency of the student's due process and the process is prolonged for several reasons for lack of parental and school district agreement, is the school district liable for the private school educational costs? Apparently not, according to a federal appeals court placement and payment are two different matters; a student has a right to placement in a public school but can alternatively be placed in a private school by the parents, at parents' discretion. If the parents, however, choose nonpublic school placement, during pendency of due process, the public school has no obligation to pay the costs. Zvi D. v. Ambach, 694 F.2d 904 (2d Cir. 1982). Where, though, a handicapped student is placed in a nonpublic facility and the facility is subsequently decertified by the state, the handicapped student is entitled to continue tuition and costs pending reevaluation and placement in another facility. Vander Malle v. Ambach, 673 F.2d 49 (2d Cir. 1982). A parent who unilaterally removes her disabled child from one school and places the child in a private school before resorting to due process hearing procedures is not entitled to tuition reimbursement. Foster v. District of Columbia Board of Education, 523 F.Supp. 1142 (D.D.C.1981).

Whether or not the public school is required to pay the full costs of maintaining a handicapped student in a private facility depends on whether the charges are made for educational or medical services. If the medical services are related to the educational needs and are necessary for the student to progress educationally, the costs must be paid. Some courts have required room and board payments when residential placement is necessary for a combination of educational and noneducational reasons. If the situation is so complex that it is difficult if not impossible for the courts to ferret out the differences, then they have generally required the public school district to pay the full costs. North v. District of Columbia Board of Education, 471 F.Supp. 136 (D.D.C.1979). Other courts have sought to directly determine whether placement was necessary in order for the child to learn. Kruelle v. New Castle County School District, 642 F.2d 687 (3d Cir. 1981). The statutory exclusion for payment for medical services does not extend to supportive services such as speech, pathology, audiology, physical therapy, recreation and psychological services which are all considered to be a part of the educational costs. Papa Coda v. State of Connecticut, 528 F.Supp. 68 (D.Conn.1981).

CHAPTER 11

SEX DISCRIMINATION

§ 11.1 INTRODUCTION

Education in America reflects the norms of society; if society is unjust then the educational system is likely to be also. Societal standards have historically assumed that women and men should play much different and carefully delineated roles in the work force. Societal stereotypes of males and females spilled over to the schools where boys played interscholastic athletics and girls were the cheerleaders or majorettes. Athletic participation by girls was generally confined to intramural sports or to physical education classes. In the classroom, boys were assumed to be more capable in mathematics and science and girls more adept at English grammar and foreign languages.

The women's rights movement of the 1970's has had an important influence on the schools; today women are advised to enter occupations which were formerly male enclaves and are being advised to enter colleges and graduate and professional schools once reserved for men only.

Court decisions and legislation have reinforced the equal treatment between women and men. Most important have been the expanding judicial interpretation of the intent of the Equal Protection Clause of the Fourteenth Amendment, Title VI of the Civil Rights Act of 1964 and Title IX of the Educational Amendments of 1972 (see: Chapter 18, Employee Discrimina-

[195]

tion), each of which affects sexual equality among students.

§ 11.2 EQUAL PROTECTION OF SEXES

The first of the modern cases involving sex discrimination was Reed v. Reed, 404 U.S. 71, 92 S.Ct. 251 (1971), in which the United States Supreme Court struck down a state statute because it gave preference to the male over the female and as such was held to violate the Equal Protection Clause. The Court, however, did not elevate sex classifications to the special category of constitutional classes, such as race, that requires strict judicial scrutiny of legislative actions. Where race is concerned the state must show a compelling interest in classifications; where sex is concerned the state need only to show that its actions are not arbitrary or capricious.

In a later case the Supreme Court appeared to add more significance to sex as a classification when it held, in Craig v. Boren, 429 U.S. 190, 97 S.Ct. 451 (1976), "that classifications by gender must serve important governmental objectives and must be substantially related to achievement of those objectives." From this case it appears that the Court has established a separated, albeit, intermediate category, of judicial scrutiny to cases involving sex discrimination. Instead of the state showing simply that its classification by sex is rational, it must now show the classification "serves important governmental objectives." Thus, the state must bear a greater burden in justifying an act which classifies persons based on gender. What this means is that actions by a school district which treat students differently because of their sex must bear the burden of showing that the rule furthers an "important governmental objective." Whether the rule will stand depends on the interpretation of what constitutes an "important" objective.

§ 11.21   Admissions

Higher admission standards for female than for male applicants to a public preparatory high school violates the Equal Protection Clause. Berkelman v. San Francisco Unified School District, 501 F.2d 1264 (9th Cir. 1974). In another case, a federal district court in Massachusetts held that the admission policy at the Boston Latin School violated equal protection because it set a different test cutoff score for boys and girls. Bray v. Lee, 337 F.Supp. 934 (D.Mass.1972). Here the school in attempting to maintain a 50–50 balance in the number of boys and girls had established separate cutoff scores. The method used for each group was to simply count down from the highest test score in each of the two groups of applicants, boys and girls, until they had accepted the total number necessary to maintain a balanced enrollment. Girls, though, scored higher on the tests, thus, the cutoff for girls was 133 while it was only 120 for boys. Several girls who scored between 120 and 133 were not admitted. The court held that this type of admissions policy violated equal protection because it created "prejudicial disparities" based on sex.

§ 11.22   Athletic Teams

Sex classifications which deny participation to female students violate equal protection. In a Minnesota case, a state athletic association league rule was challenged because it forbade girls' participation in the boys' interscholastic athletic program either as a member of a boys' team or as a member of a girls' team competing against boys. Brenden v. Independent School District 742, 477 F.2d 1292 (8th Cir. 1973). Two girls where denied the opportunity to participate as members of boys' skiing and cross-country running teams. No teams in these sports were provided for girls by their schools. The court adopted the rational basis test and said that in evaluating state actions under the Equal Protection Clause, the courts were to consider three criteria: (1) the character of the classification, (2) the individual interest affected by the classification, and (3) the governmental interest asserted in support of the classification.

In evaluating the facts of the case against these criteria, the court concluded, first, that the discrimination was based on sex of the students and as such was subject to scrutiny by the courts. In this regard the court said that discrimination based on sex can no longer be justified by "reliance on outdated images . . . of women as peculiarly delicate and impressionable creatures in need of protection from the rough and tumble of unvarnished humanity." Secondly, the interests denied were educational benefits that should be expected of all students. In particular, the court said, "discrimination in education is one of the most damaging injustices women suffer. It denies them equal education and equal employment opportunity, contributing to a second-class image. . . . Discrimination in high school interscholastic athletics constitutes discrimination in education." The court went on to point out that interscholastic activities are today recognized as an integral part of the educational process and that sterotyping of students in education has helped to perpetuate discrimination against females, generally.

Thirdly, the court queried the high school athletic league in determining its interest in maintaining the separation of the sexes in the sports activities. The league maintained that physiological differences between males and females made it impossible for girls to equitably compete with males. The court refused to accept this rationale observing that evidence had been presented indicating there was widely differing athletic ability within the classes of men and women, possibly as wide as between the classes of men and women. The record showed the schools had, in fact, adopted no cut policies allowing all male students, no matter *how untalented*, to participate in these same non-contact sports. On this basis the court had no alternative but to declare the rule unconstitutional.

When "separate but equal" teams are provided for boys and girls, girl plaintiffs cannot compel schools to allow their participation on boys' teams. O'Connor v. Board of Education, 645 F.2d 578 (7th Cir. 1981), cert. denied 454 U.S. 1084, 102 S.Ct. 641.

Some courts are of the opinion that the availability of specific sports is not critical if the overall athletic opportunities are equal. This is true particularly where boys have had extensive athletic opportunities in several sports but have sought to participate in specific sports where only girls' teams are provided. Mularadelis v. Haldane Central School Board, 74 A.D.2d 248, 427 N.Y.S.2d 458 (1980). On the other hand some courts have held that denial of opportunity to participate in a specific sport denies equal protection even when overall opportunities are equal. Attorney General v. Massachusetts Interscholastic Athletic Association, 378 Mass. 342, 393 N.E.2d 284 (1979). The prevailing view is probably best expressed by the United States Court of Appeals for the Ninth Circuit which has held denial of a specific sport to boys is not *per se* violative of equal protection. Clark v. Arizona Interscholastic Association, 695 F.2d 1126 (9th Cir. 1982).

In a case where boys of substantial prowess in volleyball sought to be included as members of the girls' volleyball team, because a team was not provided for boys, the court said the fundamental constitutional question is "whether denying boys the particular opportunity to compete on a girls volleyball team, even when boys' overall opportunity is not inferior to girls', can be justified as substantially related to an important governmental interest." The governmental interest claimed by the athletic association was one of affirmative action to overcome past discrimination against women in interscholastic sports. The court found that boys, because of their physiological differences, would be superior volleyball players to girls if allowed to compete on the same teams. The result would be that athletic opportunities for women would be diminished. Rules that advance athletic opportunity for females may distinguish between the sexes.

The court concluded that there is "clearly a substantial relationship between the exclusion of males from the team and the goal of redressing past discrimination and providing equal opportunities for women."

Girls with extraordinary athletic talent are not constitutionally entitled to participate on boys' teams when their skills exceed those of other girls who play on the girls' teams. In the case where an eleven-year-old girl had such superior ability to play basketball that she was obviously capable of participating on equal terms with boys and that participation with girls only denied her full advantage of her talents, the court ruled that utilization of sex alone as the criteria to place her on a girls only team did not violate her equal protection rights. O'Connor v. Board of Education of School District 23, 545 F.Supp. 376 (N.D.Ill.1982). The girl's parents claimed that since talents between their daughter and the boys were equivalent, that the only reason to deny her participation on the boys' team was that they were of different sexes; this they maintained was unconstitutional. The court found this sex-based criterion advanced the cause of all girls even though it may have appeared arbitrary in the case of this particular girl.

§ 11.3 TITLE IX

The Educational Amendments of 1972, 20 U.S.C.A. §§ 1681–83 (1976), contained Title IX, the popular law that forbade discrimination in interscholastic, intercollegiate, club or intramural athletics offered by a recipient of federal funds. (See Appendix B.) Although a number of lower courts determined this Act to apply to students only, the United States Supreme Court in North Haven Board of Education v. Bell, 456 U.S. 512, 102 S.Ct. 1912 (1982), interpreted the Act to apply, also, to employees. (See: Chapter 18.)

A rule of an athletic association or a high school may violate Title IX but not be offensive to the Equal Protection Clause. The statute itself provides in Section 901(a) "No person in the United States shall, on the basis of sex, be excluded from participation in, be denied the benefits of, or be subjected to discrimination under any education program or activity receiving Federal financial assistance . . .." " Certain exceptions are noted including religious schools if the act is contrary to religious tenets, United States military schools, or institutions of higher education that have historically admitted students of only one sex.

In Cannon v. University of Chicago, 441 U.S. 677, 99 S.Ct. 1946 (1979), the United States Supreme Court held that Title IX created a private remedy under which an individual could challenge discriminatory acts. Before *Cannon*, Title IX had been interpreted as establishing legal redress resulting only in termination of federal funds. The Supreme Court said: "Title IX was patterned after Title VI of the Civil Rights Act of 1964. Except for the substitution of the word 'sex' in Title IX to replace the words 'race, color, or national origin' in Title VI, the two statutes use identical language to describe the benefitted class."

Under Title IX differences in athletic ability alone is not justification for a rule denying mixed participation in noncontact sports. Haas v. South Bend Community School Corp., 259 Ind. 515, 289 N.E.2d 495 (1972).

§ 11.31. Comparability

Regulations pursuant to Title IX permit institutions to offer separate team sports, but are not intended to require boys' teams be opened to girls. Teams, however, must be offered on a "comparable" basis for students of both sexes taking into account the interests and abilities of both sexes; "an institution would be required to provide separate teams for men and women in situations where the provision of only one team would not 'accommodate the interests and abilities of both sexes.'" O'Connor v. Board of Education of School District 23, supra.

§ 11.32 One Sex Teams

Regulations under Title IX (§ 86.41) provide for operation of separate sports where selection of teams is based on "competitive skill or the activities involved is a contact sport." Where a team is offered for one sex but not for the other, members of both sexes must be allowed to try out for the team offered unless the sport involved is a contact sport. In Colorado a high school girl sued because she was denied a chance to participate on a boys' soccer team, a contact sport. A court found that denial of the girl's request violated the Equal Protection Clause even though it may not have violated Title IX. Hoover v. Meiklejohn, 430 F.Supp. 164 (D.Colo.1977). This court said that "the failure to establish any physical criteria to protect small or weak males from injurious effects of competition with larger and stronger males destroys the credibility of the reasoning urged in support of the sex classification . . . and there is no rationality in limiting this patronizing protection to females."

CHAPTER 12

CIVIL LIABILITY

§ 12.1 INTRODUCTION

One of the most frequently expressed concerns of teachers and school administrators is their potential liability. When can they be sued and, if so, what are the chances of having to pay substantial damages out of their own meager earnings. This chapter is divided into two sections: (1) common law torts and (2) constitutional torts. The first section deals with common torts, since they are of more concern to teachers.

§ 12.2 WHAT IS A TORT?

Tort is a term applied to a wide variety of civil wrongs for which a court will afford a remedy to the injured party in the form of damages. Torts are wrongs of person against person as opposed to person against the state, as in a crime. In a tort action, the injured party brings an action in law to recover compensation for damage suffered, while with a crime the state brings criminal proceedings to protect the interests of the public against the wrongdoer. A tort is to be distinguished from a breach of contract in that no special agreement exists between the parties. With a tort the person's rights are created by common law and not by the condition of a contract.

The word "tort" is a French term derived from the Latin "torquere," meaning twisted, which in English became a common synonym for "wrong." A tort may be committed by either an act or an omission to act which violates a person's right as created by law. While most are aware that to directly harm someone is deserving of damages, the more indirect nature of harm caused by an omission or failure to act creates a less discernible action. At school, the teacher and the student are placed in a special legal relationship where, if danger occurs, the teacher may, by virtue of this special relationship, be required to act to prevent harm to the student. Failure to act accordingly may result in a tort of omission.

Torts may be classified into three basic groups: (1) intentional interference, (2) strict liability, and (3) negligence. Virtually all of tort law can be divided into actions for injuries caused by intentional acts and those for negligence. Strict liability does not require a showing of "fault," but instead places the burden of damages on the actor without regard to intent or negligence. Strict liability is a developing area of tort law, but as yet has not had a great impact on teacher or school administrator liability. Therefore, the discussion here will be confined to cases of intentional interference and negligence.

§ 12.3 INTENTIONAL INTERFERENCE

Intentional torts come about as a result of voluntary action by the defendant. The defendant must intend to bring about a certain result which invades the interests of another. In schools, the most common types of intentional torts are assault and battery.

§ 12.31 Assault and Battery

Technically, a defendant may be liable if the plaintiff is placed in fear and apprehension of immediate physical contact. To hold a weapon in a threatening position, to chase in a hostile manner, or shake a fist under another's nose may all constitute assault. The key to establishing assault is the intent of the defendant and the knowledge of imminent harm by the plaintiff. No assault exists if defendant did not intend to harm the defendant; there is no such thing as negligent assault. On the other hand, there is no assault if the plaintiff is not aware of the physical threat. If a person brandishes a gun over the head of a sleeping person, there is no assault.

In order for an assault to exist, there must be an unequivocal appearance of an attempt to do some immediate physical injury to the person of another. The act must be a display of force or menace of violence of such a nature as to cause reasonable apprehension of immediate bodily harm. For example, where a man said were you not an old man I would knock you down, the court held there was no assault. There was no assault because the old man had no reason to expect immediate harm.

Therefore, the intentional tort of assault may be consummated by an act which, while not involving physical contact, places a person in immediate fear of physical attack.

While assault is apprehension, battery is the actual physical contact. Assault and battery generally go together, but it is possible for each to exist without the other. For example, if plaintiff is struck from behind and was not aware of the impending attack, battery is present, but not assault.

In a very old English case involving the meeting of two individuals in a narrow passageway, the judge explained assault and battery in this fashion. "First, the least touching of another in anger is a battery. Second, if two or more meet in a narrow passage, and without any violence or design of harm, the one touches the other gently, it will be no battery. Thirdly, if any of them use violence against the other, to force his way in a rude inordinate manner, it will be a battery; or any struggle about the passage to that degree as may do hurt will be a battery." Cole v. Turner, 6 Mod. 149 (1704).

Assault and battery in schools are most often found in actions brought against teachers for excessive punishment of pupils. As discussed elsewhere in this book, teachers and school administrators have the authority by virtue of the doctrine of *in loco parentis* to administer reasonable corporal punishment. If, though, such punishment is excessive, malicious, or in violation of school regulations, then the teacher or administrator may be subject to an assault and battery action by or on behalf of the pupil. The school's authority extends to all pupil offenses which directly affect the decorum and conduct of the school, whether on school property or not.

To be guilty of assault and battery, the teacher must not only inflict on the child immoderate chastisement, but must do so with legal malice, wicked motives or the punishment must inflict permanent injury.

The fact that a teacher administers several licks with a board fourteen to fifteen inches long, five inches wide, and one-half to two inches thick, producing reddish purple discoloration of the buttocks does not constitute excessive punishment to justify damages. LeBlanc v. Tyler, 381 So.2d 908 (La.App.1980).

This same court observed that minor bruises could be expected from a hit or a swat on the posterior and that discoloration of the skin or soreness was not sufficient to establish excessiveness to constitute assault and battery. A teacher, however, should not be misled into believing that the courts will tolerate any degree of severity.

Where a teacher took a student alone into a vacant schoolroom and claimed to have given the student a "severe shaking," bruises on the student's chest and stomach, apparently fist marks, belied the teacher's testimony and the teacher was held to be liable for battery. Thomas v. Bedford, 389 So.2d 405 (La.App. 1980).

The Supreme Court of the United States has observed that tort actions for battery of students are viable legal remedies when it can be clearly shown that a teacher exceeded bounds of propriety in punishing a child.

Technically, assault is not a very practical action for a student to bring against a teacher, since society generally assumes and accepts that teachers will on occasion frighten a child into better school performance. It is conceivable that a teacher could so intimidate or humiliate a student as to cause such mental anguish as to justify an assault action, but proof of cause and effect would be very difficult to establish.

On the other hand, the effects of physical punishment are easier to show, through photographs of the affected part of the body or by medical records; yet such evidence must clearly establish excessiveness in order to sustain an action for battery.

§ 12.32   False Imprisonment

A teacher may wonder if a student could institute an action for false imprisonment for staying after school or being confined to a certain schoolroom or space as punishment. False imprisonment is an unlawful restraint of one's physical liberty by another. A cause of action for false imprisonment must be sustained by the plaintiff's showing two things: first, that detention or restraint was against his or her will and, secondly, that the detention or restraint was unlawful.

The key word here is "unlawful." Certain persons are immune from liability because they have a special legal relationship with the person who is restrained. Judicial officers, attorneys, physicians, parents, and school teachers, generally, have such legal status. School teachers, acting *in loco parentis*, have the authority to place reasonable restraints on students' physical liberty. The word reasonable is a necessary qualifier since the teacher and even the parent could restrict a child's freedom to an extent exceeding the bounds of their special privilege. Certainly, the teacher cannot chain the child in the dark basement of the school for two days and justify such action as reasonable. To be reasonable, detention must be relatively brief, in terms of minutes or a very few hours, and such infliction must be in good faith, without malice, for the best interests of the student and/or the school. Fertich v. Michener, 111 Ind. 472, 11 N.E. 605, 14 N.E. 68 (1887). The mere fact that detention after school is an unjustified or injudicious exercise of authority on the part of the teacher does not in itself establish malice as to forego the teacher's privilege.

§ 12.4 NEGLIGENCE

The most common tort action against teachers and school administrators is negligence. Negligence torts are neither expected nor intended as opposed to the intentional tort whose result is contemplated at the time of the act. Negligence is conduct falling below a legally established standard which results in injury to another person. It is failure to exercise due care when subjecting another to a risk or danger which causes harm.

An accident is by definition unavoidable and thus does not constitute negligence, but in many instances what first appears to be an accident may be traced to someone's negligent act. Children are well known for their accident propensities and courts are well aware of this, yet teachers must be on constant guard to prevent avoidable injuries to students. Where an injury could have been prevented by a teacher or an administrator, what may appear to be an accident becomes the tort of negligence.

§ 12.41 Standard of Conduct

That which is negligence in one circumstance may not be in another. No definite result can be predicted in an action for negligence. Each case must stand on its own set of facts as applied to a rule of law. The basic rule, which is the key to negligence, is the standard of conduct of the defendant. The appropriate standard of conduct is determined by a balancing of the risks, in light of the social value of the threatened interest, and the probability and extent of harm, against the value of the interest which the actor is required to protect. *Restatement of Torts*, pp. 291–293.

This balance between the threatened harm and the utility of the actor's conduct is not, in most cases, easy to determine. In attempting better definition, the courts have developed the reasonableness theory requiring that for negligence to exist injury must have occurred from the exposure of another to "unreasonable risk". The reasonableness test has been personified in the "reasonable person."

§ 12.42   The Reasonable Person

The reasonable person is hypothetical, a community ideal of human behavior, whose conduct under the same or similar circumstances is regarded as the measure of reasonable behavior, "a fictitious person who never has existed on land or sea." William L. Prosser, *Law of Torts*, West Publishing Company, 1955, p. 124.

The reasonable person has been portrayed by different courts as a prudent person, a person of average prudence, a person of ordinary sense using ordinary care and skill, and as a reasonably prudent person. He or she is an ideal, a model of conduct and a community standard. The nature of the reasonable person, although a community ideal, varies in every case. His or her characteristics are (1) the physical attributes of the defendant, (2) normal intelligence, (3) normal perception and memory with a minimum level of information and experience common to the community, and (4) such superior skill and knowledge as the actor has or holds himself or herself out as having. As can be seen, the reasonable person formula changes with different factual situations because of the attributes or deficiencies of the defendant and because of peculiarities of beliefs, values, and customs of the individual community.

The reasonable person then has the same physical characteristics as the actor himself and the acts in question are measured accordingly. Correspondingly, the man who is crippled is not held to the same standard as the man with no physical infirmities. The courts have also made allowances for the weaknesses or attributes connected with the sex and age of the individual. The courts have not, however, been so lenient with individuals who have mental deficiencies. The courts have traditionally held that a person with less mental ability than an average person must adjust and conform to the rules of society. Where a person is actually insane, a more convincing argument can be made for allowing for the particular incapacity.

§ 12.43　A Reasonably Prudent Teacher

Teachers are specially educated and trained to teach and work with children and young adults. Teachers hold college degrees and are certified in educational methodologies. As such, teachers hold themselves out to the public as possessing superior skills and understanding of educational processes. By virtue of these attributes teachers may be held to a higher standard of conduct than the ordinary person on the street. The teacher's required conduct may be that of a reasonably prudent teacher in the same or similar circumstances rather than the lesser standard of merely a reasonably prudent person.

Too, the teacher has the additional burden of standing *in loco parentis*; a Vermont court has said that a teacher's "relationship to the pupils under his care and custody differs from that generally existing between a public employee and a member of the general public. In a limited sense the teacher stands in the parents' place in his relationship to a pupil . . . and has such a portion of the powers of the parent over the pupil as is necessary to carry out his employment. In such relationship, he owes his pupils the duty of supervision . . .." Eastman v. Williams, 124 Vt. 445, 207 A.2d 146 (1965).

This is the view which is apparently taken by most courts. Some, though, hold that a teacher should not have to bear this additional burden and charge the teacher with merely reasonable prudende of any normal person.

§ 12.5   ELEMENTS OF NEGLIGENCE

To better understand the true nature of negligence, it is necessary to break down into its component parts. These are (1) A duty on the part of the actor to protect others against unreasonable risks; (2) A failure on the part of the actor to exercise a standard of care commensurate with the risks involved; (3) The conduct of the actor must be the proximate cause or legal cause of the injury. A causal connection must exist between the act and the resulting injury; (4) Injury, actual loss, or damage must result from the act.

§ 12.51   Duty

A person has a duty to abide by a standard of reasonable conduct in the face of apparent risks. The courts generally hold that no duty exists where the defendant could not have reasonably foreseen the danger of risk involved. A duty owed by one person to another intensifies as the risk increases. In other words, the duty to protect another is proportional to the risk or hazard of a particular activity. In school functions, where risks are greater to school children, a teacher has an increased level of obligation or duty to the children. For example, whenever a teacher has children perform a dangerous laboratory experiment, he or she has a greater obligation for the childrens' safety than where he or she is merely supervising a study hall. One judge has explained the duty requirement in this way. "Every person is negligent when, without intending any wrong, he does such an act or omits to take such a precaution that under the circumstances he, as an ordinary prudent person, ought reasonably to foresee that he will thereby expose the interest of another to an unreasonable risk of harm. In determining whether his conduct will subject the interest of another to an unreasonable risk of harm, a person is required to take into account such of the surrounding circumstances as would be taken into account by a reasonably prudent person and possess such knowledge as is possessed by an ordinary reasonable person and to use such judgment and discretion as is exercised by persons of reasonable intelligence under the same of similar circumstance." Osborne v. Montgomery, 203 Wisc. 223, 234 N.W. 372 (1931).

A person is negligent when by affirmative act he injures another. However, the question often arises as to whether a person can be liable for failure to act at all. Generally the law holds that a person is not liable for an omission to act where there is no definite relationship between the parties. In other words, no general duty exists to aid a person in danger. For example, even though there is a moral duty, no legal duty exists for a bystander to aid a drowning person.

Where teachers and students are concerned, however, the situation is quite different. The greater duty of the teacher invested by the *in loco parentis* standard compels the teacher to take affirmative actions to protect students. Thus, teachers may be liable for omission to act as well as for negligent affirmative acts.

A teacher though is only required to do that which is reasonable to protect the student. For example, a female teacher's actions have been upheld as reasonable when she left the classroom to summon the principal and vice-principal from their nearby offices when a large boy menacingly entered her classroom intent on beating and ultimately injuring another student. Kim v. State, 62 Hawaii 483, 616 P.2d 1376 (1980).

§ 12.52 Standard of Care

A standard of care must be exercised commensurate with the duty owed. A legally recognized duty or obligation requires the actor to conform to a certain standard of care as the foreseeable risk involved in an act increases. The standard of care of auto mechanics shop teachers for protection of youngsters is generally greater than that of the school librarian. This is, of course, true because the risk of injury involved in handling power tools, machinery, and electrical equipment is much greater than the risk of being injured while reading a book.

The standard of care which a teacher owes a student assumes an extra duty to keep the children secure from injury. Teachers have a "special responsibility recognized by common law to supervise their charges." Miller v. Griesel, 261 Ind. 604, 308 N.E.2d 701 (1974). It is further well settled that the amount of care which the teacher owes the student increases or decreases with the relative maturity or immaturity of the student. One court has commented that even with students of seventeen or eighteen years of age, a teacher's care must be quite high, particularly where students are in groups "where the herd instinct and competitive spirit tend naturally to relax vigilance." Satarino v. Sleight, 54 Cal.App.2d 278, 129 P.2d 35 (1942).

While standards of care may differ among teachers, differences may also be found among other persons in society. Children and aged persons have generally been given substantially more leeway in their activities than is allowed a normal adult. While both children and aged persons are liable for their torts, they are not held to the same standard as are others without impairments of age. While it is difficult to pinpoint precise standards to determine the reasonableness of a child because of the great variations in age, maturity and capacity, the courts nevertheless have established a rough standard as a guideline. This subjective test for negligence in children is what it is reasonable to expect of children of like age, intelligence, and experience. As the age, intelligence, and experience of the child increases, a commensurate increase in the standard of care is required of the child. A child is generally held to a standard of care of a reasonable child of the same age, intelligence, and experience in the same or similar circumstances.

Some courts have established an arbitrary cutoff age below which a child cannot be held liable for tort. Authorities generally agree though that such arbitrary limits are not the best standard. No one can deny that, under certain circumstances, a child of six or even five years could conceivably be guilty of negligence. Some courts have said that the rule providing for a specific age cutoff, usually at six or seven years of age, is arbitrary and open to objection because one day's difference in age surely cannot determine whether a child is capable of negligence.

At any rate, children of school age are almost always capable of negligence. Thus, each child at school, as well as the teachers and administrators, may be negligent if their standard of conduct falls below that of a reasonably prudent person, of their age, physical attributes and knowledge, in the same or similar circumstances.

§ 12.53   Proximate or Legal Cause

"Proximate cause" or "legal cause" is the sequential connection between the actor's negligent conduct and the resultant injury to another person. The *Restatement of Torts* explains the necessity of adequate causal relation in this way: "In order that a negligent actor shall be liable for another's harm, it is necessary not only that the actor's conduct be negligent toward the other, but also that the negligence of the actor be a legal cause of the other's harm."

In order for proximate or legal cause to exist, there must first be a duty or obligation on the part of the actor to maintain a reasonable standard of care. In such cases the courts require that the defendant's conduct be the legal or proximate cause of the injury. In most negligence cases, however, the courts will not refer to proximate cause but will rely solely on the duty or obligation of the defendant and the standard of conduct required to avoid liability. Proximate cause as a criterion of liability has been used most often where some doubt is present as to whether the injured person was within the zone of obvious danger.

Courts require that the negligence of the defendant must be the "substantial" cause of the harm to the plaintiff—substantial enough to lead reasonable men to conclude the act is indeed the cause of injury. There must be an unbroken chain between the act and the resulting injury. If the negligence is not a substantial factor in producing the harm, then there is no liability.

The actor's negligent act must be in continuous and active force up to the actual harm, and the lapse of time must not be so great that contributing causes and intervening factors render the original negligent act to be an insubstantial or insignificant force in the harm.

Therefore, a teacher may be relieved of liability where an intervening act results in a pupil's injury. In a case illustrating this point, a teacher went home after school leaving three young boys unsupervised in her classroom. The student found a small knife left in the unlocked teacher's desk drawer and one student was cut rather severely. The teacher's leaving the boys alone in the room was adjudged not to be the proximate cause of the injury. Richard v. St. Landry Parish School Board, 344 So.2d 1116 (La.App.1977).

Proximate cause tends to overlap with the question of duty and serve in some cases as a corollary to an intervening act. Courts will sometimes say that an act is not the proximate cause of injury when what they mean is that the defendant is not negligent in the first place. Or, a court may say that an act was not the proximate cause of injury when, in fact, it meant that another's act intervened to cause the injury. Prosser has noted the elusive nature of proximate cause, thusly: " 'Proximate cause' . . . has been all things to all men. Having no integrated meaning of its own, its chameleon quality permits it to be substituted for any one of the elements of a negligence case when decision on that element becomes difficult. . . ." Prosser, § 42.

§ 12.54   Injury or Actual Loss

A defendant is not liable for injury unless he has, in fact, caused the injury. Similarly, a defendant is not liable for damages unless the plaintiff shows that he has actually suffered an injury or can show actual loss or damages resulting from the act. Nominal damages cannot be obtained where no actual loss can be shown or has occurred.

Damages for an injury may be assessed against one or more persons. If the harm suffered was caused by more than one person, then damages may be apportioned among the feasors. Also, if more than one harm is present and the harms and damages can be distinguished, there will be apportionment among the defendants.

§ 12.6　DEFENSES FOR NEGLIGENCE

Teachers or school administrators may employ one or more of several defenses if an action is brought against them in tort. In all cases involving negligence, the defendant may seek to show that the plaintiff's injury was caused by mere accident and not by anyone's fault. It may be to show, too, that no duty was owed or that there was an intervening act which broke the causal chain between the act and the injury. Or, it may be maintained that the plaintiff simply could not foresee the injurious result. These, though, are not strictly speaking defenses, but instead are elements of the tort which the plaintiff must establish in order to have a case. Assuming that the duty, foreseeability, and so forth are established by plaintiff, then defendant must respond with what are classically known as tort defenses; they are: (1) contributory negligence, (2) last clear chance, (3) comparative negligence, (4) assumption of risk, (5) act of God, and (6) immunity. Of these, contributory negligence and assumption of risk are most common in school cases where the teacher is the defendant.

§ 12.61   Contributory Negligence

Contributory negligence involves some fault or breach of duty on the part of the injured person, or failure on his or her part to exercise the required standard of care for his or her own safety. The injured party through personal negligence and fault contributes to his injury. In other words, contributory negligence is conduct on the part of the injured party which caused or contributed to the injury and which would have been done by a person exercising ordinary prudence under the circumstance. This is sometimes referred to as the "all or nothing" rule meaning that if the plaintiff is shown to be negligent at all, then defendant is completely absolved from liability. The *Restatement of Torts* defines contributory negligence as ". . . conduct on the part of the plaintiff which falls below the standard to which he should conform for his own protection, and which is legally contributing cause co-operating with the negligence of the defendant in bringing about the plaintiff's harm."

As previously pointed out, a child is capable of negligence and his failure to conform to a required standard of conduct for a child of his age, physical characteristics, sex, and training will result in the court assigning fault to his actions. If an injured child is negligent and his or her negligence contributes to the harm, then a defendant teacher, who is also negligent, may be absolved from liability.

However, since a child is not expected to perform with the same standard of care as an adult, teachers have more difficulty in showing contributory negligence than if the plaintiff were an adult. A child is by nature careless and often negligent, and knowing this, a teacher should allow for an additional margin of safety when dealing with students. This is especially true with younger children. Contributory negligence is much less reliable as a defense when dealing with children than it is with adults. In fact, courts have said that where a child is concerned, the test to be employed is whether the child has committed a gross disregard of safety in the face of known, perceived, and understood dangers.

In older cases, if a plaintiff's negligence or fault contributed to his or her injury, the court will bar recovery of any damages at all. This rule, which prevents recovery no matter how "slight" the plaintiff's negligence, has more recently been almost entirely abandoned by the "substantial factor" rule. That is, plaintiff's negligence must be a substantial factor in causing his or her own injury or defendant will be liable anyway. Some courts have, too, held that complete barring of any damages because of contributory fault is perhaps a little drastic and have, therefore, endeavored to prorate damages based on degree of fault. This results in what is known as damages for comparative negligence, which is discussed below.

§ 12.62 Last Clear Chance

The doctrine of "last clear chance" is sometimes discussed under the heading of and as a part of contributory negligence. It amounts to a defense for plaintiff against a countercharge of contributory negligence by defendant. What the doctrine of "last clear chance" does, in effect, is shift the fault or legal cause of an injury from a contributorily negligent plaintiff back to the negligent defendant. If the defendant has a "last clear chance" to avoid the harm and does not, then the plaintiff's negligence is not the legal cause of the result. Therefore, the "last clear chance" concept can probably best be explained as a counterattack against the defense of contributory negligence. As such, then, it cannot be classified as a defense for the defendant, but as a device which may be used by the plaintiff in overcoming the defense of contributory negligence.

Most courts will allow the use of the "last clear chance" doctrine where the plaintiff is either helpless or inattentive and the defendant discovers the peril in time to avoid it but does not. Last clear chance was apparently first used in 1842 where the plaintiff left his ass tied in the roadway and the defendant drove a wagon into it. The court pointed out that the plaintiff could recover, notwithstanding his own negligence, if he could show that the defendant had a last clear chance to avoid injuring the animal. Prosser says that as a result of this case, the last clear chance rule is sometimes referred to as the " 'jackass doctrine' with whatever implications that nickname may carry." Davies v. Mann, 152 Eng.Rep. 588 (Exch.1842).

Although the use of this doctrine is not common in tort cases involving teachers, its applicability is easily seen. For example, where a child is injured and both he and the teacher are negligent, the child may well claim that the sequence of events leading to the accident gave the teacher a superior opportunity or a last clear chance to avoid the harm to him.

Courts, basically, take two variables into account: (1) the nature of plaintiff's circumstance and (2) the alertness or attentiveness of the defendant. Last clear chance, though, is not readily applicable to the school setting where the teacher has a relatively high duty to protect the student. Courts will generally assume that children are most times inattentive and that teachers are expected to be observant. As such, the higher duty would probably make the teacher liable even though the "last clear chance" doctrine could conceivably apply, as well.

§ 12.63 Comparative Negligence

As previously pointed out, where contributory negligence on the part of the plaintiff is shown, the defendant is often absolved from any liability at all. This, some courts and legislatures have felt, works a hardship on the negligent plaintiff who suffers injury but can recover nothing from the negligent defendant. This concern for the injured party has led legislatures in some states to enact statutes to determine degrees of negligence and allow recovery based on the relative degree of fault. While the specific provisions of "comparative negligence" statutes vary from state to state, the concept works this way: If the plaintiff's fault is found to be about equal to the defendant's, then the plaintiff will recover one-half the damages and must bear the remainder of the loss himself. If the plaintiff's negligence amounted to one-third the fault and the defendant's two-thirds, then the plaintiff could recover two-thirds of the damages. In all states with "comparative negligence" statutes, the idea is carried forth that the plaintiff, even though he is partly to blame for his own harm, will not be totally barred from recovery. Today, over one-half the states have adopted comparative negligence in some form.

In some instances courts have not waited for legislatures to shift from contributory to comparative negligence. For example, the Florida Supreme Court in 1973 decided that it was within the province of judicial authority to make the change. In so doing the court said: "Whatever may have been the historical justification for it [contributory negligence], today it is almost universally regarded as unjust and inequitable to vest an entire accidental loss on one of the parties whose negligent conduct combined with the negligence of the other party to produce the loss." Hoffman v. Jones, 280 So.2d 431 (Fla.1973).

Where the comparative negligence standard has been adopted, last clear chance, of course, no longer has application.

§ 12.64 Assumption of Risk

Another defense against negligence is assumption of risk which, if pleaded and proved by the defendant, will absolve defendant's liability. The theory here is that the plaintiff in some manner consents to relieve the defendant of his duty or obligation of conduct. In other words, the plaintiff by expressed or implied agreement assumes the risk of the danger and thereby relieves the defendant of responsibility. The defendant is simply not under any legal duty to protect the plaintiff from normal risks. The plaintiff with knowledge of the danger voluntarily enters into a relationship with the defendant, and by so doing agrees to take his own chances.

Important to this defense is the plaintiff's knowledge and awareness of the danger. Basically, assumption of risk is plaintiff's voluntary consent to encounter a known danger. Unlike contributory negligence, which requires only unreasonable conduct on part of plaintiff, assumption of risk requires voluntary consent or a showing that plaintiff's state of mind was such that the danger was known to him. For example, a boy playing basketball was injured when his arm went through a glass pane in a door immediately behind the basketball backboard. The court later said that the boy had not assumed the risk of such an injury because the boy did not know the glass in the door was not shatterproof. Stevens v. Central School District No. 1, 25 A.D.2d 871, 270 N.Y.S.2d 23 (1966). However, another court held that a boy had assumed the risk when he suffered an injury by colliding with a doorjamb in a brick wall while playing as a voluntary member of a team in a school gymnasium. The boy had played in the gym previously and knew the location of the basket, the door, and the wall and, therefore, was aware of the danger involved in voluntarily playing in this particular gymnasium. Maltz v. Board of Education of New York City, 32 Misc.2d 492, 114 N.Y.S.2d 856 (1952).

The courts have generally established that the participant in athletic events, whether intramural or interscholastic, assumes the risk of the normal hazards of the game when he participates. This also applies to spectators attending sports or amusement activities. Spectators assume all the obvious or normal risks of being hurt by flying balls, fireworks explosions, or the struggles of combatants.

Essential to the doctrine of assumption of risk is that the plaintiff have knowledge of the risks; if he or she is ignorant of the conditions and dangers, then risk is not assumed. If plaintiff does not take reasonable precautions to determine the hazards involved, the risk is not assumed, and contributory negligence may be present instead. However, neither a participant nor a spectator assumes the risk for negligence or willful or wanton conduct of others. For example, a spectator at an athletic contest does not assume the risk of the stands falling down at a football game nor is risk assumed by attending a baseball game, where a player intentionally throws a bat into the stands and injures a spectator. Only those hazards or risks normally associated with the activity are assumed.

§ 12.65 Act of God

Man cannot, of course, be held responsible for injuries caused by natural elements or acts of God. No liability will ensue if the injury caused to a student is the result of a tornado, lightning, earthquake, volcano, etc. One should be very sure, however, that sufficient precautions are taken to protect students if natural calamities are foreseen. Slippery roads due to snowfall may result in school bus wrecks, thus, school officials should exercise reasonable care in judging whether school should be held when road conditions are bad.

When games or practices are conducted out-of-doors, coaches should be especially cognizant of weather conditions, such as thunderstorms. A coach is not normally liable if a child is struck by an unexpected burst of lightning, but liability may well accrue if the weather conditions are ignored and students are allowed to continue to play when lightning strikes repeatedly in the vicinity.

§ 12.66 Immunity

Immunity from tort liability is used in different contexts. Immunity is generally conferred on (1) national and state governments unless abrogated by statute, (2) public officials performing judicial, quasi-judicial, or discretionary functions, (3) charitable organizations granted immunity in some states, (4) infants under certain conditions, and (5) in some cases, insane persons.

Where public schools are concerned, the defense of immunity is usually employed to protect the public school district against liability. Governmental or sovereign immunity is a historical and common law precedent which protects a state agency against liability for its torts.

Teachers and other individuals are liable for their torts; in most states, however, school districts are not subject to liability for an action in tort.

A general rule of law is that government is immune from tort liability unless the legislature or the courts specifically abrogate the immunity. In other words, common law theory maintains that government cannot be sued without its consent. A school district is an arm of the state and as such has immunity. The doctrine of governmental immunity originated with the idea that "the King can do no wrong" and manifests itself today in the sovereign immunity of government in general.

Legal historians claim that sovereign immunity, as it applied to torts of the King, did not become common law until the sixteenth century. At that time, it was maintained that the King was not liable for his torts or for the torts of his ministers. Most agree that the transition was made from "the King can do no wrong" to "the government can do no wrong" in 1788 in the case of Russell v. The Men Dwelling in the County of Devon, 100 Eng.Rep. 359 (1788).

Governmental immunity with all its inherent faults evidently crossed the ocean to Massachusetts and became American law in 1812 in the case of Mower v. The Inhabitants of Leicester, 9 Mass. 237 (1812).

Courts in the United States which have sustained the immunity principle with regard to school districts have relied primarily on five criteria: (1) school districts have only those powers granted by the legislature; if the legislature has not given the school district authority to be sued in tort, then it is beyond the district's legal powers; (2) payment of tort claims is an illegal expenditure of public funds since the public receives no benefit; (3) abolition of immunity would cause a multiplicity of cases putting a financial burden on the school; (4) the doctrine of *respondeat superior*, where the master is liable for acts of his servant, does not apply to public school districts, and (5) immunity must be abolished by the legislature, not the courts.

The doctrine of governmental immunity has been severely criticized by many courts. The leading case attacking the concept is an Illinois case where a pupil was injured in a school bus accident and sued the school district. Molitor v. Kaneland Community Unit District No. 302, 18 Ill.2d 11, 163 N.E.2d 89 (1959). School districts in Illinois had prior to the case been immune from liability. The court in a sweeping opinion abrogated immunity in Illinois and, thereby, set in motion a trend toward abrogation which has been followed by about one-half the states.

In *Molitor*, the court said: "The whole doctrine of governmental immunity from liability for tort rests upon a rotten foundation. It is almost incredible that in this modern age of comparative sociological enlightenment, and, in a republic the medieval absolutism supposed to be implicit in the maxim, 'the King can do no wrong,' should exempt the various branches of the government from liability for their torts, and that the entire burden of damage resulting from the wrongful acts of the government should be imposed upon the single individual who suffers the injury, rather than distributed among the entire community constituting the government, where it could be borne without hardship upon any individual, and where it justly belongs."

§ 12.7 SAVE HARMLESS LAWS

This view has been slowly adopted by several state legislatures as well as by the courts. In Florida, for example, the state legislature abolished immunity of school districts and municipalities and, secondarily, enacted a save harmless provision which protects teachers and other school and governmental employees against liability up to a specified limit of damages.

Certain other states along with Florida have enacted save harmless laws; these include Connecticut, Iowa, Massachusetts, New Jersey, Oregon, New York, and Wyoming. The wording of the New York statute is typical; it reads in part: ". . . it should be the duty of each board of education, trustee or trustees

. . ., to save harmless and protect all teachers, practice or cadet teachers, and members of supervisory and administrative staff or employees from financial loss arising out of any claim, demand, suit, or judgment by reason of alleged negligence or other act resulting in accidental bodily injury to any person within or without the school building, provided such teacher, practice or cadet teacher, or member of the supervisory or administrative staff or employee, at the time of the accident or injury was acting in the discharge of his duties within the scope of his employment. . . ."

Such provisions are tantamount to liability insurance policies against personal liability of teachers, administrators and others, including student teachers, so long as they are acting within the scope of their employment. Where the amount of damages which a school district is authorized to pay is limited by statute, as it is in Florida at $100,000, then the teacher or other school employee is well advised to supplement the state efforts by obtaining personal liability insurance. This is particularly true where the teaching takes place in high risk areas such as shops, chemistry classes, physical education or coaching activities. Of course, in those states which have not abrogated immunity nor have a save harmless law, the entire burden of an action in tort rests on the shoulders of the teacher, administrator, or other employee, personally.

§ 12.8 CONSTITUTIONAL TORTS

Although the foundation of constitutional torts is grounded in the Civil Rights Act of 1871, codified as

Title 42 of the United States Code, Section 1983, the majority of litigation is of recent origin. The basic concept extends personal liability to public officials who violate the statutory or constitutional rights of an individual, such as a student or teacher.

The statute was enacted during the Reconstruction Era after the Civil War to protect the rights of blacks and was commonly referred to as the Ku Klux Act. In March of 1871, President Grant sent a message to Congress requesting they use their power under the Fourteenth Amendment to pass legislation to protect individuals from state officials who were abusing their power and violating the natural rights of those individuals. The President further pleaded that legislation was needed to protect the life, liberty, and property and enforcement of laws at all levels of government. Congress responded by passing the 1871 Civil Rights Act which states: "Every person who, under color of any statute, ordinance, regulation, custom, or usage, of any State or Territory, subjects, or causes to be subjected, any citizen of the United States or other person within the jurisdiction thereof to the deprivation of any rights, privileges or immunities secured by the Constitution and laws, shall be liable to the party injured in an action at, law, sent in equity, or other proper proceeding for redress." 42 U.S.C.A. § 1983.

This statute was the subject of very little litigation from the time of passage until the 1960s. With the expansion of the civil rights movement, this Act was used as a weapon to hold state officials personally liable if they violated the rights of another.

§ 12.81 Definition of Person

The Act provides that liability shall be for "every person" who infringes on the rights of another. Plaintiffs attempted to have "person" interpreted to mean an institution as well as an individual. Since an institution has more fiscal resources than the individual, greater resources would be available to pay damages. In Monroe v. Pape, 365 U.S. 167, 81 S.Ct. 473 (1961), the Supreme Court determined policemen were personally liable as individuals, but the City of Chicago was not a person and, therefore, was not liable. Some seventeen years later in Monell v. New York City Department of Social Services, 436 U.S. 658, 98 S.Ct. 2018 (1978), the Supreme Court overturned *Monroe* and declared the word "person" included local government or institution.

§ 12.82 Absolute Immunity

The Supreme Court, in a series of cases, determined that absolute immunity was available as a defense for prosecutors in initiating and presenting the state's case, Imbler v. Pachtman, 424 U.S. 409, 96 S.Ct. 984 (1976), and state legislators. Tenney v. Brandhove, 341 U.S. 367, 71 S.Ct. 783 (1951).

§ 12.83 Qualified or Conditional Immunity

Prosecutors and legislators have absolute immunity; therefore, it may appear other state officials have absolute immunity. But in Scheuer v. Rhodes, 416 U.S. 232, 94 S.Ct. 1683 (1974), the Supreme Court declared the Governor of Ohio and other state officials have only qualified or conditional immunity. Qualified or conditional immunity from civil liability means individuals would not be liable as long as they are acting clearly within the scope of their authority for the betterment of those they serve. If they venture outside the scope of their authority, and, in doing so, violate someone's rights, then they may be personally liable. Qualified immunity has been established by Supreme Court decision for superintendents of state hospitals, O'Connor v. Donaldson, 422 U.S. 563, 95 S.Ct. 2486 (1975), and for local school board members. Wood v. Strickland, 420 U.S. 308, 95 S.Ct. 992 (1975).

§ 12.84   Good Faith Immunity

Although individuals may assert good faith as a defense in a constitutional tort action, a municipality has no immunity and may not assert a good faith defense. Owen v. City of Independence, 445 U.S. 622, 100 S.Ct. 1398 (1980).

§ 12.85   Actual and Punitive Damages

Generally, actual damages will be allowed and not punitive damages. The Supreme Court ". . . had indicated that punitive damages might be awarded in appropriate circumstances in order to punish violations of constitutional rights . . ." Carey v. Piphus, 435 U.S. 247, 98 S.Ct. 1042 (1978). ". . . but it never suggested that punishment is as prominent a purpose under the statute as are compensation and deterrence." City of Newport v. Fact Concerts, Inc., 453 U.S. 247, 101 S.Ct. 2748 (1981).

CHAPTER 13

STUDENT RECORDS, DEFAMATION, AND PRIVACY

§ 13.1 INTRODUCTION

By the very nature of the educational process, educators are constantly dealing in sensitive matters involving students' private and personal affairs. Schools routinely collect and process information about students which can materially affect their future life and prosperity. Personal information which is carelessly released may well attach a stigma to a student's image in the community or establish an educational black mark which will detract from the student's success in both future educational and business pursuits. The incorrect recording of a grade or idle gossip in inappropriate places can permanently cast a very damaging shadow over one's reputation.

The law protects the student in three ways. First, school districts are required to handle and process student records in a careful and prescribed manner by federal statute, failure of which can result in the loss of federal funds. A number of states have statutes mandating procedures in protecting the student's right of privacy. Second, it allows the student protection through judicial precedents which form the law of defamation. Third, the student has a right of privacy protected by the common law right against invasion of privacy.

§ 13.2   BUCKLEY AMENDMENT

The Family Educational Rights and Privacy Act of 1974, more popularly known as the Buckley Amendment (see Appendix B), prescribes standards for schools to follow in handling student records. 20 U.S.C.A. § 1232g (Cum.Supp.1976). Parents are given the right to inspect all records that schools maintain on their children and are extended the opportunity to challenge the accuracy of the records. Parents must consent before the school can release the student's records to agencies outside designated educational categories. Consent may also be given by the student, in lieu of the parent, to release his or her own records upon the attainment of age eighteen or upon entry to postsecondary school. School districts which do not follow the procedures required risk losing federal funds administered by the United States Department of Education.

§ 13.21   Pre-Buckley

Before the Buckley Amendment, twenty-four states had statutes which gave parents or students access to records kept by the school. Only five of these states explicitly granted the right to challenge, correct, or expunge faulty information in the student files. See: Katherine Cudlipp, "The Family Educational Rights and Privacy Act Two Years Later," University of Richmond Law Review, Vol. 11, No. 1, Fall 1976, pp. 33–49.

Generally, prior to 1974, it was difficult for students to obtain access to their records. This was true, in spite of the fact that some courts had held that parents had a right of access to records unless such access was detrimental to the public interest. This right was assured by a New York court in 1961 when it ruled that "absent constitutional, legislative, or administrative permission or prohibition, a parent had the right to inspect the records of his child maintained by school authorities as required by law." Van Allen v. McCleary, 27 Misc.2d 81, 211 N.Y.S.2d 501 (1961). This court's rationale was based on the common law rule that a person with an interest in public records is entitled to inspect them.

Too, as far back as 1961, a federal district court in Alabama recognized that in dismissal cases students had a due process right of access to school records and to challenge errors and inaccuracies in them. Dixon v. Alabama State Board of Education, 294 F.2d 150 (5th Cir. 1961). Following *Dixon* other due process cases established requirements for access to student records. In *Mills*, the famous handicap case, the court clearly stated that the parents had a right to "examine the child's records before the hearing, including any texts or reports upon which the proposed action may be based." Mills v. Board of Education, 348 F.Supp. 866 (D.D.C.1972).

In other cases where parents sought to remove or suppress information in the student files or to prevent its conveyance to third parties, the precedent is not clearly on the side of the parents or the school. In one case where a school sought to send a letter to a college describing an incident in which a student had worn an armband to graduation, ignoring school authorities' request to remove it, the court held for the school saying: "School officials have the right and, we think, a duty to record and to communicate true factual information about their students to institutions of higher learning, for the purpose of giving to the latter an accurate and complete picture of applicants for admission." Einhorn v. Maus, 300 F.Supp. 1169 (E.D.Pa. 1969).

In other cases students were upheld in their attempts to have items removed from their records or communicated to third parties. In each instance, however, it required litigation to obtain redress for the parent or the student and school districts who were without knowledge of the law or other guidelines on which they could rely. Districts tended to devise their own inhouse rules which generally suited the ethical perceptions of the individual teachers or administrators who were in charge. The Buckley Amendment introduced a required uniformity to the handling of student records from district to district and with and among colleges and universities.

§ 13.22　Requirements of the Act

At the outset, the Act requires that each educational agency or institution establish procedures for granting access to student records within a reasonable period of time after the parental request. The reasonable period of time cannot exceed forty-five days. The Act provides that "directory" information, such as the student's name, address, telephone, date and place of birth, major field of study, participation in activities and sports, weight and height of members of athletic teams, dates of attendance, degrees and awards and most recent educational institution attended by the student, may be released by the school district without written consent of the parent. Nor is parental consent required for release of education records (1) to other school officials and/or teachers in the school system who have legitimate educational interests, (2) officials of other schools or school systems in which the student seeks to enroll upon the condition that the student's parents are notified of the transfer of records is given a copy, and has an opportunity to challenge the record, (3) to authorized representatives of government including state education authorities, (4) in connection with a student's application for, or receipt of, financial aid, (5) to state and local officials collecting information required by state statutes adopted before November 19, 1974, (6) to organizations conducting studies for, or on behalf of, educational agencies if personal identification of students is destroyed after no longer needed for the study, (7) accrediting organizations, (8) parents of a dependent student as defined by statute, and (9) to regulations of the Secretary of Education pertaining to health or welfare of the student or other persons.

Beyond these exceptions no personally identifiable information can be released, other than directory information, without written consent of the parent specifying the records to be released. Schools may, of course, respond to subpoenas issued by the courts for information, but must notify parents of all such occurrences.

As a broad extension of parents' rights, the law further provides that all institutional material, including teacher's manuals, films, tapes, or other supplementary instructional material used in connection with any research or experimentation program or project must be available for inspection by parents or guardians of the children engaged in the research.

The Act, then, defines the types of information, designates those who can receive information without parent permission, requires regulation allowing parent access to records, and gives the parent an opportunity to correct or expunge improper information, upon request and through a hearing process.

§ 13.23 Posting of Grades

At one time it was a common practice to post student grades on the school door or to list them in confidential ways. Today the Buckley Amendment has affected such practices. In a recent case where a parent sought to compel a board of education to release all student grades in a third-grade class containing seventy-five students, the court held that disclosure of tests scores if scrambled and with names deleted would protect the privacy of students as required under the Buckley Amendment. The parent wanted to compare scores and was not interested in their being in any particular order. Relying on this type of interpretation, it appears that teachers and school officials can continue to post grades so long as they are not individually identifiable. Kryston v. Board of Education, East Ramapo, etc., 77 A.D.2d 896, 430 N.Y.S.2d 688 (1980).

In this particular instance, a conflict was created between the parent's right to view public records under a Freedom of Information Law and the Buckley

Amendment. A public records act requires school districts to release public information, while the Buckley Amendment requires school districts to keep individual, personal student information private except upon request of the student's parent. This conflict is resolved in the definition of what is public as opposed to that which is private and personal. According to the *Kryston* decision, information which is not personally identifiable may be subject to release under public records acts.

§ 13.3   DEFAMATION

Anyone, a teacher, administrator, parent, or student, is capable of incurring liability by defaming other persons. Words are defamatory if they impute that another is guilty of dishonesty, immorality vice or dishonorable conduct which engenders an evil opinion of one in the minds of others in community. Defamation is generally understood to be injury by calumny or by false aspersion of another's reputation. Defamation is anything which tends to injure one's character or reputation.

The distinction between "criticism" and "defamation" is that criticism is addressed to public matters and does not follow a person into his or her private life. A true critic never indulges in personal ridicule but confines his or her comments to the merits of the particular subject matter under discussion.

Defamation is not a legal cause of action but encompasses the twin tort actions of libel and slander. Libel is written defamation while slander is spoken. Speaking defamatory words to a newspaper reporter may ultimately involve both slander and libel if the speaker intends his words to "be embodied forthwith in a physical form" and the words do, in fact, appear in a newspaper article. Tallent v. Blake, 57 N.C.App. 249, 291 S.E.2d 336 (1982).

§ 13.31   Libel

Libel is an accusation in writing or printing against the character of a person which affects his or her reputation and tends to hold him or her up to shame or disgrace. Stevens v. Wright, 107 Vt. 337, 179 A. 213 (1935). Libel must be false, unprivileged, and malicious to be actionable. Publication is required for libel to exist. This does not mean publication in the mass media, but may be constituted by written communication which tends to harm one's reputation in the community. A note written to a third party or a secretary typing and reading a letter may constitute publication.

Communication sufficient to establish libel may be conveyed by sign, mark, movie reel, video tape, picture, or effigy. The communication may be actionable if it holds a person up to ridicule, contempt, disgrace, obloquy, or shame in the eyes of the community.

§ 13.32   Slander

Slander is the speaking of base and defamatory words tending to create an unfavorable impression in the mind of a third party. To constitute slander there must be conveyance by words of disparagement of character of one to a third party. Plaintiff must show that there was a third party communication. Words spoken only to the offended party cannot constitute slander. If a third party overhears defamatory words, slander may be established.

There are two types of slander, slander *per se* and slander *per quod*. With slander *per se*, the plaintiff's cause of action is complete when he or she proves that the defamation has been articulated and that he or she has suffered "actual injury." In showing "actual injury," the plaintiff is not required to show out-of-pocket monetary loss but can show impairment of reputation and standing in the community, personal humiliation, and mental anguish and suffering. If "actual injury" can be shown in establishing slander *per se*, then the plaintiff can recover damages without pleading or proving that he suffered special harm or showing direct loss.

Under American common law today an action for slander *per se* will lie without proof of special harm (damage) where (1) words impute (a) a criminal offense punishable by imprisonment or (b) plaintiff is guilty of crime involving moral turpitude; (2) words impute to the plaintiff an existing venereal or other loathsome or communicable disease; (3) words impute to plaintiff conduct, characteristics, or a condition incompatible with proper conduct of his lawful business, trade, profession or public or private office; and (4) words impute unchastity to a woman.

If the plaintiff is unable to bring his case under one of these categories, he or she must resort to proving special harm or actual damages by the communication. One can see, however, how a teacher could generally bring an action under category three where a teacher's reputation in the teaching profession is harmed by false accusations.

Slander *per quod*, on the other hand, requires that the plaintiff prove actual damage. Plaintiff must show that publication of the slander was the legal cause of special harm. The distinction between slander *per se* and slander *per quod* may rest on whether a crime is imputed by the slander. For example, it is slander *per se* if one accuses a teacher of being a prostitute because prostitution violates criminal law. The law holds that it is slander *per quod* and special damages must be proven if the words imputed to a teacher appear to harm the teacher's reputation, but do not relate to conduct of a crime, moral turpitude, unchastity or damage the teacher in his or her profession. To say that a male teacher debauched a female student would, of course, be slander *per se*. On the other hand, where a defendant had accused a headmaster of committing adultery with the school custodian's wife, the court found that the words had not been uttered in the context of the school nor in reference to the plaintiff as schoolmaster; the charge could be slander *per quod*, requiring a showing of special and actual damage, a burden which the plaintiff could not sustain. Since a teacher's reputation among students and the community is so vital to performance of his or her professional responsibilities, it is easy to see how, in the majority of cases, false imputations against a teacher could fall into the category of slander *per se*.

§ 13.33 Public Figures

Since New York Times v. Sullivan, 376 U.S. 254, 84 S.Ct. 710, a 1964 United States Supreme Court decision, the law of defamation as it pertains to freedom of speech and press has changed considerably. This case, and subsequent ones, hold the interest of the publisher to be of vital importance to a free and informed society. In *Sullivan* a paid advertisement in the New York *Times* signed by a number of prominent individuals criticized the behavior of the Montgomery, Alabama, police in dealing with racial unrest. The police chief, Sullivan, claimed that the derogatory reference to police behavior amounted to defamation of him personally. The Alabama state supreme court held that the publication was libel *pe se* and that the New York *Times* was liable for one-half million dollars without the plaintiff showing special damage or fault on the part of the *Times*.

The United States Supreme Court reversed the lower court holding that the guarantee of free speech under the First Amendment prohibits a *public official* from recovering damages for a defamatory falsehood relating to his *official* conduct, unless he proves that the statement was made with malice and that the statement was made with knowledge that it was false or in reckless disregard of whether it was false or not. This protection extended to both the newspaper and to the private individuals who paid for the advertisement and signed it. Plaintiffs in the case were unable to show that the New York *Times* actually had knowledge of the falsity of portions of the statement.

Shortly after the Sullivan case, the United States Supreme Court expanded the definition of *"public officials"* to include *"public figures"* in Curtis Publishing Co. v. Butts, 388 U.S. 130, 87 S.Ct. 1975 (1967). Butts, a former University of Georgia football coach, was accused by a major news magazine of giving away football secrets to the University of Alabama football coach. The Supreme Court concluded that public figures who commanded "a substantial amount of public interest at the time of publications in question" were subject to the same burden of proof as public officials. Thus, they had to show malice and knowledge of or reckless disregard for the falsity of the publication. The Constitution requires proof of knowledge or conscious indifference to falsity when imputations are made to either public officials or public figures.

Where a private individual is offended by the press, liability may be incurred by merely showing that the statement was untruthful, not that it was made with malice nor that the newspaper knew that it was false so long as liability is not imposed without *fault*. Whenever liability is imposed against the press for false publication, the damages must be limited to the actual injury sustained; general or punitive damages are not available.

The definition of "fault" is quite important here because its use incurs a different standard than the traditional rule that "Whenever a man publishes he publishes at his peril." King v. Woodfall, 98 Eng.Rep. 914 (1774). "Fault" in this regard means that the published derogatory information was intended and directed at a certain private individual. The old view was that references in books or newspapers to fictional persons which were taken by a few readers to refer to the plaintiff were libelous *per se*. This meant that the publisher was not actually at fault, but suffered the consequences anyway.

The modern view is that it must be shown that the plaintiff was the private individual for whom the defamation was intended. This being established, the private individual can recover against the publisher actual damages.

Students and teachers are not usually considered to be public officials or public figures. Imputations against teachers by the student press would be actionable if the teacher shows that the student publisher was at fault by directing the defamation toward the teacher. Similarly, students cannot attack other students or school administrators personally without potential consequences. A former school board member running in a school board election is considered to be a public figure under the *Sullivan* precedent. Fisher v. Larsen, 138 Cal.App.3d 627, 188 Cal.Rptr. 216 (1982).

School administrators may be classified by the courts as public officials, though school superintendents are considered to be employees and not officials in several states. Assuming that the school superintendent is a public official, then newspaper articles relating to his or her *official conduct* are subject to the conditional privilege as enumerated by the *Sullivan* case. If a publication attacks or degrades the school official in the eyes of the community, in his or her "private capacity," then the offended party need only show fault and actual injury sustained by the publication.

§ 13.34   Truth

Defamation constitutes harm of reputation by denigrating a person in the minds of others by falsehood. Falsification is the basic ingredient of the tort of defamation. It follows then that conveyance of truth is not defamation. In some states courts have held that truth is a defense for libel only when published with good motives and justifiable ends. Farnsworth v. Tribune Co., 43 Ill.2d 286, 253 N.E.2d 408 (1969), ruled that a person will not be allowed to resurrect a long forgotten mistake of another and republish it. The prevailing view is, though, that truth of a defamatory statement affords a complete defense to defamation regardless of whether ill will or malice is present. "One who publishes a defamatory statement of fact is not subject to liability for defamation if the statement is true." Restatement 2d, Torts, § 581A (1977).

Under common law tort where the plaintiff is a private person, a defamatory statement is presumed to be false and the defendant must prove that the statement was true. The burden of proof is on the defendant.

If the plaintiff is a "public official" or "public figure," the burden of proof shifts. As observed above, the "public person" must present clear and convincing proof to the court that defendant published false, defamatory information with knowledge of its falsity or with reckless disregard for the truth.

Thus, if a teacher has been the brunt of a defamatory statement, then the burden of proving truth is on the defendant because a teacher is generally a private person. If, for example, a parent or student published defamatory information about a teacher, the burden would be on the parent or student to prove the statement is true.

One could probably conceive of a situation where a teacher could be a public figure if he or she had won great fame for some reason, but this is generally not the case. So long as the teacher does not acquire the esteemed status of a public personage, then the burden of proving truth would be on the defendant if the publication harmed the teacher.

§ 13.35 Privilege

Public policy requires that certain persons or officials in society be afforded absolute privilege against liability for defamation. Judges, attorneys, witnesses in court, legislators, and certain other public officials are vested with absolute protection for utterances or writings which are given in the course of conduct of public affairs: (1) judicial proceedings, (2) legislative proceedings, and (3) executive proceedings. See: Laurence H. Eldredge, *The Law of Defamation*, The Bobbs-Merrill Company, Inc., Charlottesville, Va., pp. 339–532.

§ 13.36 Conditional Privilege

Courts have found it necessary to extend limited privileges to other persons in society where the public interest requires such protection. Such *conditional* or *qualified* privileges are extended to teachers and school administrators as well as to other public servants who are charged with duties which require them to handle sensitive information, which is important to not only the individual but to the public generally. Rationale for such protection is that: "In order that the information may be freely given, it is necessary to afford protection against liability for misinformation given in an appropriate effort to protect or advance the interest in question. If protection were not given, true information that should be given or received would not be communicated because of fear of the persons capable of giving it that they would be held liable in an action of defamation if their statements were untrue." Restatement 2d, Torts, § 592A at 258, Topic 3, Scope Note.

The degree of protection afforded by the conditional or qualified privilege is determined by the courts in weighing on "one hand society's need for free disclosure without fear of civil suit, and, on the other hand, an individual's right to recover for damage to his reputation. . . ." Weissman v. Mogol, 118 Misc.2d 911, 462 N.Y.S.2d 383 (1983).

The conditional privilege negates any presumption of implied malice emanating from the defamatory statement, and places the burden on the plaintiff to show proof of actual malice. Weissman v. Mogol, supra. One can easily see that teachers would be hesitant to convey any information at all about students if no privilege existed. Without such conditional privilege reports both academic and disciplinary would hold great potential for legal actions against teachers.

In order for the privilege of the teacher or administrator to withstand challenge, the communication must have been made (1) in good faith, without malice, and within the scope of the students, teachers, or public's interest in the good conduct of the school; (2) in the honest belief that the information conveyed was true, with knowledge that any communication brought about a student was made with reasonable, or and probable grounds; and (3) in response to a legitimate inquiry by one with the right to know about a student's educational or personal qualifications and that the answer does not go beyond that which is required to satisy the inquiry.

Parents have a qualified privilege to speak publicly before a school board regarding teacher's instruction of his or her children. It is within the right of parents to oversee their children's education to make statements pertaining to a teacher's competency or inefficiency in the classroom. If, however, the statements are untrue and made with "actual or express malice, then the privilege is destroyed." Nodar v. Galbreath, 429 So.2d 715 (Fla.App.1983).

In a case where a parent, who was also a teacher, informed the school principal about male teachers allegedly fondling girl students, the court said the teacher/parent had a qualified privilege. No malice was found because the parent/teacher had been told by girls of the alleged events and written statements were obtained to that effect. Desselle v. Guillory, 407 So.2d 79 (La.App.1982).

§ 13.37 Malice

Malice is indicated where the defendant conveys false information which is not reasonably germane to the subject matter of the occasion; then the scope of the conditional privilege has been exceeded. For example, a teacher's privilege does not extend communication about a student's personal love life outside of school if it has no bearing on his or her school conduct.

In such instances, technically, a teacher does not abuse his or her privilege but, instead, exceeds the protection of the privilege. Volunteering excessive information not bearing on the school's or the student's interests is hazardous.

§ 13.38   Belief in Truth

Where a teacher conveys erroneous information about a student but believes the communication is truthful, then the privileged occasion of the teacher will not be foregone. Statements by teachers must be motivated by a desire to protect the interest of the student or the school and, if so taken, then an honest belief that the communication is true will be protected. The fact that the teacher is unintentionally mistaken is, in this case, immaterial. Too, the teacher may be compelled to show that reasonable or probable grounds were available to support the truthfulness or belief in the truthfulness of the communication.

§ 13.39   Legitimate Inquiry

Legitimate inquiry regarding a student's educational performance may be made by other teachers, school administrators within the same school or school districts, as well as by educational and employment agencies outside the school or school district proper. The Buckley Amendment discussed above gives good guidelines in this regard. At common law a teacher is protected if communication is given in response to proper inquiry.

If information were to be given about a student to a third party who had no legitimate interest in the school or student, then, if the communication is defamatory, the teacher may be liable. The teacher can then abuse the occasion of the conditional privilege by carelessly releasing false information about students.

§ 13.4 RIGHT OF PRIVACY

A legal question of privacy, however, may arise beyond statute or common law defamation. Invasion of privacy may be a separate and independent tort. As a new area of law, invasion of privacy has come into focus in recent years from hundreds of cases which have emerged in which person's privacy has been invaded and their private lives have become subject to unwanted public exposure.

According to Prosser in his *Handbook of the Law of Torts* (3rd ed. 1964), Ch. 22, p. 832, the common law right of privacy is "not one tort, but a complex of four. The law of privacy comprises four distinct kinds of invasion of four different interests of the plaintiff, but otherwise have almost nothing in common except that each represents an interference with the right of the plaintiff 'to be let alone.' " The four different kinds of invasion of privacy are: "(a) unreasonable intrusion upon the seclusion of another, . . . (b) appropriation of the other's name or likeness, . . . (c) unreasonable publicity given to the other's private life, . . . (d) publicity which unreasonably places the other in a false light before the public, . . ." Restatement 2d, Torts, § 652A, 1967. Invasion of the right of privacy may result from any of the four or there may be overlapping or concurrent invasion.

The law of invasion of privacy was relied on by plaintiffs in a Maryland case where parents claimed that the release of their child's psychological records to another school upon transfer subjected the child to unreasonable publicity and unreasonably placed her in a false light before the public. Klipa v. Board of Education of Anne Arundel County, 54 Md.App. 644, 460 A.2d 601 (1983). Parents had asked that the girl's records be transferred, but had specifically requested that the psychological portion of the records not be sent. Parents had signed a consent form to transfer the records in which no reference was made to psychological records. The school psychologist had agreed not to send the psychological records, but due to a clerical error of another employee, the records were mailed anyway.

The court in ruling for the defendant school district held that the fact that parents had signed a consent form for the records, but had not specifically released the psychological records, was irrelevant because the school district had no legal obligation to obtain parental consent for the transfer. The evidence made it clear that the records were mailed directly to the principal of the school to which the girl transferred and were delivered by him to the custody of the chief school guidance counselor, thereafter the records remained under lock and key. Further, no evidence was presented which indicated that the student was exposed to unwarranted publicity. In applying the four legal conditions under which invasion of privacy can occur, the court found that there was no invasion of something secret, secluded or private, as required by the first and second types of invasion. The school had validly obtained the information in the first instance. There was no publicity as required under the third and fourth types of invasion and there was no falsity or fiction involved as required under the third kind of invasion. Neither was the information used for the defendant's advantage as is required by the fourth condition. On the contrary, the information regarding the student's psychological background and prior behavioral pattern was vital and necessary for the school to plan for an appropriate educational program, and to address the student's social and emotional needs.

CHAPTER 14

STUDENT TESTING

§ 14.1 INTRODUCTION

The state has the authority to set standards for promotion and graduation in public school programs and to establish criteria by which students are to be evaluated. One of the most commonly used criteria is, of course, some sort of examination. A federal court has said that boards of education have the right, if not a positive duty, to develop reasonable means to determine the effectiveness of their educational programs with respect to all individual students to whom they issue diplomas, and that tests are a reasonable means of accomplishing this purpose. Brookhart v. Illinois State Board of Education, 697 F.2d 179 (7th Cir. 1983).

§ 14.2 JUDICIAL REVIEW

But while state legislatures have authority to set test standards, the courts have been reluctant to substitute their judgment in such academic matters for that of school officials. The United States Supreme Court has distinguished between judicial review of academic and disciplinary measures taken by school authorities saying that "Courts are particularly ill-equipped to evaluate academic performance." Board of Curators, University of Missouri v. Horowitz, 435 U.S. 78, 98 S.Ct. 948 (1978).

The inappropriateness of judicial intervention in student evaluations has long been documented by judicial precedent. In 1913 a Massachusetts court refused to substitute its judgment for that of school authorities who had not allowed a student to continue in school because of his poor academic performance. "The care and management of schools which is vested in the school committee includes the establishment and maintenance of standards for the promotion of pupils from one grade to another and for their continuance as members of any particular class. So long as the school committee acts in good faith their conduct in formulating and applying standards and making decisions touching this matter is not subject to review by any other tribunal." Barnard v. Inhabitants of Shelburne, 216 Mass. 19, 102 N.E. 1095 (1913).

Pupil evaluation is essential to the conduct of schools and testing is considered to be an appropriate means of determining educational effectiveness of the school and the achievement of the pupil. Unless the school enunciates a level of academic attainment for the student and measures student progress toward that level "no certification of graduation can have any meaning whatsoever." Brookhart v. Illinois State Board of Education, supra.

The general view of the courts was set out in Gaspar v. Bruton, 513 F.2d 843 (10th Cir. 1975), where it was said that "the courts are not equipped to review academic records based upon academic standards within the particular knowledge, experience, and expertise of academicians. . . . The court may grant relief, as a practical matter, only in those cases where the student presents positive evidence of ill will or bad motive."

§ 14.3　LIMITATIONS ON THE SCHOOL

A child's constitutional rights, however, may place limitations on the school's prerogatives in employing tests as standards of academic attainment. In recent years states have begun to use competency tests to gauge students' progress. Such tests have been used as the criterion by which students are advanced, remediated or placed in special educational programs. Courts have always exercised their power to overturn the determinations of school boards where a student could show that an academic decision was arbitrary or capricious or was motivated by bad faith or ill will unrelated to academic performance. The burden of proof, however, has heretofore been on the plaintiff to show that the action was taken without due regard for the welfare of the student.

More recently the Due Process and Equal Protection Clauses of the Constitution have been applied to competency tests when a student's movement from grade to grade would be affected or when graduation would be delayed or denied.

§ 14.4　COMPETENCY TESTS

Recent state legislation requiring educational accountability for minimal competency tests has been the impetus for litigation challenging testing. The purpose of such test legislation is to assure that (a) students have mastered certain skills, (b) students with deficiencies have been identified and that students are provided the appropriate types of classroom instruction. Passage of a minimum competency test means that a student has reached the prescribed level of proficiency on a series of skills.

Legislation requiring competency tests generally assumes that tests are an appropriate method of measuring the attainment of the required skills. Such tests have been used as the prerequisite for obtaining a high school diploma, promotion from grade to grade, and placement of students in remedial programs. The failure to progress normally through school or the denial of a diploma may be of such importance as to invoke strict judicial scrutiny if the student's constitutional rights are threatened. The constitutional rights which may be at stake include substantive due process and/or equal protection.

§ 14.5 DUE PROCESS INTERESTS

The United States Supreme Court has made it clear that a high school diploma is of such personal importance that its denial may be tantamount to denial of "liberty or property" under the Fourteenth Amendment. The Court observed in Board of Regents v. Roth, 408 U.S. 564, 92 S.Ct. 2701 (1972), that property interests are not bestowed lightly. "To have a property interest in a benefit, a person clearly must have more than an abstract need or desire for it. He must have more than a unilateral expectation of it. He must, instead, have a legitimate claim of entitlement to it."

The interest must be founded on a state created benefit which is available to all persons in the same cir-

[*259*]

cumstance. Such interests emanate from "rules and understandings that secure certain benefits and that support claims of entitlement to those benefits."

A person's interest in receiving a public education is beyond a mere "unilateral expectation," it is essential to success in today's society. A high school diploma is a means to social and economic mobility. Also, the high school diploma is a prerequisite to admission to higher education. Thus, public education which culminates in the all important diploma may be viewed as an entitlement to every citizen.

However, even though a person has a property interest in public education and, ultimately, in a high school diploma, this interest can be denied if a student does not perform to expectations. Public education and the diploma can be denied by following judicial requirements of procedural due process.

The student, likewise, has a liberty interest which has implications for competency testing. A "liberty" interest has at least two aspects. First, the state may not impose a stigma on a student which will effectively denigrate the student's future. Failure to achieve a certain level on a test may result in a student being branded as an intellectual inferior or even a functional illiterate. Where the potential for damage to a person is so great as to risk peer ridicule or possible public scorn, a liberty interest may well be at issue. Second, a person has an interest in pursuing further education and to be gainfully employed in a chosen field. Goss v. Lopez, supra. Any indication on a student's record that he or she is intellectually inferior "imposes a stigma . . . that forecloses freedom to take advantage of other opportunities." Grinnell v. Bailey, 519 F.2d 5 (8th Cir. 1975). Thus, the presence of both property and liberty interests requires constitutional restraints of due process be accorded. Kelley v. Johnson, 425 U.S. 238, 96 S.Ct. 1440 (1976).

§ 14.51 Objective Factors

The courts, however, have held that the nature of substantive due process review does not apply to subjective judgments about academic qualifications. Board of Curators of the University of Missouri v. Horowitz, supra. In a recent case, involving the University of Michigan, it was held that the courts could only scrutinize the objective factors which may have "tainted or otherwise affected the decision not the [subjective] propriety of the decision itself." Ewing v. Board of Regents of University of Michigan, 559 F.Supp. 791 (D.Mich.1983).

As to what factors may be objective, and thereby conducive to scrutiny, as opposed to subjective, is subject to changing definition. Earlier courts would not have questioned whether the makeup of a test was actually fair, yet, today courts may analyze both the content of the curriculum and tests and their relationship to each other.

To look behind the curriculum content and test data was justified by the United States Supreme Court in Mathews v. Eldridge, 424 U.S. 319, 96 S.Ct. 893 (1976), when the formula for invoking due process protection was laid down. The Court said "our prior decisions indicate that identification of the specific dictates of due process generally requires consideration of three distinct factors. First, the private interest that will be affected by the official action; second, the risk of an erroneous deprivation of such interest through the procedures used, and the probative value, if any, of additional or substitute procedural safeguards; and finally, the Government's interest, including the function involved and the fiscal and administrative burdens that the additional or substitute procedural requirement would entail."

Of particular relevance to the definition of that which is objective, as opposed to subjective, is reference to "the risk of erroneous deprivation." Accordingly, that students may be improperly evaluated by tests which are not valid or reliable may violate substantive due process. A test which does not measure what it purports to measure is lacking in validity. Validity may be of, at least, two kinds: (1) Predictive validity measures how well a student may function in the future as a productive member of society, while (2) concurrent validity measures how well tests correlate with norms of other current test-takers. Similarly, a test which does not measure accurately what it is intended to measure is not reliable and cannot be relied on as an objective measure of a student's academic performance. Use by the courts of such statistical techniques indicating whether tests are valid and/or reliable allows for closer judicial scrutiny. By utilizing such tools the courts are afforded the opportunity to increase their objective evaluation of, heretofore, subjective educational determinations. (See Chapter 18 Employee Testing)

Another device used by courts to apply objective standards to competency testing is the notion of "instructional matching." This standard requires that students have actual curricular exposure to the kinds of knowledge and skills over which they are to be tested. Without such instructional match a student may be denied due process.

§ 14.6 EQUAL PROTECTION

Beyond due process, students are also entitled to constitutional protection against unjustified discrimination. If a test is racially discriminatory its use is violative of the Equal Protection Clause of the Fourteenth Amendment. In 1967, a federal judge in Washington, D.C. held that the use of tests for "tracking" of students was unconstitutional. Hobson v. Hansen, 269 F.Supp. 401 (D.D.C.1967), affirmed sub nom. Smuck v. Hobson, 408 F.2d 175 (D.C.Cir. 1969). The court had found that the use of tests to assign students to ability groups resulted in black students being relegated to lower curricular levels and little opportunity was provided them to improve their position by moving upward from level to level. The court concluded with regard to testing that "teachers acting under false assumptions because of low test scores will treat the disadvantaged student in such a way as to make him conform to their low expectations . . . creating a self-fulfilling prophecy based on false assumptions that black students are intellectually inferior."

A similar decision in California in 1972 found that the use of I.Q. tests to evaluate students for placement in classes for the educable mentally retarded was unconstitutional because the school administrators could not show that there was a relationship between the I.Q. tests and the intellectual capabilities of the black students.   P. v. Riles, 343 F.Supp. 1306 (N.D.Cal.1972), affirmed 502 F.2d 963 (9th Cir. 1974).

§ 14.61   Effect vs. Intent

The two above cases rested on the judicial assumption that if the "effect" of a test was to create a racially disparate placement of students, the use of the tests was unconstitutional unless school officials could show a compelling reason to justify use of the tests.

The "effect" standard was, however, replaced by the "intent" standard in a United States Supreme Court decision in 1976, Washington v. Davis, 426 U.S. 229, 96 S.Ct. 2040 (1976).   In this case the Court upheld a written test of verbal knowledge used to select recruits for the District of Columbia police force even though the test resulted in disqualification of a much higher percentage of black applicants than whites. The Court found that racially disparate results alone were not enough to invalidate selection based on test scores.   The standard adopted by the Court was one of "intent"; plaintiffs must show that government has a racially discriminatory intent a purpose in order to have the test set aside.   (See Chapter 18 Employee Testing.)

Since the Supreme Court established the intent standard in Washington v. Davis, the lower courts have had some difficulty in determining the nature of proof necessary to show a discriminatory purpose for students.

§ 14.61a Institutional Intent. Some lower courts have adopted a compromise standard called "institutional intent" which requires school authorities to show a substantial nonracial objective if the surrounding conditions are such that one could reasonably forecast discriminatory results to an official action. This compromise test has been defined in this way: "Where the school board adopts policies that foreseeably further an illegitimate objective, and it cannot justify or adequately explain such policies in terms of legitimate educational objectives, one must presume that the school board would not have adopted such a policy but for an illegitimate purpose. Consistent with this perspective, 'institutional segregative intent' may be said to exist where a school board adopts a more, rather than a less, segregative policy and cannot justify its choice in terms of legitimate educational objectives." Note, Reading the Mind of the School Board: Segregative Intent and the De Facto/De Jure Distinction, 86 Yale L.J. 317, 330 (1976). See also: Arthur v. Nyquist, 573 F.2d 134 (2d Cir. 1978).

In applying this standard a state instituting a competency testing program has the burden of showing that the tests will further a desirable educational objective. Lewis says that: "Discriminatory purpose is established if the new competency standards further no goal of increased proficiency in basic skills, or if there exist no alternative means of ensuring attainment by students of those skills with less disparate impact on minority youngsters." Donald M. Lewis,

"Certifying Functional Literacy," *Journal of Law & Education*, Vol. 8, No. 2, April 1979, pp. 145–183.

Thus, it would appear that the "institutional intent" test would, at least, require that states institute remedial measures to assist students who fail to achieve a required level of competency. A legitimate objective of any test may be to identify those students who need additional assistance.

§ 14.61b Application of Intent Standard. Most courts have strictly adhered to the intent standard of Washington v. Davis, rejecting the "institutional intent" compromise. A good example of the direct application of the purpose (intent) standard is found in United States v. South Carolina, 445 F.Supp. 1094 (D.S.C.1977), affirmed mem. 434 U.S. 1026, 98 S.Ct. 756 (1978). In this decision a federal court sustained the state's use of the National Teacher Examination for certifying teachers and for computing state allocations for payment of teachers' salaries. The court in following Washington v. Davis required that the plaintiffs prove that the state "intended to create and use" the NTE for the purpose of racial classification. If the plaintiffs were unable to show intent the court would evaluate the classification on the basis of the rational relationship standard of the Fourteenth Amendment which merely requires that the state show that the action taken is rationally related to a reasonable state purpose. After considering the evidence presented by the plaintiffs, the court was unable to conclude discriminatory intent even though the effect of the use of the test was to classify much greater percentages of black teachers in a lower certification and pay category. Defendants rebutted allegations by presenting evidence that the NTE had content validity and that the resulting classifications were created by presence or absence of knowledge or skill and ability and in applying the knowledge. In accepting the defendants rationale the court found the tests were not used with intent to discriminate. (See Chapter 18)

§ 14.7   DEBRA P.

In 1978, the Florida Legislature enacted a law requiring that public school students pass a functional literacy examination in order to receive a high school diploma. Shortly afterward students challenged the test maintaining that it violated both the due process and equal protection clauses of the Fourteenth Amendment. A federal district court held for the students and enjoined the use of the test to withhold diplomas until the 1982–83 school year. Debra P. v. Turlington, 474 F.Supp. 244 (M.D.Fla.1979). On appeal the Fifth Circuit Court of Appeals affirmed the lower court's findings. Debra P. v. Turlington, 644 F.2d 397 (5th Cir. 1981). The Circuit Court, however, remanded the case for further factual findings on two key issues, (a) the instructional validity of the test (the Florida Student State Assessment Test, Part II) and (b) the vestiges of racial discrimination questions.

§ 14.71   Teaching What Is Tested

The validity issue was succinctly stated by the court as being whether the "test is a fair test of that which was taught." Accordingly, if the test was not fair then it could not be rationally related to a legitimate state interest and therefore would be violative of the Equal Protection Clause. The state presented evidence showing that the subjects tested parallelled the curricular goals of the state. Instructional programs of all the school districts addressed the skills for which the test was designed and the state-approved instructional materials were used in all districts to implement the state prescribed curricular objectives. Further, local school districts reported that the skills required to pass the test were included in their curriculum and that a substantial number of public school teachers responded to a questionnaire and stated that they actually taught the prescribed curriculum. The court held that this intensive verification of instructional validity, was sufficient to withstand constitutional challenge.

The court rejected the plaintiff's argument that the state must show that each teacher individually actually teaches the prescribed curriculum. "What is required," the court said, "is that the skills be included in the official curriculum and that the majority of the teachers recognize them as being something they should teach." Debra P. v. Turlington, 564 F.Supp. 177 (M.D.Fla.1983). The court further elaborated in rejecting plaintiff's contentions, that "It strains credibility to hypothesize that teachers, especially remedial teachers, are uniformly avoiding their responsibilities at the expense of their pupils."

§ 14.71a Vestiges of Segregation. Concerning the vestiges of racial discrimination issue, the court had originally deferred the effective date of the test until 1983 because Florida public schools had not been fully integrated until 1970, and the court wanted to assure that all black students would have had the opportunity to attend integrated schools for a full twelve years. With regard to racial segregation, the court enunciated the rule that the use of a particular test "can be enjoined only if it perpetuates the effects of past school segregation or if it is not needed to remedy those effects." In applying this standard the court was unable to find that the tests were offensive to equal protection; on the contrary, because the tests identified students who did not have the necessary skills and provided remedial instruction for them, the court was of the opinion that use of the basic literacy test was an important factor in eradicating vestiges of past racial discrimination.

Thus, competency tests are acceptable instruments to measure student performance, even if the effect is for higher percentages of black students than white to fail. According to *Debra P.*, however, the state must be prepared to go to substantial lengths to document the validity of the tests given and provision must be made for those students failing the test to be given remedial assistance in overcoming their deficiencies.

As yet the United States Supreme Court has not ruled on the extent of the burden which a state must bear in showing test validity for students. The range of options, at this time, extend from the strict adherence to the intent standard as espoused in United States v. South Carolina, supra, where the state must merely show that its test is rationally related to a legitimate state objective, to the more restrictive standard of Debra P. where the state must bear a substantial burden of proof to document instructional validity

and to show that the test does not perpetuate and aug-
ment the vestiges of racial discrimination.

CHAPTER 15

TERMS AND CONDITIONS OF TEACHER EMPLOYMENT

§ 15.1 INTRODUCTION

In order to qualify for employment as a public school teacher, an individual must be certified or licensed by the state. Certification signifies that an individual is competent to teach. The assurance of teacher competency, to some degree, was a response to compulsory attendance; if the state compelled children to attend school, then these children should be supervised and taught by qualified or certified teachers.

§ 15.2 CERTIFICATION

Education is a state responsibility; consequently, certification differs in each state depending on the statutory provisions and regulations. Each state has the responsibility for certification or decertification (revocation of license) and usually this responsibility is delegated to the State Board of Education and/or the Departments of Education. These agencies administer the certification process and promulgate reasonable rules and regulations. The certification process is generally less involved than decertification. A teacher who is decertified has a right to know the cause of revocation and the opportunity for a hearing since constitutional issues may be present and generally are a factor.

Most states require all teachers have a college degree for certification. Some states have made provisions for qualified or conditional certification where teachers have completed only a specified number of college units that have to be upgraded within a specified period of time. College credits usually are required in the subject area (i.e., history) in which the teacher plans to teach. Concomitantly, states usually require the appropriate professional curriculum and methodology classes. In addition to higher education training, states require individuals to be: (1) of good moral character, (2) a specified age (usually 18 or older), and (3) a citizen of the United States, or if not already a citizen, intending to become a citizen. Some states require pledging loyalty to the Constitutions of the state and United States. In recent years, some states have instituted a teacher examination prior to certification such as the National Teachers Examination. If individuals meet all of the state established standards, then they are eligible for certification or licensing, and the certifying body may not arbitrarily or capriciously refuse certification.

Some states require further academic training after initial certification, in order to maintain certification, while other states endorse teachers for life. If certification requirements are changed, grandfather clauses often cover those already certified and the new regulations apply to new applicants only.

In most states, certifying bodies are vested with some discretionary authority. This discretionary power is particularly important when applying the elusive standard of good, moral conduct or appropriate and good behavior. In one case, an Oregon policeman was convicted of breaking and entering and grand larceny. He then completed all the college requirements to apply for a teaching certificate but was denied. The crux of the question was whether he had overcome his questionable past. State certification standards required that an individual be of good, moral character. It was the determination of the State Board of Education that he had not overcome his past indiscretions and therefore, he was denied certification. The courts generally refuse to question the discretion of a Board's decisions unless it can be shown that its members acted arbitrarily or capriciously. Bay v. State Board of Education, 233 Or. 601, 378 P.2d 558 (1963).

§ 15.21   Tests

In recent years, states have reinstituted examinations prior to certification, with several states employing the National Teacher Examination. Some teachers have objected, maintaining that the "effect" of the tests is to exclude a higher percentage of blacks than of whites. (See Chapter 18, Employee testing.) The United States Supreme Court has, however, approved the use of tests so long as the tests are not used with the intent to segregate. Persons who have been excluded from teaching because of failing the test must prove that the test was designed or initiated with the "intent" to discriminate. The court said: "[a]lthough the NTE were not designed to evaluate experienced teachers, the State could reasonably conclude that the NTE provided a reliable and economical means for measuring one element of effective teaching—the degree of knowledge possessed by the teacher." United States v. State of South Carolina, 445 F.Supp. 1094 (D.S.C.1977), affirmed 434 U.S. 1026, 98 S.Ct. 756 (1978).

§ 15.22   Aliens

A New York statute provided that a teaching certificate would be denied any individual who was not a United States Citizen or who had not manifested an intention to apply for citizenship. In 1979, the United States Supreme Court upheld the New York statute. In doing so, the court relied on a 1978 case which upheld the exclusion of individuals who wanted to be policemen because of the special nature of the governmental obligation, Foley v. Connelie, 435 U.S. 291, 296, 98 S.Ct. 1067, 1070 (1978). It was maintained by the court that there was a rational governmental interest in requiring teachers to be either citizens or be in the process of becoming naturalized citizens. Ambach v. Norwick, 441 U.S. 68, 99 S.Ct. 1589 (1979).

§ 15.23   Revocation

Teaching certificates may be revoked for unprofessional conduct, which may include the violation of state law, false swearing to loyalty oaths, incompetency, and immorality. If a state is going to revoke or decertify a teacher, it may consider not only classroom ability and performance but also outside activity. The California Supreme Court upheld the decertification of a teacher who belonged to a "swingers" club and engaged in public sexual acts with numerous men and had appeared on television in disguise, espousing non-conventional sexual behavior. Pettit v. Board of Education, 10 Cal.3d 29, 109 Cal.Rptr. 665, 513 P.2d 889 (1973).

Although teachers may have their certificates revoked for good and valid reasons, the revocation may not be for an unconstitutional reason. It is unconstitutional to deny teachers freedom of speech or expression unless the teacher's actions disrupt the educational process. Reasonable questions related to job performance must be answered by teachers.

§ 15.3 LOCAL BOARD PREROGATIVES FOR EMPLOYMENT

Teacher certification, however, does not guarantee employment. State legislatures delegate the authority to employ personnel to local school boards. Although the final authority over employment rests with the school board, some states provide that a school board may employ personnel only if the superintendent has recommended the particular individual to the board. Wide latitude is vested in the board so long as the board does not violate one's constitutional or statutory rights, such as the sex, race, or religion, or if the board has acted arbitrarily, capriciously or in bad faith.

§ 15.31 Certification as a Minimum Standard

A local school board may promulgate reasonable rules and regulations relating to employment even though the teacher has already met minimum certification standards. A board may require additional training more advanced than that required for certification, such as having a Master's degree before employment. Also, a board may require a teacher to take additional courses or staff development training after being employed. A teacher may be required, as a part of the employment relationship to obtain higher levels of academic training as long as school board policy requirements do not discriminate.

§ 15.32　Residency Requirement

A board may require a teacher to establish residency within the boundaries of the school district. In recent years, urban school districts have utilized this authority to prevent mass movement of teachers. Teachers have challenged the residency requirement as violating their liberty rights. The courts have upheld the policies as rational since those teachers who live in the district have a better understanding of the students and the community and, therefore, would be more committed to the school district, and more involved in community activities. They also would be local taxpayers and, therefore, more personally involved in quality education. Some school districts have established policies that allow teachers, who lived outside of the district prior to the implementation date of the residency policy, to be exempt from the policy. These "grandfather" provisions have been attacked by new teachers claiming discrimination, but the courts have upheld the policies as reasonable if they are applied in a nondiscriminatory manner, after the initial implementation.

§ 15.33   Outside Employment

School boards have formulated policies forbidding teachers to engage in other employment during the school year. The courts have given wide latitude to local school boards in establishing employment rules and have upheld such policies. Such policies though must be applied uniformly and consistently to all teachers in like classification.

§ 15.34   Health and Physical Requirements

Within the limits of federal and state statutes and regulations, a local school board may adopt reasonable health and physical condition requirements for teachers. These standards are generally viewed favorably by the courts if they are applied uniformly and are within the scope of federal and state statutes and regulations. But, a board has to be especially cognizant of the protections and prohibitions, or conditional aspects of employment, in regard to those individuals who may be classified under various federal and state provisions for the handicapped. (See Chapter 18, Discrimination of the Handicapped.) Health and physical requirements must be rationally related to job performance and should not be promulgated to disenfranchise otherwise qualified persons.

§ 15.35   Assignment of Teaching Duties

A school board, within the provisions of state statutes, contractual terms and regulations, generally has the authority to transfer and assign teachers to best benefit the educational program. Assignments are also contingent on the certification of the teacher; if a teacher is certified to teach in the primary grades, they may be assigned courses depending on the state definition of primary. A teacher has no right to demand a particular grade or teaching position within a school district. A board may not transfer a teacher in contravention of the teacher's constitutional rights, statutory provisions, or contractual obligations. A local board may adopt reasonable rules and regulations regarding transfer but once established, they cannot be violated. To transfer a teacher to make life so uncomfortable as to force the teacher's resignation is, of course, considered to be arbitrary and violative of the teacher's rights.

§ 15.36   Extracurricular Duties and Activities

In the absence of specific contractual terms, a school board may assign reasonable extracurricular duties to a teacher. These duties may constitute such responsibilities as supervising study halls, directing a school play, coaching intramurals, conducting field trips and supervising athletic events. School officials may not assign bus driving duty, crossing guard duty or janitorial duties to teachers, as these are not reasonably related to the job performance of teachers. Extracurricular jobs must be related to the instructional activities for which the teacher is certified.

§ 15.4   RIGHT TO REMAIN SILENT

In Beilan v. Board of Education, 357 U.S. 399, 78 S.Ct. 1317 (1958) the United States Supreme Court ruled that a teacher must answer questions posed by school officials if those questions are relevant to the terms of employment. In *Beilan*, the teacher was dismissed because of refusal to answer relevant questions posed by the school superintendent regarding teaching responsibilities.

However, questions posed by a legislative committee or in a judicial proceeding may not be used as a basis for dismissing teachers. Board of Public Education, School District of Philadelphia v. Intille, 401 Pa. 1, 163 A.2d 420 (1960). Any questions asked must be balanced against the teacher's constitutional rights. The United States Supreme Court has recognized the unique position and interest teachers have in speaking out on educational issues. Pickering v. Board of Education, 391 U.S. 563, 88 S.Ct. 1731 (1968).

§ 15.5 CONTRACTS

A teacher contract contains the basic elements of contract law and must also conform to specific state statutes. The basic elements for a valid contract are: (1) offer and acceptance; (2) competent parties; (3) consideration; (4) legal subject matter; and (5) proper form. As has been said numerous times "all contracts are agreements but not all agreements are contracts."

§ 15.51 Offer and Acceptance

Only a school board may make a valid offer to contract with a teacher. The offer has to be made to the teacher and, within a reasonable time, the teacher may only accept the offer that has been tendered. If a school board tenders an offer for a specific salary and the teacher accepts the offer but requests the salary be increased, this is not a valid offer and acceptance.

In essence, the teacher has made a counter offer. There has been no meeting of the minds as to conditions and terms of the contract, thus no contract can be formed without further action by the school board.

§ 15.52 Competent Parties

Both parties must have the legal capacity to contract. A school board is a legal party under the authority vested in it by the legislature. Certification makes a teacher competent to contract.

§ 15.53 Consideration

Consideration is an essential element of a contract. Consideration is something of value received for performing an act or services for another party. In most teacher contracts, this constitutes the paying of a salary for the teaching services rendered. Consideration may be divided into three categories: (1) valuable; (2) good; and (3) a promise for an act. A teacher's salary falls into the category of a "valuable". An example of good consideration would be love and affection.

This is seldom invoked by the courts or observed in educational settings. The third category would be a promise to act and could constitute consideration in a situation where a school board is offering a reward for information. The party supplying the information requested would be entitled to the reward.

§ 15.54 Legal Subject Matter

The contract must be for a legal subject matter. Contracting for a teacher to teach a prescribed curriculum would fall in this category. If a board enters into a contract that is not of legal subject matter (such as conducting rooster fights or selling drugs) or is beyond the scope of its authority, the contract would be void.

§ 15.55   Legal Form

The contract must be in the legal form required by state statutes or regulations. Most states require contracts to be written and to include specific provisions. However, there are instances when an oral agreement may be legally binding.

§ 15.6   TENURE

Tenure is a privilege bestowed upon the teaching profession by the legislature. This privilege may be altered by legislative discretion, but not by local school boards. In 1927, the Indiana legislature worded a tenure statute in such a manner that a contract was created between the tenured teachers and the state. The United States Constitution, Article I, Section 10, provides that the obligation of a contract may not be impaired, and the United States Supreme Court invoking this provision ruled that subsequent Indiana legislatures could not alter the contractual relationship. Indiana ex rel. Anderson v. Brand, 303 U.S. 95, 58 S.Ct. 443 (1938). Although the legislature could not alter the contract of those particular teachers specifically affected by the law, it could promulgate a new statute with new requirements for new teachers.

Many reasons have been proffered as to why tenure was established. Some of these are: (1) to remove political abuse from the profession; (2) to prevent arbitrary interference by boards; (3) to provide a permanent, competent teaching force; and (4) to protect the competent, experienced professional, thereby providing job security.

Most states have established statutory provisions which grant tenure, or continuing contracts. These statutes provide that a teacher, after serving a specified probationary period, cannot be removed from a position unless the school board has established good and just cause and provided the teacher with procedural due process. The specific causes for removal vary from state to state depending on the statutory language, but include such causes as immorality, insubordination, incompetence, misconduct, neglect of duty, or other good and just cause. (See Chapter 17, Teacher Dismissal.) Generally, the tenure statutes provide specific procedures that must be followed before a teacher may be removed. Tenure is a statutory right and not a constitutional right, but once tenure is granted a "property" right is created and, thereby, requires procedural due process before removal.

Before teachers are awarded tenure status they must serve a probationary period. States require from two to five years of probation, with the majority of states requiring three years. After serving the specified period, a local school board has the discretion of granting tenure or not renewing the probationary teacher's contract. If a school board chooses not to renew a probationary teacher's contract during the probationary period, then no reasons have to be given to the teacher unless statute so requires. Even if reasons are given, by the board, and they are not constitutionally impermissible reasons, the board has no obligation to provide the teacher with a removal hearing.

Tenure may or may not be transferred from district to district, within a particular state, depending on the construction of the state statute. Some states allow, at the discretion of the local school board, the granting of tenure immediately upon moving from one district to another. In other states, an experienced teacher may be required to serve a partial probationary period such as one year rather than a full probationary period of three years.

Tenure is granted for teaching and not for extracurricular assignments such as coaching. Supplementary contracts have been interpreted by the courts to be outside tenure statutes. This rule, though, is not uniform. Not only are teaching positions encompassed by tenure laws, but statutes in a number of states provide tenure status for administrative personnel such as principals, assistant superintendents, superintendents and others.

§ 15.7 REDUCTION IN FORCE

In recent years, in many states, there has been a decline in the student population attending public schools. This has necessitated a corresponding reduction in the number of professional employees. As mentioned previously, teachers and other professionals who have acquired tenure may be dismissed only for reasonable cause. These reasons, such as incompetence, immorality, etc., reflect directly upon the teacher's abilities, whereas reduction in force does not reflect upon abilities. In school districts with declining enrollments, individuals may be laid-off or the work force reduced simply because the teachers are not needed. Reduction in force may be caused by such factors as enrollment decline, fiscal restraints, reorganization, or elimination of positions or programs. Most state tenure laws provide local school boards the flexibility to reduce the work force especially when there is a lack of financial resources.

The local school board has within its discretion the authority to adopt procedures to reduce the work force, absent contracted obligations created by statutory or collective bargaining agreements.

A local board should consider legal precedents before establishing policy in this area. Issues that have come before the courts include: (1) the necessity of reduction in force; (2) the positions eliminated; (3) the bad faith actions of school boards; and (4) seniority.

§ 15.71　Rationale for Reduction in Force

The courts will look closely at whether or not a reduction in force is necessary or is an attempt to circumvent statutory protection. Does the board have a real financial exigency requiring lay-off? The burden is upon the board or institution to establish that a financial exigency exists. In American Association of University Professors v. Bloomfield College, 129 N.J.Super. 249, 322 A.2d 846 (1974), affirmed in part 136 N.J.Super. 442, 346 A.2d 615 (1975), Bloomfield College abolished tenure for all faculty, then dismissed some eleven tenured faculty members. The union requested that the college dispose of a golf course to obtain funds for re-employment. The court found that

[*284*]

the college had a true financial crisis and need not dispose of it assets to obtain funds for faculty re-employment.

§ 15.72   Positions to be Eliminated

After it has been determined that a financial crisis exists, school boards then must decide who and what positions are to be eliminated.   In the absence of statutory or collective bargaining provisions, tenured teachers are given priority over non-tenured teachers; in other words, seniority is given greater weight. There have been some court decisions to the contrary, in which other standards besides seniority have been upheld.   However, the courts require that these standards be rational, job related, and established previously.

A board, in deciding which positions are to be eliminated, may not act in an arbitrary or capricious manner.   A board may not abolish a position, and terminate the employee, then transfer the responsibilities of the former employee to another position.   The shift of responsibilities in this manner circumvents tenure laws and is therefore illegal.

§ 15.73   Intent of the Board

A board must act in good faith and may not terminate a teacher under the guise of need to reduce the teaching force.   Some cases have arisen over whether a true financial exigency existed or whether the teacher's position was eliminated because of something the teacher said that offended the board.   In Zoll v. Eastern Allamakee Community School District, 588 F.2d

246 (8th Cir. 1978), a teacher had written letters to a local paper criticizing the school board. A jury determined the real reason for elimination of the position was something the teacher had said. The board was unable to show that a financial crisis existed. In Hagarty v. Dysart-Geneseo Community School District, 282 N.W.2d 92 (Iowa 1979) the court said ". . . we could not countenance a subterfuge by which an unscrupulous school board would use a fictitious necessity for staff reduction as a pretext for discharging a teacher."

§ 15.74   Seniority Displacement

As previously mentioned, generally, tenured teachers take precedence over non-tenured teachers in reducation in force. School board rules, however, may provide for "bumping" procedures if reduction in force is necessary. In the absence of such rules, a school board generally would take into consideration, not only seniority but also certification. If a teacher is certified in a specific area where teachers are needed then he or she may be able to replace someone with less seniority.

CHAPTER 16

CONSTITUTIONAL RIGHTS OF TEACHERS

§ 16.1 INTRODUCTION

Teachers' lives and activities have always been subject to close public interest. Since teachers were entrusted with the responsibilities of educating the children and were *in loco parentis*, they were expected to provide a role model for youth. Earlier, teachers were subject to close public scrutiny and their contracts included provisions that prohibited the use of alcoholic spirits, smoking, and in many cases required dismissal of female teachers who got married. There were also other restrictions forbidding attendance at theaters, dating, keeping late hours, and divorce. In some instances, teachers were required to teach Sunday School and perhaps more importantly, teachers were also prohibited from speaking out on political issues that might be construed as criticism of individuals in authority.

§ 16.2 PRIVILEGE DOCTRINE

School boards had unlimited control over the employment and dismissal of teachers. The dismissal of teachers was sustained by the courts based on the doctrine that employment was a privilege and not a right. In the 1960s, the courts determined that the "privilege doctrine" was inappropriate and the relationship between teacher and school board began to change.

That teaching had attendant constitutional rights that could not be arbitrarily infringed upon soon became the prevailing judicial veiw. The new view was that the interest of the government to impose restrictions on teachers must be weighed against the interests of the teachers. Neither the government's interest nor the teacher's is absolute.

§ 16.3   FREEDOM OF SPEECH AND EXPRESSION

The "privilege doctrine" was finally disposed of in Pickering v. Board of Education, 391 U.S. 563, 88 S.Ct. 1731 (1968) when it was established that teachers have constitutional rights. In *Pickering*, the Supreme Court recognized the rights of the individual teacher and correspondingly recognized the rights of the state to conduct an orderly educational process. A balance of interest test was developed whereby the rights of the individuals to express their views on public issues are constitutionally protected and the right of the state to provide an efficient and orderly educational system is also guaranteed. "The problem in any case is to arrive at a balance between the interests of the teacher, as a citizen, in commenting upon matters of public concern and the interest of the state, as an employer, in promoting the efficiency of the public services it performs through its employees."

§ 16.31   A Teacher's Right to Criticize

In the *Pickering* case, a teacher was dismissed for sending a letter to a local newspaper, criticizing the school board and superintendent in handling the distribution of funds. The school board claimed that Pickering or any teacher "by virtue of his public employment has a duty of loyalty to support his superiors." Pickering countered that he should be able to speak out, as any other citizen, on matters of public concern and, therefore, he was protected under the penumbra of the First Amendment.

§ 16.32   Balance of Interest

Justice Marshall wrote that the crux of the issue was "to arrive at a balance of interests." The court then addressed whether Pickering could be dismissed because of his critical comments. The court found the letter Pickering wrote was mainly aimed at criticizing the superintendent and board for not informing the public about the allocation of funds and that the letter was not disruptive. "So far as the record reveals, Pickering's letter was greeted by everyone but its main target, the Board, with massive apathy and total disbelief."

The second issue determined by the court was whether Pickering could be dismissed because of incorrect or false statements made in his letter to the paper. Specifically, the only false statement in the letter was that $50,000 had been spent to transport athletes when the true amount was $10,000. Since the letter had been disregarded by the public, the allegations, by the board and superintendent, that their reputations had been damaged and disruption had taken place in the community, were unsubstantiated.

In *Pickering* Justice Marshall stated, "It is possible to conceive of some positions in public employment in which the need for confidentiality is so great that even completely correct public statements might furnish a permissible ground for dismissal. Likewise, positions of public employment in which the relationship between superior and subordinate is of such a personal and intimate nature that certain forms of public criticism of the superior by the subordinate would seriously undermine the effectiveness of the working relationship between them can also be imagined."

Justice White, in a separate opinion, said if a teacher knowingly makes false and reckless statements that have a disruptive impact then these "[d]eliberate or reckless falsehoods serve no First Amendment ends and deserve no protection under that Amendment."

In another case, a principal wrote a scathing letter to two board members and their wives. In upholding the dismissal, the court said, "[h]armony between a principal and the school board is a legitimate interest of a state, and statements made to members of a school board may rationally affect adversely that harmony." Rost v. Horky, V.XVII NOLPE Rptr. No. 2 (1976).

§ 16.33   Private Criticism

In Givhan v. Western Line Consolidated School District, 439 U.S. 410, 99 S.Ct. 693 (1979), a junior high school English teacher met privately with the principal and criticized the policies of the school on racial discrimination. The principal alleged that the criticism involved "petty and unreasonable demands and were presented in an insulting, loud, hostile and arrogant manner." The Fifth Circuit Court of Appeals upheld the dismissal, citing *Pickering*, and Mount Healthy v. Doyle, 429 U.S. 274, 97 S.Ct. 568 (1977), stating "private expression by a public employee is not protected." The United States Supreme Court reversed the decision and rejected the argument that the First Amendment did not protect the teacher's criticism simply because of the close day-to-day working relationship between the principal and teacher. A teacher's First Amendment rights are not lost when the teacher ". . . arranges to communicate privately with his employer rather than to spread his views before the public."

The court refused to grant a lesser protection to private speech than to public speech, but emphasized that the teacher could be dismissed if either private or public speech impeded the proper performance of classroom duties. It was recognized that public speech is contingent upon content, whereas the impact of private speech might be judged on the time, place, and manner of the comments.

§ 16.34 Dismissal When Constitutional Issues Are Involved

In Mount Healthy v. Doyle, 429 U.S. 274, 97 S.Ct. 568 (1977), a non-tenured teacher telephoned a local radio station and criticized a dress and appearance code unilaterally issued to teachers by the administration. The teacher, Doyle, was also involved in a number of other incidents such as: a physical altercation with another teacher, an argument with school cafeteria employees, swearing at students and making obscene gestures to female students. Doyle's contract was subsequently not renewed and he requested the reasons for non renewal. In response to Doyle's request, the superintendent referred to "a notable lack of tact in handling professional matters which leave much doubt as to your sincerity in establishing good school relationships," then, he specifically referred to the radio station incident. The teacher challenged the dismissal as violative of his First and Fourteenth Amendment rights. The Sixth Circuit Court of Appeals reasoned that the telephone call was protected free speech and was the major reason for Doyle's dismissal and ordered reinstatement. The United States Supreme Court remanded the case back to the lower court to determine if the board had substantial and legitimate reasons for not renewing Doyle's contract, other than those of protected free speech. "A borderline or marginal candidate should not have the employment question resolved against him because of constitutionally protected conduct. But that same candidate ought not to be able, by engaging in such conduct, to prevent his employer from assessing his performance record and reaching a decision not to rehire on the basis of that record, simply because the protected conduct makes the employer more certain of the correctness of its decision."

The court concluded that a board could dismiss or not renew a teacher's contract even if constitutional protections are involved if there are other valid and legitimate reasons for termination. In other words, if the board had reached the same decision, even if the free speech issue had not occurred, then the dismissal would not have infringed on the constitutional rights of the teacher.

§ 16.35 Political Activity

Teachers may speak out privately on political issues and take part in partisan political activities. These political rights are cloaked with First Amendment protections. A school administrator may not use punitive measures such as transferring, dismissing or demoting a teacher for protected political activities but, at the same time, a teacher may not be involved in political activities which disrupt the educational process. A school board may reasonably expect a teacher not to use his or her position to promote a particular political outcome, or to use the classroom for political purposes, or to be involved in any activity that will interfere with or disrupt the educational environment of the school, or detract from job performance.

A California court upheld the suspension of a teacher for using his classroom for political activity Goldsmith v. Board of Education, 66 Cal.App. 157, 225 P. 783 (1924). The teacher chose to comment on the election of the superintendent and said, "I think he would be more helpful to our department than a lady, and we need more men in our schools. Sometimes your parents do not know one candidate from another; so they might be glad to be informed. Of course, if any of you have relatives or friends trying for the same office, be sure and vote for them."

§ 16.36   Political Office

It is well settled that a teacher, as a citizen of the United States, has a right to run for political office, but there is a difference between the right to run for public office and the right to continue public employment after being elected.   Common law provisions stipulate that an individual, whether a teacher or other public employee, may not hold positions simultaneously that are incompatible, and may not have a conflict of interest, or be in violation of the separation of powers of government.   These prohibitions have been determined to be of "compelling state interest," and, therefore, do not infringe on the basic political rights of teachers.

Whether or not a teacher may hold political office and serve as a teacher is dependent upon the provisions previously mentioned and individual state statutes.   Some states have "conflict of interest" statutes which provide that teachers may not serve as a state legislator, while employed as a public teacher.   But, if a state does not have a statutory provision prohibiting teachers from serving in the legislature, then, the courts have held, they may serve.   However, a board of education could reasonably request the teacher to take an unpaid leave of absence while actively serving.

Some states have passed legislation modeled after the Federal Hatch Act which prohibits participation in partisan politics.   United States Civil Service Commission v. National Ass'n of Letter Carriers, 413 U.S. 548, 93 S.Ct. 2880 (1973).   The United States Supreme Court in Broadrick v. Oklahoma, 413 U.S. 601, 93 S.Ct.

2908 (1973), upheld an Oklahoma statute prohibiting public employees from participating in partisan politics. These statutes usually limit activities such as direct fund raising for partisan candidates, becoming a candidate, starting a political party, or actively managing a campaign.

§ 16.37   Personal Appearance

School boards have promulgated dress codes, not only for students, but for teachers as well. These regulations have been challenged as a violation of the teachers' rights of free speech, expression, privacy and liberty. There is a distinct difference between the privacy rights of a governmental employee and a member of the general public. The United States Supreme Court in Kelley v. Johnson, 425 U.S. 238, 96 S.Ct. 1440 (1976), ruled that hair-grooming of police officers could be regulated. "The constitutional issue to be decided by these courts is whether petitioner's determination that such regulations should be enacted is so irrational that it may be branded 'arbitrary,' and therefore a deprivation of respondent's 'liberty' interest in freedom to choose his own hairstyle."

A Louisiana school board expanded its student dress code to prohibit employees from wearing beards. Domico v. Rapides Parish School Board, 675 F.2d 100, 102 (5th Cir. 1982). The Fifth Circuit Court of Appeals recognized the liberty interest of the individual in choosing how to wear one's hair, but ruled the school board had made a rational determination in establishing the rule as ". . . a reasonable means of furthering the school board's undeniable interest in teaching hygiene, instilling discipline, asserting authority, and compelling uniformity." This court clearly distinguished a difference between high school and college environments where hair regulations of faculty and students, in institutions of higher education, could not be justified, absent exceptional circumstances.

In Miller v. School District No. 167, Cook County, Illinois, 495 F.2d 658 (7th Cir. 1974), the Seventh Circuit Court ruled a school board ". . . undoubtedly may consider an individual's appearance as one of the factors affecting his suitability for a particular position. If a school board should correctly conclude that a teacher's style of dress or plumage, has an adverse impact on the educational process, and if that conclusion conflicts with the teacher's interest in selecting his own life style, we have no doubt that the interest of the teacher is subordinate to the public interest."

The Second Circuit Court in East Hartford Education Association v. Board of Education, etc., 562 F.2d 838 (2d Cir. 1977) recognized the liberty interest of an individual's personal appearance, but these liberty interests are "less weighty" than those of "procreation, marriage, and family life." The school board instituted a rule requiring male classroom teachers to wear a jacket, shirt and tie and female teachers a dress, skirt, blouse and pantsuits except where other teaching assignments would require more appropriate apparel, i.e., gym teachers. The court stated, "[w]e join the sound views of the First and Seventh Circuits, and follow *Kelley* by holding that a school board may, if it wishes, impose reasonable regulations governing the appearance of the teachers it employs."

[*296*]

§ 16.4 RIGHT OF PRIVACY

Teachers, historically and traditionally, have been role models, not only for students while school was in session, but these standards have flowed over into the teachers' private lives. The courts have reinforced the concept of the teacher as an exemplar and upheld school board actions regulating, within reasonable limits, the outside conduct of teachers. (See Chapter 17.) Therefore, teachers have been held to a higher standard of conduct reflecting a higher moral standard than the average citizen. This higher standard has been demanded by the public because of the trust and responsibility of teaching the young. Teachers have claimed that school board actions which intrude into their private lives is an invasion of privacy.

Most of the actions against teachers involve issues of immorality or fitness to teach, and these have included such issues as homosexual activities, heterosexual improprieties, and use of marijuana and drugs. When faced with these issues the courts seek to determine a rational nexus between the conduct in question and the professional duties being performed. The conduct of a public employee may be closely scrutinized, but before any disciplinary action may be taken, a rational nexus must be established demonstrating the outside activity has a detrimental effect upon the individual's fitness to teach. "[N]o person can be denied government employment because of factors unconnected with the responsibilities of that employment." Morrison v. State Board of Education, 1 Cal.3d 214, 82 Cal.Rptr. 175, 461 P.2d 375 (1969). Logically, a connection has to be established between the immoral ac-

[*297*]

tivity and the job. Immorality, standing alone, could be voided for vagueness, since "In the opinion of many people, laziness, gluttony, vanity, selfishness, avarice, and cowardice, constitute immoral conduct . . ." Golden v. Board of Education of County of Harrison, ___ W.Va. ___, 285 S.E.2d 665 (1982).

Golden recognized the importance of establishing a nexus between the alleged immoral conduct and its impact upon the individual's fitness to teach. "To allow dismissal of a teacher merely upon a showing of some immoral conduct without a showing of resulting impact on the teacher's fitness to teach or upon the school community would constitute an unwarranted intrusion upon the teacher's right of privacy."

The courts have developed tests to determine whether or not a teacher's conduct ceases to be private and whether or not the community is adversely affected. Two of these tests are: (1) "Does the conduct directly affect the performance of the occupational responsibilities of the teacher? or (2) Has the conduct become the subject of such notoriety as to significantly and reasonably impair the capability of the particular teacher to discharge the responsibilities of the teaching position?"

§ 16.5 FREEDOM OF RELIGION

The First Amendment of the Federal Constitution provides: "Congress shall make no law respecting an establishment of religion, or prohibiting the free exercise thereof." Separation of church and state issues have been the subject of much litigation and include: (1) aid to private and parochial schools; (2) prayer and

Bible reading in public classrooms; (3) religious instruction; (4) flag salute; and (5) curricular issues such as sex education. Although everyone has the right to religious freedom, there is a distinct difference between the rights of students and those of faculty members. Students are compelled to attend schools under compulsory attendance statutes, therefore, greater cognizance of their rights is in order. Teachers, on the other hand, are adults who, of their own volition, choose to accept a contract with compensation for services rendered. Because of these differences, the courts have interpreted issues somewhat differently.

§ 16.51   Flag Salute

In West Virginia State Board of Education v. Barnette, 319 U.S. 624, 63 S.Ct. 1178 (1943) the United States Supreme Court struck down a state statute that required students to say the Pledge of Allegiance and salute the flag. The court determined these activities to be an infringement upon the student's First Amendment rights of freedom of religion.

Cases since *Barnette* have applied this right to teachers. A teacher who did not participate in a flag ceremony, but stood silently while another conducted the program, was determined to be protected by the First Amendment. The teacher's actions were based on "personal conscience" and not disloyalty. Therefore, "we ought not impunge the loyalty of a citizen . . . merely for refusing to pledge allegiance, any more than we ought necessarily to praise the loyalty of a citizen who without conviction or meaning, and with mental reservation, recites the pledge by rote each morning." Russo v. Central School District, No. 1, 469 F.2d 623 (2d Cir. 1972), cert. denied 411 U.S. 932, 93 S.Ct. 1899 (1973). A school board may require the pledge of allegiance ceremony take place, but may not compel the teacher to participate.

§ 16.52   Teaching the Curriculum

An individual's religious beliefs are protected under the First Amendment but actions relating to those beliefs may be limited if the interest of the state is compelling. A teacher who accepts employment is expected to carry out the designated curriculum established by a local school board. In Palmer v. Board of Education of the City of Chicago, 603 F.2d 1271 (7th Cir. 1979), cert. denied 444 U.S. 1026, 100 S.Ct. 689 (1980), a teacher refused to teach the pledge of allegiance and patriotic observances and to celebrate holidays. She believed that teaching the students about Abraham Lincoln was excessive devotion to an individual. The Court acknowledged the teacher's right to freedom of belief, but also recognized a compelling state interest in the education of children for the benefit of those children and society. The court concluded that education ". . . cannot be left to individual teachers to teach what they please." Teachers have ". . . no constitutional right to require others to submit to [their] views and to forego a portion of their education they would otherwise be entitled to enjoy." In Matter of Bein, 15 Educ.Dept.Rep. 407, N.Y.Comm'r.Dec. 9226 (1976), a teacher refused to lead students in the recitation of the pledge of allegiance, the singing of holiday songs, the decorating of the classroom for holidays, the coordinating of the gift exchange at Christmas, and the singing of "Happy Birthday", because she had become a Jehovah's Witness and claimed these activities violated her religious beliefs. With the cooperation of parents, other teachers and older students, the teacher made arrangements for all curricular activities to be carried out. The teacher stated that although she did not participate, personally, in the religiously offensive activities, she provided leadership so that the children were never denied the school prescribed activities. The New York Commissioner of Education ruled the dismissal violated the teacher's right of religious freedom.

§ 16.53   The 1964 Civil Rights Act and 1972 Amendment

The Civil Rights Act of 1964, Title VII, (42 U.S.C.A. Section 2000e et seq.) prohibits any employer from discriminating against an individual because of religion. The 1972 Amendment states: "[t]he term religion includes all aspects of religious observance and practice, as well as belief, unless an employer demonstrates that he is unable to reasonably accommodate an employee's or prospective employee's religious observance or practice without undue hardship on the conduct of the employer's business." One of the key issues that has developed is, what does an employer have to do to reasonably accommodate the religious beliefs of an employee? In Trans-World Airlines, Inc. v. Hardison, 432 U.S. 63, 97 S.Ct. 2264 (1977) the Supreme Court addressed this issue. Hardison was working in a maintenance division under a negotiated agreement that allowed employees, with greater seniority, to choose what days they would work. Because of his high seniority, Hardison chose not to work on Saturdays, his religious day of observance. Later, at his own request, he was transferred to another work assignment. Hardison had little seniority in his new position, and, therefore, he could not take Saturday off.

Hardison challenged the collective bargaining agreement and the seniority rule claiming that his religious beliefs took precedent over these provisions. Justice White said that Title VII did not require TWA ". . . to carve out special exemptions." "To require TWA to bear more than a *de minimis* cost, in order to give Hardison Saturdays off, is an undue hardship."

The burden of proof is on the teacher or individual to establish that religion was a primary determinant in an employment decision. If the teacher sustains this burden and shows the primary employer motivation was religiously related, then the burden of proof shifts to the school board or employer to show that they made a good faith effort to accommodate the individual and, if this is unsuccessful, then, it must be demonstrated that the employer (board) was unable to reasonably accommodate the employee's religious beliefs without undue hardship. (See Chapter 18, Employee Discrimination.)

A member of the World Wide Church of God in Wangsness v. Watertown School District No. 14–4, etc., 541 F.Supp. 332 (D.S.D.1982) requested seven days off, without pay, to attend a religious festival. When the request was denied, he attended the festival and was subsequently discharged. The board claimed a qualified teacher could not be found to serve as a substitute. A guidance counselor had to substitute and this according to the board constituted an undue hardship on the employer. The teacher, before departing for the festival, prepared lesson plans and models to be used by the substitute teacher and consulted with the substitute about these plans. The court determined that the classes had run smoothly, and no undue hardship was suffered by the board, therefore, the teacher was due equitable relief for a violation of Title VII.

In another similar case, a school district, through a negotiated agreement, Pinsker v. Joint Dist. No. 28J, etc., 554 F.Supp. 1049 (D.Colo.1983) provided each teacher with two personal leave days. Pinsker, a Jewish teacher claimed that she needed more than two days to celebrate religious holidays. She emphasized that Christian teachers benefitted from the structure of the school calendar since school was closed in December and usually for spring vacation and these coincided with Christmas and Easter. Christian teachers could participate in religious ceremonies without being absent from school.

The court held it is unconstitutional to make an employee choose between employment and religion and if "An employer who punishes an employee by placing the latter in a position in which he or she must ignore a tenet of faith in order to retain employment it violates" Title VII. Pinsker was allowed to take unpaid leave to attend the religious ceremonies.

A New Jersey court ruled in Hunterdon Central School v. Hunterdon Central High, 174 N.J.Super. 468, 416 A.2d 980 (1980) that a negotiated agreement that allowed paid leaves of absence for religious purposes violated the establishment clause of the First Amendment. A state action must meet all conditions of the tripartite test in Lemon v. Kurtzman, 403 U.S. 602, 91 S.Ct. 2105 (1971) to be constitutional. These are: the act must (1) have a secular purpose, (2) neither inhibit nor promote religion and (3) not cause excessive entanglement. (See Chapter 5.) The provision in the negotiated agreement did not have a secular purpose since it allowed paid leave days for religious participation and benefitted those religious individuals, and even encouraged worship, while excluding non-believers. Citing Torcaso v. Watkins, 367 U.S. 488, 81 S.Ct. 1680 (1961), it is unconstitutional to ". . . impose requirements which aid all religions as against non-believers."

§ 16.54   Religious Garb

Can teachers wear religious clothing while teaching in the public schools? Although there have been contrary decisions, a school board can probably prohibit the wearing of religious uniforms. Some courts have determined that as long as the individual did not inject religious views into their teaching, then, it was permissible to wear religious uniforms. Other courts have found the wearing of religious apparel is a symbol of the teacher's dedication to religion and, therefore, a violation of the "establishment clause."

CHAPTER 17

TEACHER DISMISSAL

§ 17.1 INTRODUCTION

Conditions of employment are controlled by state statute. Whether a teacher has permanent employment, continuing contract, or tenure the conditions are defined by state statute. Procedures for nonrenewal of a probationary teacher or the dismissal of a tenured or permanent teacher are also established by statute.

There is a distinction between dismissals and nonrenewals. With nonrenewal a probationary teacher receives a contract which has a specified starting and ending date. The school board may decide the employee's services will no longer be needed. State statute stipulates the date of notification for the nonrenewal of a probationary teacher's contract.

With dismissal a teacher has served a statutory period of probation and has been granted a permanent contract or tenure. A school board, in dismissing a tenured teacher, would have to prove good cause and afford the individual an opportunity to refute the reasons for dismissal alleged by the board. To dismiss requires full procedural process, whereas nonrenewals generally require only notice by a specific date.

Teachers' rights are guaranteed by the Federal Constitution. The Fourteenth Amendment provides no state shall " . . . deprive any person of life, liber-

ty, or property, without due process of law; . . ."
The first ten amendments, when applied through the
Fourteenth Amendment, may all impact upon teacher
employment. If a school board contravenes the constitutional rights of an employee (tenured or non-tenured), such as freedom of speech, then procedural due
process must be afforded the employee.

§ 17.2 LIBERTY AND PROPERTY INTERESTS

Teachers have been granted certain liberty and
property interests by the Constitution and the extent
of these rights has been interpreted by the courts.
The United States Supreme Court has recognized that
liberty and property are broad and majestic terms and
society demands that if one of these rights is negated,
then due process is required. Property rights have
been recognized when the teacher has tenure or a permanent contract, as provided by the legislature. Also,
the contractural agreement the employee has with the
employer is a property right and cannot be breached
during the contract period. A property right is created if the individual has a legitimate claim of entitlement to continued employment as created by state law
or by the policies and procedures of a local board.

Liberty interests are involved if the employer stigmatizes the employee and jeopardizes one's opportunities for future employment. Stigmatizing the individual's good name or reputation is a violation of a
teacher's liberty interest and will require due process
of law. The following cases are landmarks in estab-

lishing and setting the parameters for teacher liberty and property rights.

§ 17.21   Board of Regents v. Roth

In Board of Regents v. Roth, 408 U.S. 564, 92 S.Ct. 2701 (1972) a professor was hired by the University of Wisconsin for a fixed term of one academic year. He subsequently was notified his contract would not be renewed for a second year. Wisconsin statute provided that after four years, tenure could be acquired and, at that time, procedural safeguards, such as due process, were provided. Mr. Roth claimed the university had deprived him of his Fourteenth Amendment rights by not giving him reasons for his nonrenewal and procedural due process. He further alleged the true reason for his nonretention was his public criticism of the university administration. The Supreme Court was presented with the question of whether a probationary teacher was entitled to procedural due process and notification of reasons for nonrenewal.

The Fourteenth Amendment requires an opportunity for a hearing if a "property" interest or a "liberty" interest is jeopardized. "But the range of interests protected by procedural due process is not infinite." Liberty and property are ". . . broad and majestic terms that are . . . purposely left to gather meaning with experience . . ." "Property interests . . . are not created by the Constitution. Rather they are created and their dimensions are defined by existing rules or understandings that stem from an independent source such as state law—rules or understandings that secure certain benefits and that support claims of entitlement to those benefits."

Property interests are established by: (1) tenure statute, (2) dismissal during the contract year, or (3) if the individual has a legitimate and objective expectation of reemployment. Liberty has not been defined with exactness and has broad meaning.

A liberty interest arises if charges are made against an individual ". . . that might seriously damage his standing and associations in his community." Therefore, if the university had made a charge that Roth was "guilty of dishonesty, or immorality" then, a liberty interest would have arisen and, correspondingly, the right to procedural due process. A charge of dishonesty or immorality would have damaged his "good name, reputation, honor, or integrity," and required a hearing to allow refutation of the charges. A liberty interest would have arisen if the university placed a "stigma" upon the individual that foreclosed his freedom to avail himself of employment opportunities in his chosen profession. The Court found that Roth had not been deprived of his property or liberty interests and was not entitled to procedural due process.

§ 17.22 Perry v. Sindermann

On the same day that Roth v. Board of Regents was issued, the Supreme Court also handed down Perry v. Sindermann, 408 U.S. 593, 92 S.Ct. 2694 (1972). This case further elaborated the property rights of individuals engaged in public employment. Sindermann had been employed in the State of Texas college system for ten years, the last four as a junior college professor at Odessa Junior College. His employment was based on a series of one year contracts. The college had not adopted a tenure system.

During his term of employment, he had public disagreements with the board of regents. In particular, he had advocated the junior college be expanded to a four year institution. This was opposed by the governing board. The college board elected not to renew his contract and issued a press release alleging insubordination on the part of the plaintiff. Sindermann brought suit, claiming his nonrenewal was based on his public criticism, a violation of his free speech rights, and he should be granted a due process hearing.

Sindermann had not established that the board had denied his free speech so the Court only looked at whether he had liberty or property interests which required a hearing. Although Sindermann did not have a property interest derived from a formal tenure system because the college had none, he claimed *de facto* tenure. To substantiate his claim of *de facto* tenure he pointed out that the faculty handbook stated that as long as the teacher is performing satisfactorily, the administration "wishes the faculty member to feel that he has permanent tenure." The Court reiterated the statement made in *Roth* that "property" denotes a broad range of interests that are secured by "existing rules and understandings." Therefore, these handbook rules constituted a legitimate claim of entitlement which created an objective expectancy of employment.

The *Roth* and *Sindermann* cases established that probationary teachers have no right to a hearing unless they can demonstrate a deprivation of liberty or property interests. A property interest may be established by state statute, policies, rules, or regulations. A property interest may be gained by either direct or "de facto" obligations. A liberty interest may be established if the institution stigmatizes the individual, damaging his good name and reputation.

§ 17.3   STIGMATIZING REASONS

§ 17.31   Public Charges

The courts have established that as long as reasons for nonrenewal are not made public, then no stigma or infringement of a liberty interest exists. In Bishop v. Wood, 426 U.S. 341, 96 S.Ct. 2074 (1976) the Supreme Court explicated the issue of a stigmatizing statement. A probationary policeman was told, in private, by his superior, he would not be reemployed because of his failure to follow orders, his poor attendance, his having and instigating low morale among fellow workers and other conduct inappropriate to being a policeman. Testimony indicated that all of the reasons given were false. The two issues litigated were: (1) whether the employee had a property interest, and (2) if the explanations for dismissal were false, did this deprive the employee of his liberty rights? The Court answered both of these in the negative.

Although a property right may be created by ordinance, the state courts had ruled that an enforceable expectation could only be claimed if provided by statute or contract. The Court ruled the plaintiff "held his position at the will and pleasure of the city" and, therefore, no liberty interest had been infringed upon since the reasons were communicated orally, in private. Since the reasons were given in private, their truth or falsity was irrelevant and did not create a liberty interest. Therefore, if reasons for a probationary teacher are given in private, then, no stigma is placed upon the individual and no deprivation of liberty occurs.

§ 17.32 Incompetence, Insubordination, Neglect of Duty

Allegations of incompetence, inadequacy, and insubordination have been alleged to be stigmatizing by non tenured teachers facing dismissal. In Gray v. Union County Intermediate Education District, 520 F.2d 803 (9th Cir. 1975) an employee was charged with insubordination, incompetence, hostility toward authority and aggressive behavior. The court stated, "[n]early any reason assigned for dismissal is likely to be to some extent a negative reflection on an individual's ability, temperament, or character. But not every dismissal assumes a constitutional magnitude. The concern is only with the type of stigma that seriously damages an individual's ability to take advantage of other employment opportunities. . . . These allegations certainly are not complimentary and suggest that [the teacher] may have problems in relating to some people, but they do not import serious character defects such as dishonesty or immorality . . . as contemplated by *Roth*." Courts have held that neglect of duty, failure to maintain discipline, improper teaching techniques, tardiness, and failure to follow orders, do not invoke liberty interests. These reasons for dismissal do not reflect on the individual's reputation or honor, nor prohibit the teacher from obtaining employment elsewhere.

§ 17.33   Stigma of Racism

In a Minnesota Community College case a nontenured professor's contract was not renewed and he claimed he had been stigmatized because of remarks accusing him of being a "racist." Charges of racism had been forwarded to the college by various campus groups, and had been entered into his personnel file. The United States Court of Appeals for the Eighth Circuit determined these charges were a deprivation of his liberty interest, reflecting on his reputation and good name. Therefore, a hearing would be required before he could be terminated, despite his nontenured status. Wellner v. Minnesota State Junior College Board, 487 F.2d 153 (8th Cir. 1973).

§ 17.34   Emotional Stability

Lack of mental or emotional stability as a reason for nonrenewal of a contract may invoke due process requirements. In a 1981 case, a school board announced the reasons for nonrenewal of a teacher were for ". . . apparent emotional instability, resentment of authority and her alleged failure to follow a written request from the administration as to reporting to school and/or attending classes." The court ruled all of the reasons except "apparent emotional instability" were not stigmatizing, but the emotional instability charge went beyond job related comments and stigmatized the teacher. This statement implied a serious personal defect and, therefore, was a violation of her liberty rights. Bomhoff v. White, 526 F.Supp. 488 (D.C.Ariz.1981).

There are cases, of a similar nature, where public comment about an individual's mental state or psychiatric condition have been held to stigmatize the teacher. See: Stewart v. Pearce, 484 F.2d 1031 (9th Cir. 1973).

§ 17.4 BURDEN OF PROOF FOR NONTENURED TEACHERS

If a nontenured teacher's contract is not renewed and no reasons are given by the board, the Constitution is not offended. If the teacher does not challenge the board and allege denial of a due process right the board has no responsibility to institute such a hearing itself. An Alabama court, citing *Roth*, stated that the employee must assert himself to protect his rights and institute the process whether school board procedures are established for such procedure or not. Stewart v. Bailey, 396 F.Supp. 1381 (N.D.Ala.1975).

If a teacher claims his or her contract has not been renewed because of constitutionally impermissible reasons, the burden of establishing the deprivation rests with the teacher. The teacher must establish a *prima facie* case that the constitutionally impermissible reason was the motivating factor for nonrenewal. If the teacher establishes that an impermissible reason for dismissal is involved, the burden shifts to the school board to show, by a preponderance of evidence, "that [the board] would have reached the same decision as to [plaintiff's] reemployment even in the absence of the protected conduct." Mount Healthy City Board of Education v. Doyle, 429 U.S. 274, 97 S.Ct. 568 (1977).

§ 17.5   DISMISSAL OF TENURED TEACHERS FOR INCOMPETENCY

Incompetency has been given broad interpretation by the courts. Incompetency is defined as "want of physical, intellectual, or moral ability; insufficiency; inadequacy; specific want of legal qualifications or fitnesses," (Webster's New International Dictionary) Beilan v. Board of Education, School District of Philadelphia, 357 U.S. 399, 78 S.Ct. 1317 (1958). It generally concerns a fitness to teach which contains a broad range of factors. The courts have included in incompetency, lack of knowledge of subject matter, lack of discipline, unreasonable discipline, unprofessional conduct, and willful neglect of duty.

A teacher who has been certified by the state is assumed to be competent and it is the responsibility of the school board to prove incompetency. As long as school boards are not arbitrary or capricious, the courts will generally not interfere. The Fifth Circuit Court of Appeals stated that "[f]or sound policy reasons, courts are loathe to intrude upon the internal affairs of local school authorities in such matters as teacher competency." Blunt v. Marion County School Board, 515 F.2d 951 (5th Cir. 1975).

The manner of offering evidence in incompetency cases is generally through testimony. Both the quantity and quality of evidence is important. The courts have liberally allowed opinions of principals, curricular supervisors, and other supervisory personnel to stand as expert testimony. Other testimony by students and parents may be important, but the actual observations, by supervisors, of what transpired in the classroom, are very significant. One court said, "This court, in absence of proof of an abuse of discretion, cannot substitute its opinion for the decision of the school board and of the district court where both of these tribunals were presented with substantial evidence upon which to base their decisions." Frank v. St. Landry Parish School Board, 225 So.2d 62 (La.App.1969).

§ 17.51 Lack of Discipline

Although failure to maintain discipline has been a major factor in dismissing teachers for incompetency, it is usually coupled with other charges. A teacher's dismissal notification listed fourteen specific reasons and included inadequate maintenance of discipline during class, excessive and ineffective use of films, ineffective classroom teaching, and failure to cooperate with school administrators. The court upheld the dismissal because the preponderance of evidence showed that this teacher's students were disruptive, daydreamed in class, wandered around the room, and left the room without permission. The evidence also showed that these same students behaved properly in other classes. Board of Directors of Sioux City v. Mroz, 295 N.W.2d 447 (Iowa 1980).

In Louisiana, a teacher was charged with failure to maintain discipline and to prepare lesson plans. The teacher exhibited a negative attitude toward teaching and did not institute suggested improvement strategies. The failure to maintain discipline was confirmed by the principal, the supervisor of child welfare, the coordinator of special education, and another teacher. The children were allowed to roam around the room and read aloud when the teacher was attempting to read. The assistant principal testified that the teacher did an adequate job and the disciplinary problems arose because of the disparity of student ages in the room. Even so, the court said, "[o]ur review of the record convinces us there is no foundation for holding that the action of the School Board was arbitrary, capricious or an abuse of the Board's discretion." Mims v. West Baton Rouge Parish School Board, 315 So.2d 349 (La.App.1975).

§ 17.52   Excessive Discipline

Dismissal of a tenured teacher for excessive discipline has been upheld where it was shown that the teacher punished students by making them stay in the bathroom, pulling their hair, pinching them, and pulling their ears. Gwathmey v. Atkinson, 447 F.Supp. 1113 (D.Va.1976).

Dismissal of a tenured teacher for incompetency has also been upheld where on three separate occasions, he administered excessive physical punishment when disciplining students. Kinsella v. Board of Education, etc., 64 A.D.2d 738, 407 N.Y.S.2d 78 (1978).

[*316*]

§ 17.53 Teacher's Ability

Incompetence also includes a lack of knowledge of subject matter, using incorrect standard English, poor teaching methods, and not following required methodology. The U.S. Court of Appeals for the Fifth Circuit upheld the dismissal of a teacher who had been teaching for twenty-five years and was discharged for incompetency for using poor grammar, making spelling errors, both written and spoken, including misspelled words on the blackboard, which students copied, having instructional deficiencies in math, English (phonics) and reading, and using poor writing techniques. The teacher also attempted to teach spelling before the children had mastered the alphabet. Three supervisors presented substantial and credible evidence that the teacher lacked the necessary academic skills to teach and was hostile toward criticisms aimed at improvement. Blunt v. Marion County School Board, 515 F.2d 951 (5th Cir. 1975).

In Louisiana, a teacher was held properly discharged for incompetency where the specific charges were that she could not adapt to the new instructional program, and misspelled and mispronounced words. She lacked the ability to organize and carry out constructive instructional programs and had serious discipline problems in class. Jennings v. Caddo Parish School Board, 276 So.2d 386 (La.App.1973).

The courts have allowed the dismissal of teachers for acts inappropriate to the educational environment or where there was evidence of unfitness to teach. Some states, through statute, require that teachers be given a chance to improve or remediate themselves before dismissal. If a state statute requires remediation, the school board must show that a good faith effort has been made to improve the instructional capabilities of the teacher before proceeding with dismissal.

In Gilliland v. Board of Education of Pleasant View, 67 Ill.2d 143, 8 Ill.Dec. 84, 365 N.E.2d 322 (1977), a teacher was charged with incompetency for allegedly ruining pupils' attitudes toward school, lacking rapport with pupils, and giving irregular homework assignments. Charges of cruelty were also charged because the teacher had grabbed childrens' hair, arms and shoulders, and had hit one child with a book. The teacher claimed she should be allowed to remediate the problems, but the court stated " . . . many causes, when standing alone, may be remediable, whereas those same causes in combination with others may well be irremediable. Here, we think it clear that the combination of a number of causes plus the continuous nature of the conduct were sufficient bases for a finding of irremediability."

Although one act may be remediable, another act may be irremediable, particularly if it is of a nature that offends the senses of the community or endangers the health and safety of children. A sixth grade tenured teacher used high amperage batteries in a cattle prod to discipline children. The court said the "manifest weight of evidence" showed the actions of the teacher were irremediable. Rolando v. School Directors of District No. 125, 44 Ill.App.3d 658, 3 Ill.Dec. 402, 358 N.E.2d 945 (1976).

§ 17.6 DISMISSAL OF TENURED TEACHERS FOR INSUBORDINATION

Courts have defined insubordination as "a willful disregard of express or implied directions of the employer and a refusal to obey reasonable orders." School District No. 8, Pinal County v. Superior Court, 102 Ariz. 478, 433 P.2d 28 (1967). Charges of insubordination are not supportable if: "(1) the alleged misconduct was not proved; (2) the existence of a pertinent school rule or a superior's order was not proved; (3) the pertinent rule or order was not violated; (4) the teacher tried, although unsuccessfully, to comply with the rule or order; (5) the teacher's motive for violating the rule or order was admirable; (6) no harm resulted from the violation; (7) the rule or order was unreasonable; (8) the rule or order was invalid as beyond the authority of its maker; (9) the enforcement of the rule or order revealed possible bias or discrimination against the teacher; or (10) the enforcement of the rule or order violated the First Amendment rights to free speech or academic freedom." (78 ALR 3d 83, 87).

§ 17.61 Insubordination Not Proven

Insubordination is refusal or repeated refusal to follow directions. In a case where a teacher was charged with insubordination for inappropriate punishment of students and allowing card games to be played in study hall, the court ruled that there was no insubordination, though the conduct was highly questionable, because the teacher no longer continued the activities after being admonished by the principal. Thompson v.

Wake County Board of Education, 31 N.C.App. 401, 230 S.E.2d 164 (1976), see: 292 N.C. 406, 233 S.E.2d 538 (1977).

In another insubordination case a teacher was told not to use J.D. Salinger's "Catcher in the Rye" in his classroom and had agreed not to use the novel. Subsequently, he started to use the novel again and was requested to meet with the principal concerning the issue. The teacher walked out of the meeting after five minutes and was charged with two counts of insubordination: (1) breaking the previous agreement, and (2) walking out of the conference. The school board upheld the charges and dismissed the teacher. Upon appeal, the court determined the dismissal was too severe. Although the courts will not generally review administrative sanction, this decision was disproportionate to the offense and was not fair since students were not harmed and there was no indication of lack of fitness to teach. Harris v. Mechanicville Central School District, 45 N.Y.2d 279, 408 N.Y.S.2d 384, 380 N.E.2d 213 (1978).

§ 17.62　Insubordination Proven

Two cases reflect the right of a school board to dismiss an employee for willful disregard of school policies, rules or regulations. In the first case, a teacher of twenty-four years requested leave for five days to attend an out-of-state reading conference. The board denied the request, whereupon, the teacher obtained a well qualified substitute and attended the conference. The teacher was charged with insubordination and dismissed. The act was held to be irremediable because of the damage done to the faculty and school district by willful violation of a reasonable rule. Christopherson v. Spring Valley Elementary School, 90 Ill.App.3d 460, 45 Ill.Dec. 866, 413 N.E.2d 199 (1980).

The second case involved a tenured teacher who informed the superintendent she planned to take a week off to take a trip to Jamaica with her husband. The superintendent denied the leave. When the teacher did not appear at school, the superintendent recommended she be dismissed for insubordination. After a hearing, the school committee dismissed the teacher, whereupon the teacher filed suit. The court stated, "[i]n wake of plaintiff's conduct come grave doubts among school administrators, recriminations and jealousy among teachers, and an attitude of laxity and self-indulgence, possibly affecting the entire school community. These are consequences which the law does not require school administrators to condone." Fernald v. City of Ellsworth Superintending School Committee, 342 A.2d 704 (Me.1975).

§ 17.7 DISMISSAL OF TENURED TEACHERS FOR IMMORALITY

Immorality is specified by statute in numerous states as grounds for dismissal. Although the term immorality has been attacked as unconstitutionally vague, Kilpatrick v. Wright, 437 F.Supp. 397 (M.D.Ala.1977) it generally has been upheld by the courts, especially when it relates to fitness to teach and where there is a rational nexus between the prohibited activity and the individual's position as a teacher. Immorality may include both heterosexual and homosexual activities, but does not pertain to exclusively sexual activities. In Horosko v. Mount Pleasant Township School District, 335 Pa. 369, 6 A.2d 866 (1939), cert. denied, 308 U.S. 553, 60 S.Ct. 101, immorality was defined as "[a] course of conduct as offends the morals of the community and is a bad example to the youth whose ideals a teacher is supposed to foster and elevate".

In one case, a tenured teacher was elected to the school board in the school district where she resided. In that capacity she attended a conference after being denied paid personal leave as a teacher in the district where she taught. Upon her return, she submitted a request for excused absences because of illness and the board dismissed her based on immorality. The court determined ". . . questions of morality are not limited to sexual conduct, but may include lying." Bethel Park School District v. Krall, 67 Pa.Cmwlth. 143, 445 A.2d 1377 (1982).

§ 17.71   Heterosexual Conduct

17.71a   With Students. Because of the exemplary nature of teaching, the courts have left little question about the seriousness of sexual involvement with students. In one instance, a tenured teacher, while on a field trip, tickled and touched female students on various parts of their bodies including between the legs. He was observed lying on a motel bed with one of the female students, watching television. The teacher made sexual remarks and innuendos to the female students and was subsequently dismissed for immorality. Upon being charged with immorality, the teacher responded that the activities were "good natured horse-play." Later, some students apologized to the field trip coordinator because they considered their behavior was "pretty gross." The teacher, who had enjoyed a reputation as a good teacher with excellent rapport, contended there was no nexus between his classroom effectiveness and his conduct. The court determined his activities constituted unfitness to teach. Weissman v. Board of Education of Jefferson City School District, 190 Colo. 414, 547 P.2d 1267 (1976).

Another teacher had females sit between his legs, kissed them on the cheek, stuck his tongue in one's ear and placed his hand on another's breast. Although the teacher testified he did not touch the students, the girls accusations were corroborated by a male student. The court upheld the dismissal as supported by evidence. Lombardo v. Board of Education of School District No. 27, 100 Ill.App.2d 108, 241 N.E.2d 495 (1968).

A high school teacher was dismissed for allegedly attempting to seduce a student, telling vulgar jokes in classes, and making comments about sexual intercourse in class. Two former female students testified to the allegations, while eight former students, another teacher, the principal, and assistant principal testified they had never observed such behavior, nor received complaints of such a nature. The dismissal was held improper because the testimony did not support the allegations. Chandler v. East St. Louis School District, 35 Ill.App.2d 317, 182 N.E.2d 774 (1962).

17.71b With Nonstudents. The courts, when dealing with cases of sexual activity by teachers with nonstudents, attempt to determine if there has been an impact on the teacher's fitness to teach and whether the activities were public or private. In a California case, a 48 year old elementary school teacher had her life certificate revoked by the State Board of Education for immorality. The plaintiff was arrested at a private club by an undercover police officer after he watched her commit three separate acts of oral copulation, a violation of the Penal Code. After plea bargaining, the charges were reduced to a misdemeanor, outraging public decency. The teacher and her husband had also appeared previously on television, in disquise, discussing non-conventional sexual life styles. Even though the teacher introduced into evidence her classroom evaluations, which were satisfactory, and a contract from the local board offering to rehire her, the court held that the state board was correct in revoking her certificate. The evidence showed that the sex acts were witnessed by several strangers in a semi-public atmosphere and "[p]laintiff's performance certainly reflected a total lack of concern for privacy, decorum or preservation of her dignity and reputation." The court said a teacher " . . . in the public school system is regarded by the public and pupils in the light of an exemplar, whose words and actions are likely to be followed by children coming under her care and protection." Obviously participation in sex orgies fell short of this standard. Pettit v. State Board of Education, 10 Cal.3d 29, 109 Cal.Rptr. 665, 513 P.2d 889 (1973).

In a Florida case, a teacher who had an unblemished record performed cunnilingus with his 9 year old step-daughter and was dismissed by the school board for immorality. Although expert testimony stated it was an isolated act, and would probably never happen again, the court upheld the dismissal. The act reflects a ". . . perverse personality which makes (the teacher) a danger to school children and unfit to teach them." Tomerlin v. Dade County School Board, 318 So.2d 159 (Fla.1975).

The mores of a small rural community are usually quite different than large cosmopolitan areas. The norms and expectations of the community have much to do with acceptability of teacher conduct. In a South Dakota case, a teacher's boyfriend moved in to live with her about two months after she became a teacher in a small rural community. The community became aware of the situation and several persons became offended. School officials trying to stem the initial protest, sought to resolve the situation by talking to the teacher at which time she advised the school officials that her living arrangements were private. The school officials then sought to dismiss her for gross immorality and incompetence. The teacher responded that the dismissal violated her rights of privacy and freedom of association, as well as substantive due process and equal protection of the Fourteenth Amendment. The court ruled for the school board concluding that the state is entitled to maintain a "properly moral scholastic environment" and in this circumstance the dismissal was proper. Sullivan v. Meade Independent School District No. 101, 530 F.2d 799 (D.S.D.1976).

17.71c Unwed Pregnant Teachers. School boards have attempted to dismiss unwed pregnant teachers on charges of immorality and teachers have challenged these actions, based on their rights of privacy, denial of due process and equal protection, violation of Title VII of the 1964 Civil Rights Act, and Title IX of the Education Amendments Act of 1972.

In a case involving equal protection a pregnant, unmarried, elementary, remedial reading teacher was discharged for immorality because the school board felt that being unwed and pregnant is proof *per se* of immorality. Since the school board offered no proof to support the contentions, the court held the dismissal was in violation of the teacher's equal protection rights. Avery v. Homewood City Board of Education, 674 F.2d 337 (5th Cir.1982).

In another case where the superintendent learned, through rumor, that a teacher was pregnant and unmarried, the school board dismissed her for immorality. "The Board made no findings that [the teacher's] claimed immorality had affected her competency or fitness as a teacher, and no such nexus was developed in the evidence. No 'compelling interest' . . . was established by the evidence which would justify the invasion of [the teacher's] constitutional right of privacy." Drake v. Covington County Board of Education, 371 F.Supp. 974 (M.D.Ala.1974).

Where a teacher was dismissed for being pregnant and unwed, but no action had been taken against other pregnant and unmarried teachers who were employed in the district, the court held that the board had acquiesced in allowing unwed pregnant teachers to remain employed and, therefore, was foreclosed from arguing that unwed pregnant teachers were unfit to teach.

New Mexico State Board of Education v. Stoudt, 91 N.M. 183, 571 P.2d 1186 (1977).

A federal court refused to allow a school board to dismiss a pregnant, unwed teacher when it held that no constitutional rights had been violated because [t]here was no rational connection between the plaintiff's pregnancy out of wedlock and the school board's interest in conserving marital values even though the board thought the teacher's acts were destructive of community values. Brown v. Bathke, 566 F.2d 588 (8th Cir. 1977).

§ 17.72 Homosexuality

Two factors are considered by the courts when a school board takes action to dismiss a teacher for homosexuality, (1) the degree to which the teacher's sexual preferences have become public knowledge; and (2) the recognition that an individual is a practicing homosexual, even if there is no specific act. Throughout, not only homosexual but also heterosexual cases, the courts have attempted to determine if a school board can establish a rational nexus between the private activity and the professional responsibility, and if the private activity manifests an unfitness to teach.

17.72a Public Homosexual Acts. Dismissal of a teacher who had his teaching certificate revoked because he was convicted of disorderly conduct for having touched and rubbed another man's genitalia on a public beach was upheld by a California court because the action demonstrated unfitness to teach. The court held that a nexus did exist between the private action and the teacher's professional responsibilities. Sarac

v. State Board of Education, 249 Cal.App.2d 58, 57 Cal.Rptr. 69 (1967).

17.72b Private Homosexual Acts. In determining fitness to teach or the nexus between the homosexuality and teaching, a number of questions should be considered: (1) Are the students and other teachers adversely affected? (2) Could you anticipate a high degree of adversity from the situation? (3) Was the conduct or act of a recent nature or substantially in the past? (4) What type of teaching certificate did the teacher hold; elementary, secondary, etc.? (5) Are there any extenuating factors surrounding the situation? (6) What were the motives of the individual? (7) What is the probability of the situation being replicated? and (8) Are any constitutional rights involved? All of these factors are important when considering the teacher's impact on the students and the educational environment. The school board must balance the constitutional interests of the teacher against the right to have an orderly and appropriate educational environment for the school children.

In a case where a teacher was not a practicing homosexual and had engaged in only one such act, with another teacher, the state board of education revoked his certificate. The revocation took place three years after the incident and two years after the teacher had voluntarily related the incident to the school superintendent. The court held that the certificate must be restored unless the board could show actual unfitness to teach. Morrison v. State Board of Education, 1 Cal.3d 214, 82 Cal.Rptr. 175, 461 P.2d 375 (1969).

Where a former student told the vice-principal he believed a teacher to be a homosexual and the teacher was dismissed because evidence was adduced that the teacher was an active member of a homosexual society, responded to blind advertisements for homosexual company, and actively sought out other males, the court held that the teacher's homosexuality must be considered within the context of his position as a teacher, and it would be unreasonable to assume that his ability as a teacher was not damaged or impaired. Likewise, the court concluded that the school board does not have to wait for an overt act before exercising fiduciary responsibilities for the children and the school district. Gaylord v. Tacoma, 88 Wn.2d 286, 559 P.2d 1340 (1977).

§ 17.73 Transsexuality

The rule of law with regard to transsexuals is the same as with homosexuals, that is, if it is detrimental to the educational environment, the transsexual teacher can be dismissed. In one such case, a 54 year old tenured, male elementary teacher, who was married with three children, requested leave for surgery in early spring. Upon returning in May, after surgery, he had become a she/he. The board on becoming aware of the situation, had a series of meetings with the teacher, and submitted a proposal to the teacher, including, *inter alia*, teaching electives at the high school and resigning after one more year. The teacher rejected these options. Although testimony presented by psychiatrists conflicted, as to the psychological harm the teacher would cause to children in the

[*329*]

school, the court concluded that the " . . . teacher's presence in the classroom would create a potential for psychological harm to the students, the teacher is unable properly to fulfill his or her role and his or her incapacity has been established within the purview of the statute". The court emphasized the conclusions only related to teaching in that specific district, but expressed no opinion on fitness to teach elsewhere, under different circumstances. In re Grossman, 127 N.J.Super. 13, 316 A.2d 39, 49 (1974).

§ 17.8 PUBLIC LEWDNESS

Public lewdness is, of course, objectionable behavior in civilized society and is generally presumed to be inappropriate behavior for a school teacher. In a case where a tenured teacher caressed, undressed and made lewd gestures with a mannequin in a well-illuminated vacant lot and the activity became public knowledge and was observed by the school superintendent one evening; the teacher claimed his private conduct is constitutionally protected and his psychiatrist testified, although he had a personality disorder, it would not impair his classroom effectiveness. The court held that because the actions had already gained notoriety it was likely the conduct would damage his effectiveness as a teacher and "his working relationship within the educational process." "The right to be left alone in the home extends only to the home and not to conduct displayed under the street lamp on the front lawn." Wishart v. McDonald, 500 F.2d 1110 (1st Cir. 1974).

§ 17.9 CRIMINAL CONVICTION

State statutes, in a number of states, provide that teachers may be dismissed for "a felony or a crime of moral turpitude." A felony is "[a] crime of a graver or more atrocious nature than those designated as misdemeanors . . . Generally an offense punishable by death or imprisonment in the penitentiary." *Black's Law Dictionary*, Fourth Edition, West Publishing Company, 744.

§ 17.91 Felony

A teacher may not be convicted of a felony in the courts, but, may be dismissed by a school board for the same act. A teacher may be unfit to teach, but may not have been convicted of a crime. In a case where a teacher was charged with a criminal act of engaging in oral copulation with another man and was acquitted of criminal charges, the school board dismissed the teacher for immorality and unfitness. The state code provided that school boards may dismiss teachers for sex offenses. The court held for the board and said that it was the responsibility of the board to determine the fitness of the employee even if they had been acquitted of criminal charges. The key is whether the act is a detrimental influence to the pupils of the district. Board of Education v. Calderon, 35 Cal.App.3d 490, 110 Cal.Rptr. 916 (1973), cert. denied and appeal dismissed 419 U.S. 807, 95 S.Ct. 19 (1974).

In a California case where a teacher pleaded guilty to possession of narcotics and was placed on probation for two years for the conviction of a felony, the school board placed him on indefinite suspension and started dismissal proceedings. By the time his dismissal had reached the courts, his probation had ended and his charges had been reduced to a misdemeanor. However, during this time the California legislature significantly reduced the criminal penalty for possession of marijuana. The Supreme Court said: "since the school board's authority to dismiss the teacher rests solely on statutory grounds and the statute no longer existed the teacher could not be dismissed." Governing Board of Rialto Unified School District v. Mann, 135 Cal.Rptr. 526, 18 Cal.3d 819, 558 P.2d 1 (1977).

§ 17.92   Moral Turpitude

Moral turpitude is "[a]n act of baseness, vileness, or depravity in the private and social duties which a man owes to his fellow men, or to society in general, contrary to the accepted and customary rule of right and duty between man and man." (*Black's Law Dictionary*, 1160). Moral turpitude is difficult to clearly define because it is premised on the moral standards of the community.

Revocation of the teaching certificate of two teachers for growing 52 marijuana plants in a greenhouse has been upheld by a Florida court. The court concluded that since teachers are in a leadership capacity, and are obligated to maintain a high moral standard in the community, the possession of marijuana plants, and the ensuing publicity, seriously impaired their abilities to be effective teachers. Adams v. State Professional Practices Council, 406 So.2d 1170 (Fla.App.1981), petition denied 412 So.2d 463. In an earlier decision, a teacher was found not to be guilty of moral turpitude where he was cultivating only one marijuana plant out of curiosity. Board of Trustees v. Judge, 50 Cal.App.3d 920, 123 Cal.Rptr. 830 (1975).

§ 17.93 Misdemeanor

Included in the area of criminal convictions is the dismissal of a teacher for a misdemeanor. Misdemeanors are "[o]ffenses lower than felonies and generally those punishable by a fine or imprisonment otherwise than in a penitentiary." (*Black's Law Dictionary*, 1150).

A teacher was charged with theft, assault and battery, and fleeing a police officer and as a result was dismissed from his teaching position. The court upheld his dismissal and stated "[i]t cannot be said that a teacher's conduct outside the classroom bears no reasonable relation to his qualifications for employment." Gary Teachers Union, Local No. 4, American Federation of Teachers v. School City of Gary, 65 Ind.App. 314, 332 N.E.2d 256 (1975).

In another case where a tenured teacher was arrested and charged with " . . . disturbing the peace by being under the influence of intoxicants, attempting to fight, and display of a gun," his dismissal was upheld for good and just cause and the board's action was held not to be arbitrary, irrational or unreasonable. Williams v. School District No. 40 of Gila County, 4 Ariz.App. 5, 417 P.2d 376 (1966).

§ 17.10　DRUGS

Teachers, in recent years, have been dismissed for possession and use of controlled substances. Since state statutes usually do not specify dismissal for drugs, teachers who have been involved with drugs have been dismissed under statutory provisions of fitness to teach, moral turpitude, immorality, misdemeanor, and felony convictions, plus other good and sufficient cause.

An example is found in Georgia where a tenured teacher was arrested for possession of cocaine, glutethimide, and marijuana and pleaded guilty to violating that state's Controlled Substances Act. Since it was a first offense, the teacher was placed on probation. Because of the publicity, she was transferred to two other teaching positions during the remainder of the year. Finally, the board dismissed her for "immorality" and "other good and sufficient cause" based on her guilty plea. The court said, "the proven fact of the teacher's possession of three dangerous drugs is evidence from which 'immorality' may be inferred, even in the absence of criminal purpose or intent." Dominy v. Mays, 150 Ga.App. 187, 257 S.E.2d 317 (1979). A similar result was reached in Chicago Board of Education v. Payne, 102 Ill.App.3d 741, 58 Ill.Dec. 368, 430 N.E.2d 310 (1981).

A different result, however, was reached in a case where a teacher was charged with sale and possession of a controlled substance. The teacher pleaded guilty and was charged by the school board with misconduct. A hearing panel recommended the teacher merely be reprimanded and the teacher brought suit, claiming the reprimand was excessive. The court felt to merely reprimand the teacher, instead of imposing a more severe penalty, was far too lenient and not commensurate with the actions of the teacher. The court remanded the case back to the administrative agency for reconsideration and a determination which would impose a more rigorous penalty on the teacher. The court said, "[T]his penalty is so disproportionate to the misconduct proved by the evidence in the record, an abuse of discretion is manifest and the determination may not stand." Riforgiato v. Board of Education of City of Buffalo, 86 A.D.2d 757, 448 N.Y.S.2d 74 (1982).

§ 17.11 PROCEDURAL DUE PROCESS

The basic concept of procedural due process is an opportunity to be heard, in a manner that promotes fairness and establishes the accuracy of the charges. Procedural due process is a flexible concept and has been referred to by the courts as "fundamental fairness." An individual has a right to refute the charges brought against him, by government, before a liberty or property right is taken away. The more serious the deprivation, the more formal the procedure for due process. (See Chapter 3.) Therefore, an administrative hearing to remove a teacher from his/her position is not as serious as a criminal offense and would require less stringent procedural due process.

The procedures to be followed in dismissing a teacher are generally specified by statute. Some of the elements of procedural due process are: There must be fair and reasonable notice of the charges; there must be an opportunity for a hearing; the hearing must be conducted by an impartial tribunal; there must be sufficient time to prepare for the hearing; the decision should be based on the evidence presented at the hearing; and there must be an opportunity to appeal a negative decision.

Although the specific elements of hearings are not set forth, the hearing must adhere to the minimal requirements of fair play to allow the teacher the opportunity to refute the charges. The Supreme Court of Missouri in Valter v. Orchard Farm School District, 541 S.W.2d 550 (Mo.1976) suggested these minimal elements for a hearing. They may not necessarily be the same as provided for students since circumstances may be quite different. (See Chapter 3.) According to Valter the requirements for teachers are:

1. The opportunity to be heard.

2. The opportunity to present evident to refute the charges.

3. The opportunity to present witnesses.

4. Representation by legal counsel.

5. The opportunity to cross-examine witnesses.

6. Access to all evidence, such as written reports, in advance.

School boards, generally, are the tribunal hearing the evidence and making the decision to dismiss or retain a teacher. This procedure has been challenged as a violation of due process because the school board is said not an impartial tribunal and therefore, fundamental fairness of procedural due process is allegedly hindered.

The Supreme Court addressed this issue of impartiality in Hortonville Joint School District No. 1 v. Hortonville Education Association, 426 U.S. 482, 96 S.Ct. 2308 (1976). Negotiations between teachers and the school board failed to produce an agreeable contract and the teachers went on strike. Wisconsin statutes prohibited teacher strikes, and, after a period of time, when the teachers were asked to return to work and did not, they were notified that disciplinary hearings would take place. The teachers appeared before the board, as a group, with counsel. The day after the hearing, the board terminated the teachers, but invited any who wished to reapply for a teaching position. A teacher reapplied and was rehired. The teachers claimed the Due Process Clause of the Fourteenth Amendment was violated because the board was not sufficiently impartial. The Supreme Court found that board members who were public servants, and who had no personal or financial stake in the negotiations had no conflict of interest. In the words of the Court, "[M]ere familiarity with the facts of a case gained by an agency in the performance of its statutory role does not, however, disqualify a decisionmaker."

CHAPTER 18

EMPLOYMENT DISCRIMINATION

§ 18.1 INTRODUCTION

Social and political movements of the 1960's and 1970's contributed to change in employment practices. The Civil Rights Act of 1964, The Equal Pay Act, the Age Discrimination in Employment Act, The Pregnancy Discrimination Act, The Rehabilitation Act all addressed issues, some more successfully than others. What resulted was a change in laws, rules and regulations governing race, sex, age and handicapped discrimination. This chapter addresses these issues from a legal perspective.

§ 18.2 RACE DISCRIMINATION

§ 18.21 Testing and Hiring

In Griggs v. Duke Power Co., 401 U.S. 424, 91 S.Ct. 849 (1971) the use of tests and high school diplomas were challenged as being unrelated to job requirements in making personnel decisions. These criteria excluded a high percentage of minorities, which was a violation of Title VII. (See Appendix B.) The Duke Power Company required a high school education or the successful completion of a standardized intelligence test as a condition of employment. Neither the degree, nor the test, were significantly related to job success. A higher percentage of blacks either failed the test or did not have high school educations, there-

[338]

fore, they were excluded from the labor force, and whites were given preference.

Tests which appear to be neutral on their face may not be used to "freeze" the status quo. Duke Power Company had a history of racial discrimination. Congress did not intend Title VII to guarantee every person, who has suffered past discrimination, a job, but the purpose of the act was to remove artificial and unnecessary barriers which discriminated against race or some other protected classification. The lower court determined the company had established the diploma and test requirements without the intent to discriminate. But, good intent is not enough when there are "built-in head winds" for minorities. Congress was interested in the consequences of what actually happened, the effect, and not simply the motivation. "Nothing in the Act precludes the use of testing or measuring procedures; obviously they are useful. What Congress has forbidden is giving these devices and mechanisms controlling force unless they are demonstrably a reasonable measure of job performance. Congress has not commanded that the less qualified be preferred over the better qualified simply because of minority origins. Far from disparaging job qualifications as such, Congress has made such qualifications the controlling factor, so that race, religion, nationality, and sex become irrelevant. What Congress has commanded is that any tests used must measure the person for the job and not the person in the abstract." The Supreme Court ruled the practice in violation of Title VII and initiated the use of the effect test.

[*339*]

The Supreme Court in Albemarle Paper Co. v. Moody, 422 U.S. 405, 95 S.Ct. 2362 (1975) clarified the degree of relationship which is required to exist between the test and the job. A class action suit was filed by black employees, alleging a violation of Title VII because of policies relating to seniority, employment testing and back pay. The lower court ordered the implementation of a new seniority system. Two issues were presented to the Supreme Court, back pay and testing.

If the company had discriminated against a class then ". . . backpay should be denied only for reasons that, if applied generally, would not frustrate the central statutory purposes manifested by Congress in enacting Title VII of eradicating discrimination throughout the economy and making persons whole for injuries suffered through past discrimination." Since Title VII is not concerned with good intent, or the absence of discriminatory intent, the absence of bad faith is not a reason to deny back pay. "Congress directed the thrust of the Act to the consequences of employment practices, not simply the motivation."

The Court affirmed the *Griggs* finding. Testing may be used in employment hiring, but it must be related to the job. If the employee can show a *prima facie* case of discrimination, and there is a significant difference in results between groups, (the effect test), then the burden shifts to the employer to prove the test is job related. Like the company in *Griggs*, Albemarle used two tests; the Beta Examination, to test nonverbal intelligence and the Wonderlic Test, the same test used in *Griggs*. When the Wonderlic Test was added to the testing program, no attempt was made to validate the test, and the national norms were used to determine who would be hired. As in *Griggs* "discriminatory tests are impermissible unless shown, by professionally acceptable methods, to be 'predictive of or significantly correlated with important elements of work behavior which comprise or are relevant to the job or jobs for which candidates are being evaluated'." Before the case went to trial, the company engaged an expert to validate the job relatedness of the test. After spending one-half of a day at the plant a "concurrent validation" study was designed which was later conducted by plant officials. There were one hundred three employees tested, four of whom were blacks. The test scores were correlated with the subjective ranking of the supervisors. Departments which required greater skills had the higher ranking employees, and were the subjects of the validation study. The test was validated on job-experienced white workers, even though the tests were actually used to screen new applicants. The Court found this attempt at validation fell far short of a standard job relatedness study, and declared the use of the tests violative of Title VII.

In Washington v. Davis, 426 U.S. 229, 96 S.Ct. 2040 (1976), the Supreme Court decided whether the effect test, which was applied to Title VII also applied to constitutional issues. In *Washington*, a higher percentage of blacks failed a test used to screen individuals for police officer training. The test was designed to measure verbal ability, vocabulary, reading, and comprehension, but had never been validated for job relatedness. A group of policemen alleged a violation of the due process clause of the Fifth Amendment because of the higher percentage of black failures. The Court of Appeals, "held that the statutory standards elucidated in . . . Griggs v. Duke Power Company, supra were to govern the due process question." The Supreme Court disagreed with the Court of Appeals; "[w]e have never held that the constitutional standard for adjudicating claims of invidious racial discrimination is identical to the standards applicable under Title VII, and we decline to do so today." Therefore, the disproportionate impact test for statutory scrutiny should not be used for constitutional challenges, the proper standard must prove discriminatory purpose showing the test was designed with the intent or purpose of discriminating. Therefore where the effect test is appropriate for Title VII cases the intent test must be used for constitutional challenges.

The United States brought suit against the State of South Carolina for alleged violations of the Fourteenth Amendment and Title VII of the Civil Rights Act of 1964. The allegation was made pursuant to discrimination against minorities who had failed the National Teacher Examination (NTE) which was used to certify teachers and determine salary levels. The plaintiffs claimed there was a disparate racial impact on minorities which violated the Fourteenth Amendment and Title VII. When determining whether the intent of the test was discriminatory the court cited Village of Arlington Heights v. Metropolitan Housing Development Corp., 429 U.S. 252, 97 S.Ct. 555 (1977) which ruled that to determine the intent or purpose of the test it must be evaluated in a total context, such as, (1) reviewing the historical background, (2) the legislative history, and (3) testimony of officials. The plaintiffs failed to prove the test was implemented with the intent to discriminate. The court then applied the lesser "rational relationship" standard. State officials articulated that a rational relationship existed between the test and education in South Carolina since the test determined whether the applicant had a minimum knowledge necessary to teach and the purpose of the test was to improve the quality of education in South Carolina. These reasons were held to be rationally related to a legitimate governmental interest.

The Court then turned to the question of whether the test and compensation scales violated Title VII. Claims under Title VII were dismissed because the act gave no authority to the Attorney General to pursue an action except by referral from the Equal Employment Opportunity Commission (EEOC). Therefore, the claims of the United States under Title VII were dismissed.

"The remaining claims under Title VII must be tested under statutory standards." Since the plaintiffs had established a disparate impact, then it should be determined whether the tests were job related. The government had to establish a rational relationship between the test and the legitimate objectives of government.

A group of four hundred fifty-six individuals, with professional credentials, assessed the content validity of the National Teacher Examination. This group reviewed the curriculum of South Carolina to determine if the test measured what was being taught. "The design of the validity study is adequate for Title VII purposes." The Supreme Court made clear once again in *Washington v. Davis* that "a content validity study that satisfies professional standards also satisfies Title VII."

The business necessity standards were determined not to be a "compelling interest" as a part of "strict scrutiny" but only an examination of alternatives which the employer might have available which would lessen the disparate impact but achieve the objective of the employer. Plaintiffs contended that simply graduating from an accredited approved college program would be sufficient. This alternative was rejected since there are great variations in admission requirements and academic standards among the teacher training institutions. Since the standardized test (NTE) reflected the individual's knowledge of subject matter, which is directly related to teaching, the business necessity standard was satisfied. United States v. State of South Carolina, 445 F.Supp. 1094 (D.S.C.1977).

§ 18.22   *Prima Facie* Case

Because of the difficulties of proving intent, most litigation has been concerned with disparate impact under Title VII. The plaintiffs, in establishing a *prima facie* case must show four basic factors are true: "(i) that he belongs to a racial minority; (ii) that he applied and was qualified for a job for which the employer was seeking applicants; (iii) that, despite his qualifications, he was rejected; and (iv) that, after his rejection, the position remained open and the employer continued to seek applicants from persons of complainant's qualifications." McDonnell Douglas Corp. v. Green, 411 U.S. 792, 93 S.Ct. 1817 (1973).

The McDonnell Douglas standards for establishing a *prima facie* case are flexible. Facts will vary from case to case and specifications for *prima facie* proof will not necessarily be the same in every aspect. "A prima facie case under *McDonnell Douglas* raises an inference of discrimination only because we [the Courts] presume these acts, if otherwise unexplained, are more likely than not based on the consideration of impermissible factors." Furnco Construction Corp. v. Waters, 438 U.S. 567, 98 S.Ct. 2943 (1978).

Therefore, to dispel the adverse inference from a *prima facie* showing, all the employer needs to do is "articulate some legitimate, nondiscriminatory reason for the employee's rejection." McDonnell Douglas v. Green, 411 U.S. 792, 93 S.Ct. 1817 (1973). After the employer has articulated some legitimate reason, the plaintiff must be afforded the opportunity to present evidence that this is no more than a pretext for discrimination.

A female teacher established a prima facie case of discrimination in Board of Trustees of Keene State College v. Sweeney, 439 U.S. 25, 99 S.Ct. 295 (1978). The Appeals Court required the defendant university "to prove [the] absence of [a] discriminatory motive", the Supreme Court reaffirmed *Furnco* and distinguished between "articulate", "show", and "prove". "[W]e think that there is a significant distinction between merely 'articulating some legitimate, non-dis-

[*345*]

criminatory reason' and 'proving absence of discriminatory motive.' "   The case was remanded to the lower court to allow the university to articulate a legitimate reason as established and defined by the Supreme Court.

§ 18.23   Reverse Discrimination

Reverse discrimination is a term used, in recent years, referring to the use of remedial legislation, such as Title VII, to discriminate against non-minorities.   Title VII "does not impose a duty to adopt a hiring procedure that maximizes hiring of minority employees" (*Furnco*, supra).   It prohibits an employer from discriminating against any employee, therefore, making the job requirements neutral.   The Supreme Court in McDonald v. Santa Fe Trail Transportation Co., 427 U.S. 273, 96 S.Ct. 2574 (1976) stated, "Title VII, whose terms are not limited to discrimination against members of any particular race, prohibits racial discrimination in private employment against white persons upon the same standards as racial discrimination against non-whites."

The Medical School of the University of California at Davis established two admission programs.   The regular admission program took into consideration grade point averages, the Medical College Admission Test, recommendations and other standards.   Students were allowed to apply in the regular admission program whether they were minorities or not, and each year a small number of minorities were accepted through the regular admissions process.   A special program for blacks, Chicanos, Asians, and American Indians, screened candidates on similar standards, considering their disadvantaged backgrounds, both economically and educationally. Minority candidates who did not qualify for the regular admissions program were nominated for the sixteen special admission positions.

A white applicant filed suit alleging discrimination based on the Equal Protection Clause of the Fourteenth Amendment and Title VI of the Civil Rights Act of 1964. The applicant contended he was only allowed to apply for eighty four slots while the minority candidates could apply for the regular admissions, 84 slots, plus the sixteen allocated to minorities. If the minority candidate did not qualify in the regular program of eighty four positions, he could then come under the special admission category.

The case was originally filed on both constitutional equal protection grounds and Title VI of the Civil Rights Act of 1964. The Supreme Court decided the case on Title VI after requesting supplementary information. The Title VI (See Appendix B) decision obviated a constitutional interpretation by the Court.

The Court ruled the use of "quotas" are not allowable and that the present admission system was quota based. It was determined that race may be used as a factor in admission programs and it may even be a "plus", but it cannot be the sole, decisive factor. Regents of University of California v. Bakke, 438 U.S. 265, 98 S.Ct. 2733 (1978).

Reverse discrimination was the subject of a suit when the United Steelworkers of America and Kaiser Aluminum and Chemical Corporation negotiated a collective bargaining agreement. This agreement provided for the elimination of racial imbalance in employment. Since the craftwork force was almost exclusively white, fifty percent of the craft-training positions, by agreement, were reserved for blacks until the percentage of blacks in craft positions approximated the percentage of blacks in the local labor market. In 1974, the first year of the affirmative action plan, thirteen individuals were selected for craft training. Seven were black and six were white. The most senior black of the group had less seniority than a number of white workers who were not selected. These white workers filed suit claiming discrimination based on Title VII of the Civil Rights Act of 1964. The Supreme Court determined Title VII was not violated since all private, voluntary, race-conscious, affirmative action plans are not prohibited. The Court left open the question of what is a voluntary, private, affirmative action program that violates Title VII. "We need not today define in detail the line of demarcation between permissible and impermissible affirmative action plans. It suffices to hold that the challenged Kaiser-USWA affirmative action plan falls on the permissible side of the line." United Steelworkers, etc. v. Weber, 443 U.S. 193, 99 S.Ct. 2721 (1979).

A white female applied to a traditionally black institution the Florida Agricultural and Mechanical University (FAMU) and the Dean requested a professor, Dr. Davis, to select a search committee. The professor responded by sending a letter to the Dean on December 3, 1976, giving the names of the search committee. The letter also stated that the committee could adequately evaluate another candidate, Mr. Thompson, and went on to suggest that Mr. Thompson and two other faculty members attend a meeting together in January, in another state. The letter appeared to presume that Mr. Thompson would be hired.

Dr. Davis discussed housing arrangements with Mr. Thompson on the telephone on December 6, 1976. Thompson was interviewed on December 9, 1976. On December 10, 1976, the chairman, Dr. Davis, in a letter to the Dean, recommended Mr. Thompson be employed, although his application and recommendations were not completed until December 23, 1976.

Dr. Schwartz, the white female candidate, was interviewed on December 13, 1976 for the same position. Dr. Schwartz filed suit alleging discrimination and established a *prima facie* case. FAMU had the burden of articulating a legitimate non-discriminatory reason for the employment action. The chairman of the search committee stated that the black male candidate had more college teaching and professional experience. After closely scrutinizing the vita of each candidate, it was determined that the male candidate had a large number of inaccuracies. The end result was that the white female had both more college teaching and experience and it was questionable whether the male candidate had the minimum experience required as advertised.

The reasons for hiring Thompson rather than Schwartz, given by the University, were merely pretexts for racial and sexual discrimination. The court ordered the female be hired in a tenured position, with hiring retroactive to January 1, 1977, and back pay was awarded for the time she was illegally denied employment, along with attorney fees and costs. "In the court's opinion she [Dr. Schwartz] was better qualified than was the black [Mr. Thompson] male selected for employment." Schwartz v. State of Florida, 494 F.Supp. 574 (N.D.Fla.1980).

§ 18.3 SEX DISCRIMINATION

§ 18.31   Pregnancy

California's Unemployment Compensation Disability Fund was established to pay persons, in private employment, who temporarily were unable to work because of a disability not covered by workman's compensation. The unemployment fund received financial support from a percentage deducted from the worker's wages. Limits were established on the amount an individual received and the program contained certain exclusions. No funds were paid for disabilities of less than eight days or more than twenty-six weeks, and "disability is not compensable if it results from the individual's court commitment as a dipsomaniac, drug addict or sexual psychopath . . ." or for pregnancy.

Four women challenged the pregnancy exclusion. Of these four, only one had a normal pregnancy. The State of California modified the plan to pay for pregnancies with complications, therefore, only normal pregnancy was excluded. The exclusion of normal pregnancy was determined not to be invidious discrimination under the Fourteenth Amendment. No evidence was produced establishing the program discriminated against any definable group because, "[t]he program divides potential recipients into two groups—pregnant women and non-pregnant persons. While the first group is exclusively female, the second includes members of both sexes. The fiscal and actuarial benefits of the program thus accrue to members of both sexes." Geduldig v. Aiello, 417 U.S. 484, 94 S.Ct. 2485 (1974).

A General Electric Company disability plan for all employees paid a weekly rate for non-occupational sickness and accidents except disabilities arising from pregnancy. The plan was challenged as a violation of Title VII, of the Civil Rights Act of 1964. (78 Stat. 253, as amended, 42 U.S.C.A. §§ 2000e et seq.) The lower court had ruled that *Geduldig* was not controlling since it was an Equal Protection case and this case was litigated under Title VII. The Supreme Court disagreed and stated, "[w]e think, therefore, that our decision in *Geduldig v. Aiello,* . . ., dealing with a strikingly similar disability plan, is quite relevant in determining whether or not the pregnancy exclusion did discriminate on the basis of sex." The Court again determined there was no gender discrimination, only a classification between pregnant and non-pregnant persons.

The Supreme Court concluded that no clear definition for sex existed for Title VII and this was compounded by the conflicting regulations published by ". . . the EEOC, . . ., and the Wage and Hour Administrator . . ." Since the guidelines were in conflict and no definition had been established, it was questionable whether Congress meant pregnancy to be covered under the term sex. General Electric Co. v. Gilbert, 429 U.S. 125, 97 S.Ct. 401 (1976).

Because of the *Geduldig* and *Gilbert* cases, Congress made it quite evident it intended Title VII to cover pregnancy. Title VII was amended on October 31, with the passage of the Pregnancy Discrimination Act. (P.L. 65–535, amended section 701 of Title VII). The Act prohibits discrimination based on pregnancy, childbirth, or related medical conditions. The woman who is affected by pregnancy, childbirth or other related medical conditions must be treated the same for fringe benefits purposes as others are treated for employment-related purposes. The Act does not mandate the employer's health insurance program cover abortions unless the life of the mother would be endangered, or if medical complications arise. If the employer wishes to provide abortion programs, then this act would not preclude such arrangements.

On April 27, 1979 an insurance company sent a memorandum to all employees explaining Title VII. The memorandum stated that to be covered for disability benefits, the employee must be working effective April 30, 1979, and, if an employee was on leave on April 30, 1979, they would not receive benefits until they returned to work. The court ruled the policy violated Title VII since disabled men on leave on April 30, 1979 continued to receive disability benefits. Therefore, denial of benefits to females constituted discrimination because of unequal treatment of males and females. Equal Employment, etc. v. Group Hospital Service, 539 F.Supp. 185 (N.D.Tex.1982).

Mandatory leave policies for pregnant teachers have been challenged by pregnant teachers as a violation of their constitutional rights. The Supreme Court, in deciding companion cases, resolved some of the issues concerning pregnancy policies. The school board policy in *LaFleur* required all pregnant teachers to take leave, without pay, five months before the birth of the child. Teachers had to apply two weeks in advance of leaving. Teachers were not allowed to return to teaching until the start of a regular semester when the child reached three months of age. Reemployment was not guaranteed and the individual would only be put on a priority list, after certification by a physician attesting to her physical health.

In the second case the Chesterfield County School Board policy required teachers to leave work four months before the child's birth. Notice was required six months before birth was expected. The teacher was guaranteed employment after the birth of the child, the following school year, if a physician attested she was physically fit. Furthermore, the teacher had to give the school board assurance that child care would not interfere with her teaching.

The Court acknowledged that the advance notice requirements were rational rules to maintain continuity of instruction. However, the arbitrary cut-off dates were not rationally related to preserving continuity of instruction and could even work to the detriment of that goal. This goal was deemed unconstitutional because it presented an *irrebuttable presumption* that all females who are pregnant become physically in-

[*353*]

competent at a specified date and "[p]ermanent irrebuttable presumptions have long been disfavored
under the Due Process Clauses of the Fifth and Fourteenth Amendments. We conclude, therefore, that
neither the necessity for continuity of instruction nor
the states' interest in keeping physically unfit teachers
out of the classroom can justify mandatory leave regulations."

The Court determined the rule requiring the child to
be three months old before the mother returned to
school violated due process and was arbitrary and irrational. It created an irrebuttable presumption that a
person cannot be an effective teacher until her child is
three months old. However, the Chesterfield County
rule, requiring a teacher to be certified by a physician
before returning to work, did meet all due process requirements. Cleveland Board of Education v. La-
Fleur; Cohen v. Chesterfield County School Board,
414 U.S. 632, 94 S.Ct. 791 (1974).

A leave policy of the Nashville Gas Company required all pregnant employees to take leave, without
sick pay. Sick pay was allowed for nonoccupational
disabilities, but not for pregnancy. The policy further
stipulated that an individual who is pregnant loses all
accumulated seniority. "Petitioners policy of denying
employees returning from pregnancy leave their accumulated seniority acts both to deprive them 'of employment opportunities' and 'to adversely effect
[their] status as an employee' because of their sex in
violation of" Title VII. Nashville Gas Co. v. Satty, 434
U.S. 136, 98 S.Ct. 347 (1977).

§ 18.32 Equal Pay Act

In 1963, the Fair Labor Standards Act of 1938 (See Appendix B) was amended to include what is commonly called the Equal Pay Act. The intent of the act was to eliminate discrimination in wages based on sex where equal work, equal skills and effort are performed under the same working conditions (29 U.S.C.A. § 206(d)(1)). Exceptions are provided when differential pay is based on: (1) a seniority system; (2) a merit system; (3) where quantity and quality of production is a factor; and (4) where pay differences are based on any factor except sex.

Title VII of the Civil Rights Act of 1964 (42 U.S.C.A. § 2000e–2(h)) was amended to incorporate the Equal Pay Act. The language of Title VII is similar to that of the Equal Pay Act, except, not only is sex covered, but also race, color, religion or national origin. Title VII provides; it is not unlawful to provide different compensation, "or different terms, conditions, or privileges of employment pursuant to a bona fide seniority or merit system, or a system which measures earnings by quantity or quality of production or to employees who work in different locations, provided that such differences are not the result of an intention to discriminate because of race, color, religion, sex or national origin." (42 U.S.C.A. § 2000e–2(h)).

When a claim of unequal pay for equal work is analyzed, the standard is essentially the same for the Equal Pay Act and Title VII. "To establish a claim of unequal pay for equal work a plaintiff has the burden to prove that the employer pays different wages to

[*355*]

employees of opposite sexes for equal work on jobs the performance of which requires equal skill, effort and responsibility, and which are performed under similar working conditions." Odomes v. Nucara, Inc., 653 F.2d 246 (6th Cir. 1981); see: Corning Glass Works v. Brennan, 417 U.S. 188, 94 S.Ct. 2223 (1974). It was not the intent of Congress that the jobs must be identical. To effectuate the Equal Pay Act and its remedial remedies, "only substantial equality of skills, effort, responsibility and working conditions is required." *Odomes*, supra. Whether the work is equal must be established on a case by case basis. In the *Odomes* case, it was shown by the plaintiff nurse's aide uncontradicted testimony, that orderlies do little or nothing that the nurse's aide did not do, therefore, equal pay should be received.

Once the plaintiff has established that he or she is being paid unequally for the same work "the burden shifts to the employer to show that the differential [pay scale] is justified under one of the Act's four exemptions. Corning Glass Works v. Brennan, supra.

In Usery v. Columbia University, 568 F.2d 953 (2d Cir. 1977) the Secretary of Labor commenced an action against the university for discriminating against female "light cleaners" who receive lower pay than male "heavy cleaners". The district judge declared that the Secretary had not sustained the burden of proof since heavy cleaners exerted greater effort than light cleaners. On appeal, the circuit court applied the criterion of "equal effort." The "mere fact that two jobs call for effort different in kind will not render them unequal, nor will effort expended on additional tasks assigned to male employees necessarily suffice to justify pay differential; if additional tasks do not consume significant total amount of all employee's time, or if female employees also perform duties which require additional effort or if third persons who perform additional tasks as their primary job are paid less than male employees in question, in these situations additional effort is insufficient to differentiate male positions under the Act." Since the heavy cleaners job required substantially more effort, the unequal pay was justified under the Equal Pay Act.

§ 18.33 Benefits

For years insurance companies and others have been using actuarial tables in calculating payments and benefits for insurance and other types of benefit plans. These data indicate females live longer than males on the average. These types of programs have been challenged as a form of sex discrimination under Title VII especially when averages are used since Title VII refers to the individual.

The Los Angeles Department of Water and Power required female employees to make a larger contribution to a pension plan than males. Females and males who were the same age, seniority and earned equal salaries received equal monthly benefits upon retirement. To provide equal benefits the department established differential contributions, since females live longer than males; they would receive a monthly amount over a longer period of time. The females challenged the differential contributions claiming it violated Section 703(a)(1) of the Civil Rights Act of 1964,

Title VII.   City of Los Angeles, Department of Water v. Manhart, 435 U.S. 702, 98 S.Ct. 1370 (1978).

As mentioned, a significant aspect of Title VII is that it provides for the individual. It is a violation of the Act "to discriminate against any individual with respect to his compensation, terms, conditions or privileges of employment, because of such individual's race, color, religion, sex or national origin" (42 U.S.C.A. § 2000e–2(a)(1)). The importance of the statute, focusing on the individual, is significant. One example is, on the average, women are shorter than men. The statute would prohibit a tall woman from being refused a job if height is a requirement. The salient issue is the qualifications of the individual must be considered and an employer may not use an arbitrary classification. In *Manhart* sex was being used as the exclusive measure of longevity when it is known that longevity has a statistically significant positive correlation, with other factors such as race and national origin. Therefore, using the single measure of sex was an arbitrary standard in determining monthly contributions for the department's pension plan.

The department countered that the difference was not based on sex but on longevity. When Title VII was amended to incorporate the Equal Pay Act (Fair Labor Standards Act of 1938, as amended, 29 U.S.C.A. § 206(d)) pay differentials were allowable if based on several factors. These factors are: (1) a seniority system; (2) a merit pay system; (3) a pay system based on quality and quantity of production; or (4) a differential based on any factor other than sex. It was contended the contributions should be allowed under factor four, since it was based on longevity and not on sex. Life expectancy could be based on a number of factors, such as weight, past medical history, smokers versus non-smokers, and alcohol consumption, but since only sex was used, it was an attempt to disguise it as longevity. Since no evidence was presented that other factors were taken into account the Supreme Court agreed "with the [District Judges'] observation that one cannot say that an actuarial distinction based entirely on sex is 'based on any other factor other than sex.' Sex is exactly what it is based on."

The only issue addressed by the court was whether it was legal to make women and men contribute unequal amounts to an employee-operated pension fund. "Nothing in our holding implies that it would be unlawful for an employer to set aside equal retirement contributions for each employee and let each retiree purchase the largest benefit which his or her accumulated contributions could command on the open market. Nor does it call into question the insurance undustry's practice of considering the composition of an employer's work force in determining the probable cost of a retirement or death benefit plan."

The Supreme Court, previously, in Albemarle Paper Co. v. Moody, 422 U.S. 405, 95 S.Ct. 2362 (1975) established a presumption for retroactive back pay relief. The district court in *Manhart* awarded retroactive relief for the class of females offended, although Title VII does not require retroactive relief. Title VII provides that if unlawful discrimination has taken place retroactive relief may be an integral part of "appropriate" relief. The Supreme Court found retroactive pay was inappropriate in *Manhart* since this was the first case challenging contribution to pension funds. Also, the department administrators assumed the actuarial tables were valid and, therefore could not have foreseen the marked departure from past practice based on sex-differentiation determined in this case. The department was not required to refund to female employees all contributions that were in excess of what males contributed.

The State of Arizona, in Arizona Governing Committee v. Norris, ___ U.S. ___, 103 S.Ct. 3492 (1983) offered its employees a voluntary tax deferred annuity plan. Here, an employee could voluntarily join the plan and have three options: (1) a single lump-sum payment when the employee retired; (2) payments at a specified amount for a fixed period of time; or (3) monthly annuity payments for the remainder of the employees life. The first two options treated males and females equally and were not in dispute. But, option three, the monthly annuity plan, was determined by sex-based mortality tables. If a males and females retired at the same age with the same contributions, males received a greater payment per month than females. Sex was the only factor used to classify the individuals. No other factors were used such as smoking, weight, family history, and medical history.

"[C]lassifications of employees on the basis of sex is no more permissible at the pay-out stage of a retirement plan than at the pay-in stage." The plan proposed by Arizona, although voluntary, was determined to be the equivalent of the plan litigated in *Manhart*.

"If a woman participating in the Arizona plan wishes to obtain monthly benefits equal to those obtained by a man she must make greater monthly contributions than he, just as female employees in *Manhart* had to make greater contributions to obtain equal benefits."

The basic arguments raised in *Manhart* were again presented in Arizona Governing Committee v. Norris only with insignificant differences. "Our ruling today was clearly foreshadowed by *Manhart*. That decision should have put petitioners on notice that a man and a woman who make the same contributions to a retirement plan must be paid the same monthly benefits."

The court did not require benefits be made retroactive, as this would be costly to firms offering employer sponsored pension plans. Instead, the court established a date, August 1, 1983, when all such plans must be sex-neutral. Two other cases Teachers Insurance and Annuity Association v. Spirit, ___ U.S. ___, 103 S.Ct. 3565 (1983) and Peters v. Wayne State University and TIAA–CREF, ___ U.S. ___, 103 S.Ct. 3566 (1983) were remanded to the lower courts to render decisions consistent with the court's ruling in Arizona Governing Committee v. Norris.

§ 18.34   Title IX and Employment Discrimination

Title IX (Education Amendment of 1972, Pub.L. 92–318, 86 Stat. 373, 20 U.S.C.A. §§ 1681 et seq.) (See Appendix B) prohibits discrimination based on gender in any educational programs or activities receiving federal funds. This act closely patterned after Title VI of the Civil Rights Act of 1964 (Pub.L. 88–352, 78 Stat. 252, 42 U.S.C.A. §§ 2000d et seq.) states:

> "No person in the United States shall, on the basis of sex, be excluded from participation in, be denied the benefits of, or be subjected to discrimination under any education program or activity receiving Federal financial assistance . . ." (Section 901(a)).

Section 902 authorizes the promulgation of regulations ensuring that recipients are in compliance with Section 901(a). Since Title IX is patterned after Title VI some individuals believed it pertained only to students. The act does not contain the term student but rather "person." Interpreting the term "person" to include employees, the Department of Health, Education and Welfare (HEW) promulgated regulations pertaining to employment. Subpart E (See: C.F.R. §§ 106.51–106.61, 1980) provides:

> "No person shall, on the basis of sex be excluded from participation in, be denied the benefits of, or be subjected to discrimination in employment, or recruitment, consideration, or selection therefor[e], whether full-time or part-time, under any education program or activity operated by a recipient which receives or benefits from Federal financial assistance." Section 106.51(a)(1).

A number of educational institutions challenged the provision that Title IX applied to employees. See: North Haven Board of Education v. Bell, 456 U.S. 512, 102 S.Ct. 1912, 1913 note 9 (1982). The United States Supreme Court in *North Haven* determined "while Section 901(a) does not expressly include employees within its scope or expressly exclude them, its broad directive that 'no person' may be discriminated against on the basis of gender, on its face, includes employees as well as students." Therefore, any educational program or activity receiving federal funds may not discriminate against employees or students.

§ 18.4 AGE DISCRIMINATION

The federal government passed the Age Discrimination in Employment Act in 1967 (as amended in 1978, Title 29 U.S.C.A. § 621, Age Discrimination in Employment Act Amendments of 1978) which prohibits discrimination against any individuals who are at least 40, but less than 70 years of age. The act was designed not to maximize the number of elderly in the workforce, but to prohibit discrimination based on age. This act prohibits discrimination when hiring or discharging individuals with respect to: compensation, terms, conditions, privileges, retirement, and demotion.

Mandatory retirement statutes have been challenged as a violation of equal protection and due process of law. However, the courts, with few exceptions, have upheld the right of employers to establish mandatory retirement ages. The United States Supreme Court upheld a Massachusetts statute requiring uniformed police to retire at age 50. It was determined that government employment is not a fundamental right, nor is age a suspect classification. Therefore, the proper standard of judicial review for equal protection consideration, is the rational interest test. The purpose of the statute is to assure physical preparedness through having younger uniformed officers and this was rationally related to the state objective of providing proper police protection. Massachusetts Board of Retirement v. Murgia, 427 U.S. 307, 96 S.Ct. 2562 (1976).

The rational interest test was used again when the Court upheld a statute requiring Foreign Service employees to retire at 60 years of age, while other Civil Service employees were allowed to retain employment until 70 years of age. The rational rationale given for this early retirement policy was: "Congress . . . was legitimately intent on stimulating the highest performance in the Foreign Service by assuring that opportunities for promotion would be available despite [the] limits on [the] number of personnel in the Service, and plainly intended to create [a] relatively small, homogeneous and particularly able corps of foreign service officers . . ." Vance v. Bradley, 440 U.S. 93, 99 S.Ct. 939 (1979).

The Seventh Circuit Court of Appeals determined that a teacher who had reached the mandatory retirement age could not be forced to retire unless the reason for retirement was rationally related to the teacher's fitness to teach. No evidence was presented to substantiate any relationship existed between age and the teacher's fitness to teach. The court distinguished this case from *Murgia* supra. Evidence in *Murgia* showed a relationship between age and physical fitness, whereas here, the relationship was between age and mental fitness. Since teaching is more mental than physical and the older you get the more experience and knowledge you acquire, then, theoretically you become a better teacher. Gault v. Garrison, 569 F.2d 993 (7th Cir. 1977).

The Second Circuit Court questioned the *Gault* decision, see also: Lamb v. Scripps College, 627 F.2d 1015 (9th Cir. 1980), in a factually similar situation and upheld the constitutionality of a mandatory retirement age for teachers. The court determined the rational test for mental fitness in *Gault* was too restrictive and reasoned the state may have other rational reasons for mandatory retirement, which are appropriate, such as opening up opportunities for young teachers and minorities, and instilling fresh ideas and techniques. Therefore, the mandatory retirement age for teachers was approved. Palmer v. Ticcione, 576 F.2d 459 (2d Cir. 1978).

The Commissioner of New York presented evidence that school bus drivers over 65 have a higher accident rate. Therefore, because of health and safety, it is reasonable to require retirement at 65 years of age. Kerwick v. New York State Board of Equalization, 114 Misc.2d 928, 453 N.Y.S.2d 151 (1982).

The party claiming age discrimination will be evaluated under the same factors as established for race discrimination in McDonnell Douglas Corp. v. Green, 411 U.S. 792, 93 S.Ct. 1817 (1973). If the action is a private, non-class action then ". . . the complainant has the burden of establishing a *prima facie* case, which he can satisfy by showing that (i) he belongs to a special minority; (ii) he applied and was qualified for a job the employer was trying to fill; (iii) though qualified, he was rejected; and (iv) therefore, the employer

continued to seek applicants with complainant's qualifications."

After the plaintiff has established a *prima facie*
case, the burden shifts to the employer, who must articulate legitimate, nondiscriminatory reasons for not
employing the individual or individuals.

§ 18.5 DISCRIMINATION OF THE HANDICAPPED

A blind female certified by the Philadelphia Department of Education attempted to obtain employment in
the Philadelphia School District. The district's policy
prevented anyone with a "chronic or acute physical defect," including blindness, from taking the Philadelphia Teacher's Examination. The teacher persisted in
attempting to take the examination and in 1974,
passed. The reason for allowing her to take the examination was apparently in response to the passage
of the Rehabilitation Act of 1973 which became effective in December, 1973. (P.L. 93–112 Section 500(a),
29 U.S.C.A. § 790(a)). The school district offered her
several jobs which she refused because seniority was
not also granted from the date of the original application. The teacher filed suit seeking retroactive seniority. The court not only granted retroactive seniority,
but determined the school district's policy, not allowing blind or other handicapped people to teach was
unconstitutional because it made the irrebuttable presumption that all blind or handicapped individuals are
incompetent. This violated the individual's due process rights. Gurmankin v. Costanzo, 556 F.2d 184 (3d
Cir. 1977). The court made seniority retroactive to

September, 1970, but noted it would not apply to pre-1974 injuries to the new Rehabilitation Act. Therefore, it required relief based on constitutional grounds. The teacher was denied back pay and tenure and appealed the decision based on these two issues. Back pay is an appropriate relief in a Title VII, employment discrimination case, see: Albemarle Paper Co. v. Moody, 422 U.S. 405, 95 S.Ct. 2362 (1975) but this was not an employment discrimination case but rather a statutory deprivation of a civil right under Title 42 U.S.C.A. § 1983. The court denied tenure.

Not awarding of tenure might be appropriate in some situations. In Kunda v. Muhlenberg College, 621 F.2d 532 (3d Cir. 1980) the court said "determination about such matters as teaching ability, research scholarship, and professional stature are subjective, and unless they can be shown to have been used as the mechanism to obscure discrimination, they must be left for evaluation by the professionals". *Gurmankin*, supra. In *Kunda*, the teacher had a record of scholarship and was granted tenure. But in *Gurmankin*, the teacher had never taught or been evaluated, thus granting tenure would have been an inappropriate remedy. Gurmankin v. Costanzo, supra.

A blind tenured teacher filed suit, Upshur v. Love, 474 F.Supp. 332 (N.D.Cal.1979) charging discriminatory policies and procedures had prevented him from being promoted to an administrative position. Each prospective administrator was required to take a written and oral test. The plaintiff took the written examination, with the assistance of a reader, and scored in the lowest quartile. After being evaluated on both the oral and written tests, the administrative committee declined to place the plaintiff on the preferred list for prospective administrators.

The court agreed with *Gurmankin* that physical handicaps are analogous to age and are not a suspect classification. Since handicap is not a suspect classification, the strict scrutiny test is inapplicable and the appropriate test is the rational basis test. Using the rational basis test, it was determined that the defendants did not violate the teacher's equal protection rights. The committee found, separate from his handicapping condition, that the plaintiff did not have the skills and qualifications to be placed on the administration list. The committee was seeking competent and talented people, and therefore, was justifiably concerned with the plaintiff's blindness. When questions were presented to the blind teacher as to how he would cope with difficulties, his answers were superficial, at best. There was no irrebuttable presumption in the school district's policies that handicapped people could not function in such a position, each individual was assessed on his or her abilities.

When determining the merits of a Rehabilitation Act claim, Section 504 is violated if the handicapped person is denied a position "solely by reason of his handicap." The plaintiff was not qualified, even if he were not blind. The act also specifies the employer must "reasonably accommodate" an individual, but this standard applies only if the individual is "otherwise qualified."

The disparate treatment test is inapplicable for Section 504 claims. The Rehabilitation Act has established these criteria: "First, the individual is required to show that he is otherwise qualified for the position sought; second, the individual must show that even though he is otherwise qualified, he was rejected for the position solely on the basis of his handicap. The two factors are interrelated, since if the individual is not otherwise qualified he cannot be said to have been rejected solely because of his handicap." Pushkin v. Regents of University of Colorado, 658 F.2d 1372 (10th Cir. 1981).

*

APPENDIX A

SELECTED CONSTITUTIONAL PROVISIONS

THE CONSTITUTION OF THE UNITED STATES

Amendment I

Congress shall make no law respecting an establishment of religion, or prohibiting the free exercise thereof; or abridging the freedom of speech, or of the press; or the right of the people peaceably to assemble, and to petition the Government for a redress of grievances.

Amendment IV

The right of the people to be secure in their persons, houses, papers, and effects, against unreasonable searches and seizures, shall not be violated, and no Warrants shall issue, but upon probable cause, supported by Oath or affirmation, and particularly describing the place to be searched, and the persons or things to be seized.

Amendment V

No person shall be held to answer for a capital or otherwise infamous crime, unless on a presentment of indictment of a Grand Jury, except in cases arising in the land or naval forces, or in the Militia, when in time of War or public danger; nor shall any person be subject to the same offense to be twice put in jeopardy of life or limb; nor shall be compelled in any criminal case to be a witness against himself, nor be deprived of life, liberty or property, without due process of law; nor shall private property be taken for public use, without just compensation.

Amendment VIII

Excessive bail shall not be required, nor excessive fines imposed, nor cruel and unusual punishments inflicted.

Amendment X

The powers not delegated to the United States by the Constitution, nor prohibited by it to the States, are reserved to the States respectively, or to the people.

Amendment XIV

Section 1. All persons born or naturalized in the United States, and subject to the jurisdiction thereof, are citizens of the United States and of the State wherein they reside. No state shall make or enforce any law which shall abridge the privileges or immunities of citizens of the United States; nor shall any State deprive any person of life, liberty, or property, without due process of law; nor deny to any person within its jurisdiction the equal protection of the laws.

Section 2. Representatives shall be apportioned among the several States according to their respective number, counting the whole number of persons in each state, excluding Indians not taxed. But when the right to vote at any election for the choice of electors for President and Vice President of the United States, Representatives in Congress, the Executive and Judicial officers of a State, or the members of the Legislature thereof, is denied any of the male inhabitants of such State, being twenty-one years of age, and citizens of the United States, or in any way abridged, except for participation in rebellion, or other crime, the basis of representation therein shall be reduced in the proportion which the number of such male citizens shall bear to the number of male citizens twenty-one years of age in such State.

Section 3 and 4. (Omitted)

Section 5. The Congress shall have power to enforce, by appropriate legislation, the provisions of the article.

APPENDIX B

SELECTED FEDERAL STATUTES
CIVIL RIGHTS ACT OF 1964
TITLE VI
(Selected Parts)

42 U.S.C.A. §§ 2000d—d–1

FEDERALLY ASSISTED PROGRAMS

§ 2000d. Prohibition against exclusion from participation in, denial of benefits of, and discrimination under Federally assisted programs on ground of race, color, or national origin

No person in the United States shall, on the ground of race, color, or national origin, be excluded from participation in, be denied the benefits of, or be subjected to discrimination under any program or activity receiving Federal financial assistance.

Pub.L. 88–352, Title VI, § 601, July 2, 1964, 78 Stat. 252.

. . .

§ 2000d–1. Federal authority and financial assistance to programs or activities by way of grant, loan, or contract other than contract of insurance or guaranty; rules and regulations; approval by President; compliance with requirements; reports to Congressional committees; effective date of administrative action

Each Federal department and agency which is empowered to extend Federal financial assistance to any program or ac-

[373]

tivity, by way of grant, loan, or contract other than a contract of insurance or guaranty, is authorized and directed to effectuate the provisions of section 2000d of this title with respect to such program or activity by issuing rules, regulations, or orders of general applicability which shall be consistent with achievement of the objectives of the statute authorizing the financial assistance in connection with which the action is taken. No such rule, regulation, or order shall become effective unless and until approved by the President. Compliance with any requirement adopted pursuant to this section may be effected (1) by the termination of or refusal to grant or to continue assistance under such program or activity to any recipient as to whom there has been an express finding on the record, after opportunity for hearing, of a failure to comply with such requirement, but such termination or refusal shall be limited to the particular political entity, or part thereof, or other recipient as to whom such a finding has been made and, shall be limited in its effect to the particular program, or part thereof, in which such noncompliance has been so found, or (2) by any other means authorized by law: *Provided, however,* That no such action shall be taken until the department or agency concerned has advised the appropriate person or persons of the failure to comply with the requirement and has determined that compliance cannot be secured by voluntary means. In the case of any action terminating, or refusing to grant or continue, assistance because of failure to comply with a requirement imposed pursuant to this section, the head of the Federal department or agency shall file with the committees of the House and Senate having legislative jurisdiction over the program or activity involved a full written report of the circumstances and the grounds for such action. No such action shall become effective until thirty days have elapsed after the filing of such report.

Pub.L. 88–352, Title VI, § 602, July 2, 1964, 78 Stat. 252.

CIVIL RIGHTS ACT OF 1964
42 U.S.C.A. § 2000e—e–2
TITLE VII
(Selected Parts)
EQUAL EMPLOYMENT OPPORTUNITIES

§ 2000e–2. Unlawful employment practices
Employer practices

(a) It shall be an unlawful employment practice for an employer—

(1) to fail or refuse to hire or to discharge any individual, or otherwise to discriminate against any individual with respect to his compensation, terms, conditions, or privileges of employment, because of such individual's race, color, religion, sex, or national origin; or

(2) to limit, segregate, or classify his employees or applicants for employment in any way which would deprive or tend to deprive any individual of employment opportunities or otherwise adversely affect his status as an employee, because of such individual's race, color, religion, sex, or national origin.

Employment agency practices

(b) It shall be an unlawful employment practice for an employment agency to fail or refuse to refer for employment, or otherwise to discriminate against, any individual because of his race, color, religion, sex, or national origin, or to classify or refer for employment any individual on the basis of his race, color, religion, sex, or national origin.

. . .

Training programs

(d) It shall be an unlawful employment practice for any employer, labor organization, or joint labor-management

[*375*]

committee controlling apprenticeship or other training or re-training, including on-the-job training programs to discrimi-nate against any individual because of his race, color, relig-ion, sex, or national origin in admission to, or employment in, any program established to provide apprenticeship or oth-er training.

Businesses or enterprises with personnel qualified on basis of religion, sex, or national origin; educational institutions with personnel of particular religion

(e) Notwithstanding any other provision of this sub-chapter, (1) it shall not be an unlawful employment practice for an employer to hire and employ employees, for an em-ployment agency to classify, or refer for employment any individual, for a labor organization to classify its member-ship or to classify or refer for employment any individual, or for an employer, labor organization, or joint labor-manage-ment committee controlling apprenticeship or other training or retraining programs to admit or employ any individual in any such program, on the basis of his religion, sex, or na-tional origin in those certain instances where religion, sex, or national origin is a bona fide occupational qualification reasonably necessary to the normal operation of that partic-ular business or enterprise, and (2) it shall not be an unlaw-ful employment practice for a school, college, university, or other educational institution or institution of learning to hire and employ employees of a particular religion if such school, college, university, or other educational institution or institu-tion of learning is, in whole or in substantial part, owned, supported, controlled, or managed by a particular religion or by a particular religious corporation, association, or society, or if the curriculum of such school, college, university, or other educational institution or institution of learning is di-rected toward the propagation of a particular religion.

. . .

Seniority or merit system; quantity or quality of production; ability tests; compensation based on sex and authorized by minimum wage provisions

(h) Notwithstanding any other provision of this subchapter, it shall not be an unlawful employment practice for an employer to apply different standards of compensation, or different terms, conditions, or privileges of employment pursuant to a bona fide seniority or merit system, or a system which measures earnings by quantity or quality of production or to employees who work in different locations, provided that such differences are not the result of an intention to discriminate because of race, color, religion, sex, or national origin, nor shall it be an unlawful employment practice for an employer to give and to act upon the results of any professionally developed ability test provided that such test, its administration or action upon the results is not designed, intended or used to discriminate because of race, color, religion, sex or national origin. It shall not be an unlawful employment practice under this subchapter for any employer to differentiate upon the basis of sex in determining the amount of the wages or compensation paid or to be paid to employees of such employer if such differentiation is authorized by the provisions of section 206(d) of Title 29.

. . .

Preferential treatment not to be granted on account of existing number or percentage imbalance

(j) Nothing contained in this subchapter shall be interpreted to require any employer, employment agency, labor organization, or joint labor-management committee subject to this subchapter to grant preferential treatment to any individual or to any group because of the race, color, religion, sex, or national origin of such individual or group on account of an imbalance which may exist with respect to the total number or percentage of persons of any race, color, religion, sex, or national origin employed by any employer, referred or classified for employment by any employment agency or labor organization, admitted to membership or classified by any labor organization, or admitted to, or employed in, any apprenticeship or other training program, in comparison with the total number or percentage of persons of such race, color, religion, sex, or national origin in any community, State, section, or other area, or in the available work force in any community, State, section, or other area.

Pub.L. 88–352, Title VII, § 703, July 2, 1964, 78 Stat. 255; Pub.L. 92–261, § 8(a), (b), Mar. 24, 1972, 86 Stat. 109.

DISCRIMINATION BASED ON SEX

TITLE IX

(Selected Parts)

20 U.S.C.A. § 1681

§ 1681. Sex

Prohibition against discrimination; exceptions

(a) No person in the United States shall, on the basis of sex, be excluded from participation in, be denied the benefits of, or be subjected to discrimination under any education program or activity receiving Federal financial assistance, except that:

Classes of educational institutions subject to prohibition

(1) in regard to admissions to educational institutions, this section shall apply only to institutions of vocational education, professional education, and graduate higher education, and to public institutions of undergraduate higher education;

Educational institutions commencing planned change in admissions

(2) in regard to admissions to educational institutions, this section shall not apply (A) for one year from June 23, 1972, nor for six years after June 23, 1972, in the case of an educational institution which has begun the process of changing from being an institution which admits only students of one sex to being an institution which admits students of both sexes, but only if it is carrying out a plan for such a change which is approved by the Commissioner of Education or (B) for seven years from the date an educational institution begins the process of changing from being an institution which admits only students of only one sex to being an institution which admits students of both sexes, but only if it is carrying out a plan for such a change which is approved by the Commissioner of Education, whichever is the later;

Educational institutions of religious organizations with contrary religious tenets

(3) this section shall not apply to an educational institution which is controlled by a religious organization if the application of this subsection would not be consistent with the religious tenets of such organization;

Educational institutions training individuals for military services or merchant marine

(4) this section shall not apply to an educational institution whose primary purpose is the training of individuals for the military services of the United States, or the merchant marine;

Public educational institutions with traditional and continuing admissions policy

(5) in regard to admissions this section shall not apply to any public institution of undergraduate higher education which is an institution that traditionally and continually

from its establishment has had a policy of admitting only students of one sex;

Social fraternities or sororities; voluntary youth service organizations

(6) this section shall not apply to membership practices—

(A) of a social fraternity or social sorority which is exempt from taxation under section 501(a) of Title 26, the active membership of which consists primarily of students in attendance at an institution of higher education, or

(B) of the Young Men's Christian Association, Young Women's Christian Association, Girl Scouts, Boy Scouts, Camp Fire Girls, and voluntary youth service organizations which are so exempt, the membership of which has traditionally been limited to persons of one sex and principally to persons of less than nineteen years of age;

Boy or Girl conferences

(7) this section shall not apply to—

(A) any program or activity of the American Legion undertaken in connection with the organization or operation of any Boys State conference, Boys Nation conference, Girls State conference, or Girls Nation conference; or

(B) any program or activity of any secondary school or educational institution specifically for—

(i) the promotion of any Boys State conference, Boys Nation conference, Girls State conference, or Girls Nation conference; or

(ii) the selection of students to attend any such conference;

Father-son or mother-daughter activities at educational institutions

(8) this section shall not preclude father-son or mother-daughter activities at an educational institution, but if such

activities are provided for students of one sex, opportunities for reasonably comparable activities shall be provided for students of the other sex; and

Institution of higher education scholarship awards in "beauty" pageants

(9) this section shall not apply with respect to any scholarship or other financial assistance awarded by an institution of higher education to any individual because such individual has received such award in any pageant in which the attainment of such award is based upon a combination of factors related to the personal appearance, poise, and talent of such individual and in which participation is limited to individuals of one sex only, so long as such pageant is in compliance with other non-discrimination provisions of Federal law.

Preferential or disparate treatment because of imbalance in participation or receipt of Federal benefits; statistical evidence of imbalance

(b) Nothing contained in subsection (a) of this section shall be interpreted to require any educational institution to grant preferential or disparate treatment to the members of one sex on account of an imbalance which may exist with respect to the total number or percentage of persons of that sex participating in or receiving the benefits of any federally supported program or activity, in comparison with the total number or percentage of persons of that sex in any community, State, section, or other area: *Provided*, That this subsection shall not be construed to prevent the consideration in any hearing or proceeding under this chapter of statistical evidence tending to show that such an imbalance exists with respect to the participation in, or receipt of the benefits of, any such program or activity by the members of one sex.

Educational institution defined

(c) For purposes of this chapter an educational institution means any public or private preschool, elementary, or secondary school, or any institution of vocational, professional, or higher education, except that in the case of an educational institution composed of more than one school, college, or department which are administratively separate units, such term means each such school, college, or department.

Pub.L. 92–318, Title IX, § 901, June 23, 1972, 86 Stat. 373; Pub.L. 93–568, § 3(a), Dec. 31, 1974, 88 Stat. 1862; Pub.L. 94–482, Title IV, § 412(a), Oct. 12, 1976, 90 Stat. 2234.

EQUAL PAY ACT
(Selected Parts)
29 U.S.C.A. § 206

§ 206. Minimum wage

Prohibition of sex discrimination

(d)(1) No employer having employees subject to any provisions of this section shall discriminate, within any establishment in which such employees are employed, between employees on the basis of sex by paying wages to employees in such establishment at a rate less than the rate at which he pays wages to employees of the opposite sex in such establishment for equal work on jobs the performance of which requires equal skill, effort, and responsibility, and which are preformed under similar working conditions, except where such payment is made pursuant to (i) a seniority system; (ii) a merit system; (iii) a system which measures earnings by quantity or quality of production; or (iv) a differential based on any other factor other than sex: *Provided*, That an employer who is paying a wage rate differential in violation of this subsection shall not, in order to comply with the provisions of this subsection, reduce the wage rate of any employee.

(2) No labor organization, or its agents, representing employees of an employer having employees subject to any provisions of this section shall cause or attempt to cause such an employer to discriminate against an employee in violation of paragraph (1) of this subsection.

(3) For purposes of administration and enforcement, any amounts owing to any employee which have been withheld in violation of this subsection shall be deemed to be unpaid minimum wages or unpaid overtime compensation under this chapter.

(4) As used in this subsection, the term "labor organization" means any organization of any kind, or any agency or employee representation committee or plan, in which employees participate and which exists for the purpose, in whole or in part, of dealing with employers concerning grievances, labor disputes, wages, rates of pay, hours of employment, or conditions of work.

June 25, 1938, c. 676, § 6, 52 Stat. 1062; June 26, 1940, c. 432, § 3(e), (f), 54 Stat. 616; Oct. 26, 1949, c. 736, § 6, 63 Stat. 912; Aug. 12, 1955, c. 867, § 3, 69 Stat. 711; Aug. 8, 1956, c. 1035, § 2, 70 Stat. 1118; May 5, 1961, Pub.L. 87–30, § 5, 75 Stat. 67; June 10, 1963, Pub.L. 88–38, § 3, 77 Stat. 56; Sept. 23, 1966, Pub.L. 89–601, Title III, §§ 301–305, 80 Stat. 838, 839, 841; Apr. 8, 1974, Pub.L. 93–259, §§ 2–4, 5(b), 7(b)(1), 88 Stat. 55, 56, 62; Nov. 1, 1977, Pub.L. 95–151, § 2(a)–(d)(2), 91 Stat. 1245, 1246.

FAMILY RIGHTS AND PRIVACY ACT
(BUCKLEY AMENDMENT)
(Selected Parts)
20 U.S.C.A. § 1232g

§ 1232g. Family educational and privacy rights

Conditions for availability of funds to educational agencies or institutions; inspection and review of education records; specific information to be made available; procedure for access to education records; reasonableness of time for such access; hearings; written explanations by parents; definitions

(a)(1)(A) No funds shall be made available under any applicable program to any educational agency or institution which has a policy of denying, or which effectively prevents, the parents of students who are or have been in attendance at a school of such agency or at such institution, as the case may be, the right to inspect and review the education records of their children. If any material or document in the education record of a student includes information on more than one student, the parents of one of such students shall have the right to inspect and review only such part of such material or document as relates to such student or to be informed of the specific information contained in such part of such material. Each educational agency or institution shall establish appropriate procedures for the granting of a request by parents for access to the education records of their children within a reasonable period of time, but in no case more than forty-five days after the request has been made.

.   .   .

(2) No funds shall be made available under any applicable program to any educational agency or institution unless the parents of students who are or have been in attendance at a

school of such agency or at such institution are provided an opportunity for a hearing by such agency or institution, in accordance with regulations of the Secretary, to challenge the content of such student's education records, in order to insure that the records are not inaccurate, misleading, or otherwise in violation of the privacy or other rights of students, and to provide an opportunity for the correction or deletion of any such inaccurate, misleading, or otherwise inappropriate data contained therein and to insert into such records a written explanation of the parents respecting the content of such records.

. . .

Release of education records; parental consent requirement; exceptions; compliance with judicial orders and subpoenas; audit and evaluation of Federally-supported education programs; record-keeping

(b)(1) No funds shall be made available under any applicable program to any educational agency or institution which has a policy or practice of permitting the release of education records (or personally identifiable information contained therein other than directory information, as defined in paragraph (5) of subsection (a) of this section) of students without the written consent of their parents to any individual, agency, or organization, other than to the following—

(A) other school officials, including teachers within the educational institution or local educational agency who have been determined by such agency or institution to have legitimate educational interests;

(B) officials of other schools or school systems in which the student seeks or intends to enroll, upon condition that the student's parents be notified of the transfer, receive a copy of the record if desired, and have an opportunity for a hearing to challenge the content of the record;

(C) authorized representatives of (i) the Comptroller General of the United States, (ii) the Secretary, (iii) an administrative head of an education agency (as defined in section 1221e–3(c) of this title), or (iv) State educational authorities, under the conditions set forth in paragraph (3) of this subsection;

(D) in connection with a student's application for, or receipt of, financial aid;

(E) State and local officials or authorities to whom such information is specifically required to be reported or disclosed pursuant to State statute adopted prior to November 19, 1974;

(F) organizations conducting studies for, or on behalf of, educational agencies or institutions for the purpose of developing, validating, or administering predictive tests, administering student aid programs, and improving instruction, if such studies are conducted in such a manner as will not permit the personal identification of students and their parents by persons other than representatives of such organizations and such information will be destroyed when no longer needed for the purpose for which it is conducted;

(G) accrediting organizations in order to carry out their accrediting functions;

(H) parents of a dependent student of such parents, as defined in section 152 of Title 26; and

(I) subject to regulations of the Secretary, in connection with an emergency, appropriate persons if the knowledge of such information is necessary to protect the health or safety of the student or other persons.

Nothing in clause (E) of this paragraph shall prevent a State from further limiting the number or type of State or local officials who will continue to have access thereunder.

(2) No funds shall be made available under any applicable program to any educational agency or institution which has a policy or practice of releasing, or providing access to, any personally identifiable information in education records oth-

er than directory information, or as is permitted under paragraph (1) of this subsection unless—

(A) there is written consent from the student's parents specifying records to be released, the reasons for such release, and to whom, and with a copy of the records to be released to the student's parents and the student if desired by the parents, or

(B) such information is furnished in compliance with judicial order, or pursuant to any lawfully issued subpoena, upon condition that parents and the students are notified of all such orders or subpoenas in advance of the compliance therewith by the educational institution or agency.

. . .

(B) With respect to this subsection, personal information shall only be transferred to a third party on the condition that such party will not permit any other party to have access to such information without the written consent of the parents of the student.

. . .

Students' rather than parents' permission or consent

(d) For the purposes of this section, whenever a student has attained eighteen years of age, or is attending an institution of post-secondary education the permission or consent required of and the rights accorded to the parents of the student shall thereafter only be required of and accorded to the student.

. . .

Pub.L. 90–247, Title IV, § 438, as added Pub.L. 93–380, Title V, § 513(a), Aug. 21, 1974, 88 Stat. 571, and amended Pub.L. 93–568, § 2(a), Dec. 31, 1974, 88 Stat. 1858.

§ **1232h.** **Protection of pupil rights**

**Inspection by parents or guardians of
instructional material**

(a) All instructional material, including teacher's manuals, films, tapes, or other supplementary instructional material which will be used in connection with any research or experimentation program or project shall be available for inspection by the parents or guardians of the children engaged in such program or project. For the purpose of this section "research or experimentation program or project" means any program or project in any applicable program designed to explore or develop new or unproven teaching methods or techniques.

**Psychiatric or psychological examinations,
testing, or treatment**

(b) No student shall be required, as part of any applicable program, to submit to psychiatric examination, testing, or treatment, or psychological examination, testing, or treatment, in which the primary purpose is to reveal information concerning:

(1) political affiliations;

(2) mental and psychological problems potentially embarrassing to the student or his family;

(3) sex behavior and attitudes;

(4) illegal, anti-social, self-incriminating and demeaning behavior;

(5) critical appraisals of other individuals with whom respondents have close family relationships;

(6) legally recognized privileged and analogous relationships, such as those of lawyers, physicians, and ministers; or

(7) income (other than that required by law to determine eligibility for participation in a program or for receiving financial assistance under such program), without

[*388*]

the prior consent of the student (if the student is an adult or emancipated minor), or in the case of unemancipated minor, without the prior written consent of the parent.

(Jan. 2, 1968, P.L. 90–247, Title IV, Part C, Subpart 2, § 439, as added Aug. 21, 1974, P.L. 93–380, Title V, § 514(a), 88 Stat. 574; Nov. 1, 1978, P.L. 95–561, Title XII, Part D, § 1250, 92 Stat. 2355.)

EDUCATION OF HANDICAPPED CHILDREN

(Selected Parts)

20 U.S.C.A. §§ 1400–1461

§ 1400. Congressional statements and declarations

. . .

§ 1401. Definitions

. . .

Purpose

(c) It is the purpose of this chapter to assure that all handicapped children have available to them, within the time periods specified in section 1412(2)(B) of this title, a free appropriate public education which emphasizes special education and related services designed to meet their unique needs, to assure that the rights of handicapped children and their parents or guardians are protected, to assist States and localities to provide for the education of all handicapped children, and to assess and assure the effectiveness of efforts to educate handicapped children.

Pub.L. 91–230, Title VI, § 601, Apr. 13, 1970, 84 Stat. 175, amended Pub.L. 94–142, § 3(a), Nov. 29, 1975, 89 Stat. 774.

APPENDIX B

As used in this chapter—

. . .

(15) The term "children with specific learning disabilities" means those children who have a disorder in one or more of the basic psychological processes involved in understanding or in using language, spoken or written, which disorder may manifest itself in imperfect ability to listen, think, speak, read, write, spell, or do mathematical calculations. Such disorders include such conditions as perceptual handicaps, brain injury, minimal brain dysfunction, dyslexia, and developmental aphasia. Such term does not include children who have learning problems which are primarily the result of visual, hearing, or motor handicaps, of mental retardation, of emotional disturbance, or of environmental, cultural, or economic disadvantage.

(16) The term "special education" means specially designed instruction, at no cost to parents or guardians, to meet the unique needs of a handicapped child, including classroom instruction, instruction in physical education, home instruction, and instruction in hospitals and institutions.

(17) The term "related services" means transportation, and such developmental, corrective, and other supportive services (including speech pathology and audiology, psychological services, physical and occupational therapy, recreation, and medical and counseling services, except that such medical services shall be for diagnostic and evaluation purposes only) as may be required to assist a handicapped child to benefit from special education, and includes the early identification and assessment of handicapping conditions in children.

(18) The term "free appropriate public education" means special education and related services which (A) have been provided at public expense, under public supervision and direction, and without charge, (B) meet the standards of the State educational agency, (C) include an appropriate preschool, elementary, or secondary school education in the

State involved, and (D) are provided in conformity with the individualized education program required under section 1414(a)(5) of this title.

(19) The term "individualized education program" means a written statement for each handicapped child developed in any meeting by a representative of the local educational agency or an intermediate educational unit who shall be qualified to provide, or supervise the provision of, specially designed instruction to meet the unique needs of handicapped children, the teacher, the parents or guardian of such child, and, whenever appropriate, such child, which statement shall include (A) a statement of the present levels of educational performance of such child, (B) a statement of annual goals, including short-term instructional objectives, (C) a statement of the specific educational services to be provided to such child, and the extent to which such child will be able to participate in regular educational programs, (D) the projected date for initiation and anticipated duration of such services, and (E) appropriate objective criteria and evaluation procedures and schedules for determining, on at least an annual basis, whether instructional objectives are being achieved.

(20) The term "excess costs" means those costs which are in excess of the average annual per student expenditure in a local educational agency during the preceding school year for an elementary or secondary school student, as may be appropriate, and which shall be computed after deducting (A) amounts received under this subchapter or under title I or title VII of the Elementary and Secondary Education Act of 1965, and (B) any State or local funds expended for programs which would qualify for assistance under this subchapter or under such titles.

(21) The term "native language" has the meaning given that term by section 703(a)(2) of the Bilingual Education Act.

(22) The term "intermediate educational unit" means any public authority, other than a local educational agency,

which is under the general supervision of a State educational agency, which is established by State law for the purpose of providing free public education on a regional basis, and which provides special education and related services to handicapped children within that State.

Pub.L. 91–230, Title VI, § 602, Apr. 13, 1970, 84 Stat. 175; Pub.L. 94–142, § 4(a), Nov. 29, 1975, 89 Stat. 775.

§ 1415. Procedural safeguards

Establishment and maintenance

(a) Any State educational agency, any local educational agency, and any intermediate educational unit which receives assistance under this subchapter shall establish and maintain procedures in accordance with subsection (b) through subsection (e) of this section to assure that handicapped children and their parents or guardians are guaranteed procedural safeguards with respect to the provision of free appropriate public education by such agencies and units.

Required procedures; hearing

(b)(1) The procedures required by this section shall include, but shall not be limited to—

(A) an opportunity for the parents or guardian of a handicapped child to examine all relevant records with respect to the identification, evaluation, and educational placement of the child, and the provision of a free appropriate public education to such child, and to obtain an independent educational evaluation of the child;

(B) procedures to protect the rights of the child whenever the parents or guardian of the child are not known, unavailable, or the child is a ward of the State, including the assignment of an individual (who shall not be an employee of the State educational agency, local educational agency, or intermediate educational unit involved in the education or care of the child) to act as a surrogate for the parents or guardian;

(C) written prior notice to the parents or guardian of the child whenever such agency or unit—

(i) proposes to initiate or change, or

(ii) refuses to initiate or change,

the identification, evaluation, or educational placement of the child or the provision of a free appropriate public education to the child;

(D) procedures designed to assure that the notice required by clause (C) fully inform the parents or guardian, in the parents' or guardian's native language, unless it clearly is not feasible to do so, of all procedures available pursuant to this section; and

(E) an opportunity to present complaints with respect to any matter relating to the identification, evaluation, or educational placement of the child, or the provision of a free appropriate public education to such child.

(2) Whenever a complaint has been received under paragraph (1) of this subsection, the parents or guardian shall have an opportunity for an impartial due process hearing which shall be conducted by the State educational agency or by the local educational agency or intermediate educational unit, as determined by State law or by the State educational agency. No hearing conducted pursuant to the requirements of this paragraph shall be conducted by an employee of such agency or unit involved in the education or care of the child.

Review of local decision by State educational agency

(c) If the hearing required in paragraph (2) of subsection (b) of this section is conducted by a local educational agency or an intermediate educational unit, any party aggrieved by the findings and decision rendered in such a hearing may appeal to the State educational agency which shall conduct an impartial review of such hearing. The officer conducting such review shall make an independent decision upon completion of such review.

Enumeration of rights accorded parties to hearings

(d) Any party to any hearing conducted pursuant to subsections (b) and (c) of this section shall be accorded (1) the right to be accompanied and advised by counsel and by individuals with special knowledge or training with respect to the problems of handicapped children, (2) the right to present evidence and confront, cross-examine, and compel the attendance of witnesses, (3) the right to a written or electronic verbatim record of such hearing, and (4) the right to written findings of fact and decisions (which findings and decisions shall also be transmitted to the advisory panel established pursuant to section 1413(a)(12) of this title).

INDEX

References are to Pages

✧